Sams Teach Yourself

Microsoft® Windows Me Millennium Edition

Jennifer Fulton

in **10** Minutes

SAMS

A Division of Macmillan USA
201 West 103rd St., Indianapolis, Indiana, 46290 USA

Sams Teach Yourself Windows® Me Millennium Edition in 10 Minutes

Copyright © 2000 by Sams Publishing

International Standard Book Number: 0-672-31951-9

Library of Congress Catalog Card Number: 00-103848

Printed in the United States of America

First Printing: June 2000

01   00   99   4   3   2   1

Trademarks

All terms mentioned in this book that are known to be trademarks or service marks have been appropriately capitalized. Sams Publishing cannot attest to the accuracy of this information. Use of a term in this book should not be regarded as affecting the validity of any trademark or service mark.

Warning and Disclaimer

Every effort has been made to make this book as complete and as accurate as possible, but no warranty or fitness is implied. The information provided is on an "as is" basis. The author and the publisher shall have neither liability nor responsibility to any person or entity with respect to any loss or damages arising from the information contained in this book or from the use of the CD or programs accompanying it.

ASSOCIATE PUBLISHER
Mark Taber

ACQUISITIONS EDITOR
Betsy Brown

DEVELOPMENT EDITOR
Laura N. Williams

MANAGING EDITOR
Charlotte Clapp

PROJECT EDITOR
Dawn Pearson

COPY EDITOR
Sean Medlock

INDEXER
Chris Barrick

PROOFREADERS
Katherin Bidwell
Pat Kinyon

TECHNICAL EDITOR
Dallas Releford

TEAM COORDINATOR
Amy Patton

INTERIOR DESIGNER
Gary Adair

COVER DESIGNER
Aren Howell

COPY WRITER
Eric Borgert

PRODUCTION
Ayanna Lacey
Heather Hiatt Miller
Stacey Richwine-DeRome

Contents

Introduction 1

1 Introducing Windows 5

Starting Windows 5
Using the Mouse 7
Using the Start Button 10
Shutting Down Windows 14

2 Navigating the Windows Desktop 19

Understanding the Windows Desktop 19
Web Integration and the Active Desktop 20
Using the Taskbar 22
Using the Windows Toolbars 24
Displaying the Desktop Quickly 27

3 Working with Windows 28

What's a Window? 28
Opening a Window 30
Switching Between Windows 30
Sizing a Window with Maximize, Minimize, and Restore 31
Sizing a Window's Borders 34
Using Scrollbars 35
Moving a Window 36
Arranging Windows on the Desktop 37
Closing a Window 38

4 Using Toolbars and Menus 40

Using Toolbars 40
Using Menus 46
Using Shortcut Menus 48

5   Using Dialog Boxes   50

When a Dialog Box Appears 50
Selecting Dialog Box Options 50

6   Getting Windows Help and Support   54

Getting Help in Windows 54
Finding Help from the Home Page..55
Using the Index Feature 59
Using the Search Feature 60
Displaying a Tour or Tutorial 61
Getting Assisted Support 62
Using the What's This? Feature 62

7   Customizing Windows   64

Arranging Icons on the Desktop...64
Adding Shortcuts to the Desktop 65
Adding a Screen Saver 68
Changing the Screen Resolution...75

8   Changing the Appearance of Windows   77

Changing the Background of the Desktop 77
Changing the Appearance (Colors) of Windows 80
Adding Special Effects 82
Using Themes for a Coordinated Look 83

9   Customizing Other Attributes of Windows   86

Changing the Taskbar 86
Reorganizing the Start Menu 87
Changing the Sounds Associated with System Events....................90
Changing the Date and Time 91
Adjusting the Volume 91
Modifying Mouse Settings 93
Changing How AutoUpdate Works 94

10 Accessing Your Drives, Folders, and Files   97

Understanding Drives, Folders, and Files...97
Using My Computer 99

Using Windows Explorer 102
Turning on Classic View..103
Turning on the Single-Click Option 105

11 Viewing Drives, Folders, and Files   106

Changing the Display in My Computer and Windows Explorer 106
Replacing the Folders List 110
Viewing Graphic Files 111
Customizing Web View Folders 118

12 Accessing Resources on Your Home Network   120

What Is a Network? 120
Installing a Home Network..121
Setting Up Multiple Users for One Computer 126
Accessing Shared Resources 128
Sharing Your Resources 129
Sending Notes Over the Network...131

13 Selecting, Copying, and Moving Files and Folders   134

Selecting Multiple Files and Folders 134
Copying and Moving Files and Folders 136

14 Compressing and Uncompressing Files   141

What Is File Compression?...141
Compressing Files into a Folder..142
Extracting Files from a Compressed Folder...................................146

15 Creating, Deleting, Renaming, and Finding Files and Folders   148

Creating a Folder 148
Deleting a File or Folder...149
Renaming Files and Folders 152
Searching for a File...152

16   Formatting, Naming, and Copying Floppy Disks   157

How to Tell How Much Room Is on a Disk.....................................157
Formatting a Floppy Disk..158
Copying a Disk 160

17   Performing Disk Management   162

Using the Maintenance Wizard to Improve Performance 162
Creating a System Startup Disk 169
Backing Up Your Files 169
Performing a System Restore 170

18   Installing and Uninstalling Applications   175

Installing Software 175
Uninstalling Software..182
Using the CD-ROM Sampler to Preview Microsoft
    Applications..184

19   Using Your Applications   186

Starting an Application..186
Creating and Opening Documents 189
Copying and Moving Information 190
Saving and Closing Documents 193
Exiting an Application 195

20   Printing in Windows   196

Installing a Printer..196
Printing from an Application 200
Controlling the Print Job...201

21   Editing Video with Movie Maker   204

Importing and Recording Video and Audio 205
Editing a Project 208
Previewing the Finished Project.......................................212
Saving or Sending Video 212

22   Using Windows Media Player   215

Playing Audio CDs 215
Creating Playlists 218
Playing Videos 220
Listening to Streaming Audio..222
Applying a New Skin 223

23   Working with WordPad and Paint   225

Creating and Editing a Document with WordPad 225
Creating Graphics with Paint 228

24   Using Other Accessories   234

Using the Sound Recorder 234
Using the Calculator 235
Using Phone Dialer..236

25   Using Internet Explorer   239

Internet Basics...239
Creating Your Internet Connection 240
Connecting to an Online Service 244
Disabling Call Waiting 244
Starting Internet Explorer 245
Going to a Specific Site 246
Following a Link..247
Returning to a Previously Viewed Page 248
Using History to Revisit a Page 249
Playing Internet Radio Broadcasts 250

**26   Searching for Web Pages and Saving Your
       Favorites   252**

Understanding Web Searches 252
Using the Favorites Folder 258

27   Displaying Internet Content on the Desktop 261

Displaying Web Content on Your Desktop.........................261
What Is a Subscription? 263
Subscribing to a Channel 264

28   Customizing the Active Desktop   270

Working Offline 270
Synchronizing Subscriptions 270

**29   Sending and Receiving Mail with Outlook
      Express   274**

Entering Email Addresses..274
Sending an Email Message..277
Checking for New Messages 281
Replying to Messages..283
Deleting Old Messages...284

30   Using Outlook Express News   285

Viewing and Subscribing to a Newsgroup 285
Posting a Message..288

**A   Configuring Hardware and Adding/
     Removing Windows Components   291**

Configuring the Modem 291
Adding Other New Hardware...294
Changing the Properties of an Object.............................294
Adding or Removing Windows Components....................295

Index   299

About the Author

Jennifer Fulton, iVillage's Computer Coach, is a consultant, trainer, and best-selling author of over 75 books covering many areas of computing, including DOS and Windows. Jennifer is a self-taught computer guru, which means that if something *can* happen to a computer user, it *has* happened to her at one time or another. After working with computers all day, Jennifer brings what's left of her sense of humor to her many books, including *Sams Teach Yourself Windows 98 in 10 Minutes*, *Easy Outlook 2000*, *Sams Teach Yourself Excel 2000 in Ten Minutes*, *How to Use Publisher 2000*, *Office 2000 Cheat Sheet*, *Complete Idiot's Guide to Upgrading and Repairing PCs*, *Sams Teach Yourself Quicken 99 in 10 Minutes*, and *Computers: A Visual Encyclopedia*.

Jennifer began her writing career as a staff writer for Macmillan Computer Publishing before escaping to the life of a freelance author, trainer, and consultant. She lives in Indianapolis with her husband, Scott, who is also a computer book author, and her daughter, Katerina, author-to-be. They live together in a small home filled with many books, some of which they have *not* written themselves.

Dedication

To my wonderful husband, Scott, and my little angel, Katerina.

Acknowledgments

I would like to thank everyone for their involvement in this project, including Acquisitions Editor Betsy Brown, Development Editor Laura Williams, Project Editor Dawn Pearson, Copy Editor Sean Medlock, and Technical Editor Natasha Knight. I always appreciate the opportunity to write for Sams and to collaborate with the wonderful people who work there.

Tell Us What You Think!

As the reader of this book, *you* are our most important critic and commentator. We value your opinion and want to know what we're doing right, what we could do better, what areas you'd like to see us publish in, and any other words of wisdom you're willing to pass our way. As an Associate Publisher for Sams, I welcome your comments. You can fax, email, or write me directly to let me know what you did or didn't like about this book—as well as what we can do to make our books stronger.

Please note that I cannot help you with technical problems related to the topic of this book, and that due to the high volume of mail I receive, I might not be able to reply to every message.

When you write, please be sure to include this book's title and author as well as your name and phone or fax number. I will carefully review your comments and share them with the author and editors who worked on the book.

> Fax: 317-581-4770
>
> Email: *office_sams@macmillanusa.com*
>
> Mail: Mark Taber
>   Associate Publisher
>   Sams Publishing
>   201 West 103rd Street
>   Indianapolis, IN 46290 USA

Introduction

What's New in Windows Me

Windows is the world's most popular operating system. One reason for this is its graphical user interface (GUI), which lets users issue commands by clicking icons and work with programs within easily manipulated screens called (appropriately) *windows*.

 Operating System This lets your computer interpret requests for applications and commands from you, the user. The operating system is the brain of your PC, enabling it to manage data.

Windows Me represents a marriage of form and function. It makes your everyday tasks—such as locating files, viewing graphics, compressing files, and keeping your system up to date with the latest improvements—almost as easy as breathing. In addition, Windows Me is the first Windows operating system devoted entirely to the needs of the home user. So if you're using Windows Me at home, you'll find all the tools you need to work and have fun. If you're using it at work, you'll find some extras that might just make your work time more playful.

 Compatibility Issues Windows Me will run both 16-bit applications (Windows 3.1) and 32-bit applications (Windows 95 and 98). This means that any program you use on an older version of Windows is compatible with Windows Me.

In short, Windows Me offers you these advantages:

- **Performance improvements** that make Windows faster, such as a streamlined System Registry that keeps better track of the programs you actually have installed.

- **An improved online experience** with a streamlined online setup, the latest version of Internet Explorer (version 5.5), and improved connectivity.

- **Home network support** using a simple-to-use installation wizard, as well as easy file and application sharing.

- **A more trouble-free environment**, thanks to a System Restore feature that enables you to return to a previous version of your Windows setup with the touch of a button, as well as automatic Windows Update, system file protector, easier installation of Plug and Play devices, and silent installation of USB peripherals.

- **Integration of common tasks into Windows Explorer**, such as viewing graphics, compressing files, and locating files and folders.

- **State-of-the-art multimedia and game support**, including Movie Maker, which enables you to easily record, edit, and publish your audio or video creations, and Media Player, which allows you to play and organize all your video and audio files.

- **Simpler, friendlier Help and Support system** that uses HTML and e-support to provide you with the help you need when you need it, even at 3 a.m.

How to Use This Book

This book is designed for the reader who doesn't have a lot of time to learn about a new operating system. Each lesson in this book will take only 10 minutes to complete. So even in a busy workday, you can still find the time to learn what you need.

The book is divided into five parts. Part One concentrates on graphical operations, such as the organization of the Windows desktop, using the windows, dialog boxes, menus, and toolbars you find in Windows programs, and getting help. Part Two deals with making your Windows environment more compatible with your needs. Here you'll learn how to customize icons, add a screen saver, change system sounds, reorganize the **Start** menu, and more. Part Three presents file and directory management, including accessing resources on a home network. Part Four discusses the general operation of Windows applications, printing, and using the Windows accessories. Part Five shows you how to use Internet Explorer (a Web browser), send and receive electronic mail, and use the Active Desktop to display Web content.

You should probably complete the lessons in order, but feel free to skip around after you complete the first part (Lessons 1 to 6).

Conventions Used in This Book

This book uses the following conventions:

- Information you type appears in `monospace`.

- Menus and menu options, dialog box options, keys you press, and names of buttons and dialog box tabs appear in **boldface**.

When instructing you to choose menu commands, I use two different formats. Shorter menu options look something like this: "From the **File** menu, choose **Open**." Longer menu options look something like this: "Click **Start**, and then select **Programs**, **Accessories**, **Communications**, **Phone Dialer**."

In addition to these conventions, this book uses the following sidebars to identify helpful information:

 Plain English   These sidebars define new terms or terms that might be unfamiliar to you, such as technical terminology, jargon, and so on.

Timesaver Tips   These sidebars include keyboard and mouse shortcuts, as well as hints that can save you time and energy.

 Caution   These sidebars identify areas where new users often run into trouble and offer practical solutions to these problems.

LESSON 1

Introducing Windows

In this lesson, you'll learn how to start and shut down Windows. You'll also learn how to use the mouse (including the new Microsoft IntelliMouse) and the Windows Start button.

Starting Windows

To start Windows, simply turn on your computer. Windows then prepares your computer for use, a process called *booting* the computer.

 I See a Startup Menu If you see the Windows Startup Menu, you're being asked to choose from one of several configurations that your system administrator has set up for you. Contact your administrator to find out which number you should choose in this instance. Most Windows users (especially home users) won't see this menu. If you want to display the Startup menu because you're experiencing problems, press and hold the **Ctrl** key during reboot.

After a moment, you see the Welcome to Windows or Enter Network Password dialog box. The User Name box should already contain your name or the name under which your computer is presently registered. The bottom box, marked Password, should be blank except for a blinking cursor. Type your password and press **Enter**. As you type, Windows inserts asterisks into the Password box. This is to keep your password secure, in case anyone is peeking over your shoulder.

Remember Your Password   You must know your password to start Windows, and to connect and share any network resources.

After a few moments, you see the Windows desktop, which should be similar (although perhaps not identical) to Figure 1.1. The term *desktop* is used metaphorically to describe how the objects you work with are arranged and managed, like the everyday papers and other objects on your desk.

FIGURE 1.1   The Classic Windows Desktop.

 The Other Desktop   Windows offers you a choice of two different Desktops: the Classic Desktop and the Active Desktop. You'll learn more about the Active Desktop in Lesson 2, "Navigating the Windows Desktop."

Using the Mouse

The *mouse* is a device that you use to manipulate objects in Windows. As you move the mouse on its pad, the mouse pointer onscreen moves in tandem. The *mouse pointer* (or simply *pointer*) is the small symbol (such as an arrow) that moves on the screen when you move the mouse.

The mouse is a simple device, mechanically speaking, so there are only a few gestures you'll ever need to perform with it:

- To *point* to an object on the screen, move the mouse pointer so that it's directly over that object. You point to an object when you're preparing to do something to it.

- To *click* an object to which your mouse pointer is currently pointing, press the left mouse button once and quickly release it. Generally, you click an object to issue a command, open a program, or select the object.

- To *right-click* an object, point to it and then press and release the right mouse button. When you right-click an object, Windows and many applications display a menu called a *shortcut menu,* which lists commands that pertain to that object.

- To *drag* an object from place to place, first point to it. Then click and hold down the mouse button—don't release it yet. Next, move the pointer in the direction you want to drag the object. When the pointer is in the position where you want the object to appear, release the mouse button. (If you want to drag a word or paragraph, you have to select it first.) This process is called *drag-and-drop.* You might use it to move a file from one directory to another, or to move a paragraph within a word processing document. Normally, a drag-and-drop operation involves the left mouse button. However, Windows Me and some Windows programs employ so-called *right-drags* that bring up a context menu after the button is released.

- To *double-click* an object, point to it and then rapidly press and release the left mouse button twice. Double-clicking is the standard method in Windows for starting an application or selecting an object from a dialog box and immediately closing the box (dismissing it).

A Better Mousetrap   Some mouses, such as those from Logitech, can be programmed to perform a double-click action whenever you click the middle, right, or thumb button—whichever you choose.

Too Slow or Too Fast?   If you're having trouble clicking and double-clicking with the mouse, you might want to adjust its speed. For help, see Lesson 9, "Customizing Other Attributes of Windows." If you're not accustomed to using a mouse, a good way to practice is to play one of the games that come with Windows, which you'll find on the **Start** menu under **Programs, Games.**

Using the Single-Click Option

Turning on Windows' single-click option dramatically changes the way your mouse operates. For instance, instead of left-clicking an object to select it, you point to it, hold the mouse completely still, and wait for Windows to recognize that the pointer has stopped (about a third of a second by default). Windows then highlights the object you've selected.

Also, double-clicking is replaced by single-clicking, thus treating each object as though it were a hyperlink. For example, with the single-click option turned on, you simply click a file to open it. You'll learn how to turn on the single-click option in Lesson 10, "Accessing Your Drives, Folders, and Files."

Using an IntelliMouse

Microsoft is the manufacturer of both Windows and the IntelliMouse pointer device, so naturally it provides extra support for the IntelliMouse in Windows. This mouse has a small gray vertical wheel between its two buttons. The wheel is used for scrolling, and it can also be clicked to act as a third button of sorts.

Windows applications that are compatible with the IntelliMouse work as follows:

- To scroll slowly, simply rotate the wheel up or down.

- To scroll more quickly, click the wheel once and then move the mouse in the direction you want to scroll. Click the wheel again to turn off the automatic scrolling.

- To zoom in or out, press the **Ctrl** key as you rotate the wheel up (to zoom in) or down (to zoom out).

For instance, with Microsoft Excel, you can rotate the wheel to scroll down a worksheet. Or, using the wheel more like a button, you can hold it down and then move the mouse in the direction you want to scroll. Or you can press the **Ctrl** key while rotating the wheel up or down to increase or decrease the zoom factor of the active worksheet.

Me Too!   Logitech, another manufacturer of pointing devices for PCs, offers several alternatives to the IntelliMouse, all with the tiny scroll wheel. These devices work in a similar manner.

Using the Start Button

Almost every operation you initiate in Windows begins with the **Start** button in the lower-left corner of the screen. You can start programs, change Windows features, locate files, shut down Windows, and perform other operations with the commands you'll find on the **Start** menu (see Figure 1.2).

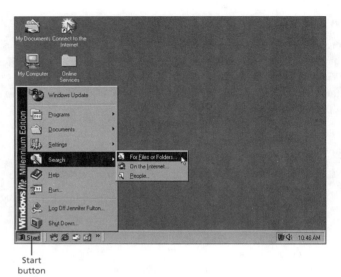

Start
button

FIGURE 1.2   The Start menu, which is displayed when you click the
Start button.

 Why Do My Menus Look Different?   Windows uses
personalized menus, so the menus you see on your
system might be slightly different than the ones
shown in this book. You'll learn more about personalized menus later in this section.

Here are some brief descriptions of the commands that are displayed
when you click the **Start** button:

- If you have a connection to the Internet, you can use the
  Windows Update command periodically to update your version
  of Windows. This command connects you to the Microsoft Web
  site, where you can select various updates for your system.

- The **Programs** command displays a categorized listing of the
  programs available on your system. Simply navigate through the
  various categories or *submenus* until you find the program you
  want to start.

Windows Update Is Now AutoUpdate   Although the **Windows Update** command is located at the top of the **Start** menu, you'll probably never use it. That's because in Windows, the **Windows Update** feature, now called **AutoUpdate**, is *completely automatic*. Whenever you connect to the Internet, **AutoUpdate** updates your system as needed without troubling you. If you like, you can configure **AutoUpdate** to notify you of updates before downloading and installing them. You can also turn **AutoUpdate** off completely and use **Windows Update** to update your system instead. You'll learn more about **AutoUpdate** in Lesson 9.

- The **Documents** command brings up a list of the documents, channels, and Internet links you use most frequently, either on your local system or on the World Wide Web. Click one of these entries to open the document in the associated application, to display the Web page in Internet Explorer, or to open a channel on the desktop. Quick access to the My Documents and My Pictures folders is also provided through the **Documents** menu.

- The **Settings** command allows you to quickly change your Windows settings, such as customizing the **Start** menu or taskbar, changing display properties, adjusting the mouse, installing a printer, and so on.

- The **Search** command helps you locate files or folders on your system or your company's network. You can also use **Search** to locate Web pages or email addresses.

- The **Help** command brings up the Windows Help system, which provides quick pointers on using the operating system. You'll learn how to use **Help** in Lesson 6, "Getting Windows Help and Support."

My Documents and My Pictures The My Documents and My Pictures folders have been provided by Windows for your use. The My Documents folder typically contains files you create yourself, such as Word documents, Excel worksheets, and the like. The My Pictures folder usually contains scanned images, graphics downloaded from the Web, digital pictures, and graphics you create yourself using Paint or a similar program. You'll find the My Pictures folder within the My Documents folder, which is located in the main directory of drive C:.

- The **Run** command lets you manually enter a program's executable filename, along with its path and any switches that it might require. For example, you might use the **Run** command to initiate the setup command for a new software program.

- The **Log Off** command lets you log off your business or home network so that you can log back on as a different user. Use this command when you share your computer with a coworker or another member of the family and you each have a set of preferred Windows settings you want to use. Later in this lesson, you'll learn how to log on as a different user without shutting down the computer.

- The **Shut Down** command allows you to shut down Windows safely. You can also use this command to restart (*reboot*) your computer when needed. You'll learn how to shut down your computer later in this lesson.

Turn Off Log Off!   If your computer isn't connected to a business or home network, you can remove the **Log Off** command and shorten the **Start** menu. See Lesson 9 for help.

Selecting Commands from the Start Menu

To select a command from the **Start** menu, simply click the **Start** button, point to the command you want, and click again. When you select a command, additional menus are displayed. For example, when you select **Programs**, a listing of your favorite programs is displayed, along with your program groups. To select a command from one of these menus, slide the mouse pointer onto the menu (which holds the menu open) and click the command.

Personalized Menus

Windows Me has *personalized menus* that display the commands you use the most. When you select commands from the **Start** menu, Windows makes a note of them. The next time you display the **Start** menu, Windows presents you with the commands you use most often. If you want to select a command that isn't currently displayed, first you need to expand the **Start** menu by resting the mouse pointer on the expand button, as shown in Figure 1.3. Once the menu is expanded, all of its commands are displayed and you can click the one you want. You may notice that some commands on the expanded menu are indented; these are the commands that don't appear unless the menu is expanded.

Although personalized menus are easier to use because they display only a short list of commands, you may want to use fully expanded menus all the time. If you decide not to use personalized menus, you can turn them off by following the steps in Lesson 9.

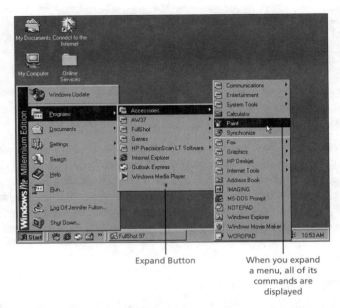

Expand Button

When you expand
a menu, all of its
commands are
displayed

FIGURE 1.3   To expand a menu, rest the mouse pointer on the
expand button.

Shutting Down Windows

When it's time to turn your computer off, don't just flip the OFF switch;
that isn't good for Windows or your data. Instead, you need to shut down
Windows and then let the system tell you when it's okay to flip the OFF
switch:

1. Close all your open applications, making sure that any docu-
    ments you're currently working on are saved.

2. Click the **Start** button.

3. From the **Start** menu, select **Shut Down**. Windows displays the
    dialog box shown in Figure 1.4.

FIGURE **1.4** The Shut Down Windows dialog box.

4. Choose **Shut down** from the **What do you want the computer to do?** list box, and then click **OK**. Windows initiates its shutdown procedure.

5. If Windows tells you it's safe to turn off your computer, turn off both your computer and monitor. (On most newer computers, you won't see this message because Windows will power down the computer and its monitor automatically.)

Other Shutdown Options

The **Shut Down** menu provides several additional options:

- **Stand By**   Some computers let you suspend their operations, maintaining power to the central processor but not the peripherals, hard drive, or display. This allows you to keep what you're currently doing on your computer with the minimum amount of power necessary. This is especially nice if you have a laptop computer running on batteries only. In Stand By mode, you can bring your computer up with a quick press of the **Spacebar** and begin working again. Stand By mode is an alternative to shutting down your computer and reloading everything when you want to work again. However, if the power to your computer is interrupted while it's in Stand By mode, you'll lose any data that hasn't been saved to the hard disk. If your computer supports Stand By mode, the **Stand By** command will appear on the **What do you want the computer to do?** list. For more information on power management, see Lesson 7, "Customizing Windows."

- **Hibernate**   This is an alternative to Shut Down mode that allows Windows to shut down properly, while saving any data in memory, and turn off the computer. Unlike Shut Down mode, your desktop will be restored as it was before hibernation (it won't be reset to Start Up condition). Like Stand By mode, this option appears only if your computer supports it.

- **Restart**   You might need to restart your computer after making a system configuration change (such as changing the screen resolution), or to simply refresh Windows' internal resources. You'll find that running multiple applications in Windows at once often causes a severe drain on your system's resources. By restarting your PC, you can remove all programs from memory and refresh your system.

The Old Ctrl+Alt+Delete   It used to be that you restarted your PC by pressing **Ctrl+Alt+Delete**. Now, this "three-finger salute" is used to bring up a dialog box that lets you end a task without shutting down the entire system. Or you can use it to initiate an emergency shutdown when your system freezes and refuses to respond.

Where's MS-DOS Mode?   In Windows ME, there's no DOS mode per se. If you want to run a DOS program, do so within Windows just as you'd start any Windows program. If your program requires you to display a DOS prompt first, click **Start, Programs, Accessories, MS-DOS Prompt**.

Logging On as a Different User

Windows allows multiple users to share the same computer while maintaining each user's individual preferences. This is especially handy in a household with three children and two adults sharing the same computer. It's accomplished by setting up passwords for the users. Then each user enters his password, thus *logging on,* when Windows is started. Logging on also affects your network connection—you're logged off the network and then logged back on as a different user.

By the way, logging on again doesn't require a complete shutdown of the system, but it will close all running applications. Make sure you save your work and shut down your programs before proceeding. To log on as a different user, follow these steps:

1. Click the **Start** button.

2. From the **Start** menu, select **Log Off**, as shown in Figure 1.5. The **Log Off Windows** dialog box appears.

FIGURE **1.5**   Logging off your network or changing user configurations.

3. Click **Yes**. The Welcome to Windows dialog box appears.

4. Enter the user name and password you want to use, and then click **OK**. The Windows desktop reappears—it may look different if the user name you entered is associated with a different configuration.

Setting Up Users   You can establish several users for your computer, each with his own desktop, My Documents and Favorites folders, and so on. See Lesson 12, "Accessing Resources on Your Home Network," for help with setting up users and configuring their preferences.

In this lesson, you learned about the major components of the Windows Desktop and how the mouse is used to manipulate those components. You also saw how to start, restart, and shut down Windows. In the next lesson, you'll learn the difference between the Classic and Active Desktops, along with how to use the taskbar and toolbars.

LESSON 2

Navigating the Windows Desktop

In this lesson, you'll learn the differences between the Active Desktop and the Classic Desktop. You'll also learn how to use the Windows taskbar and the toolbars.

Understanding the Windows Desktop

The Windows Desktop appears when you start Windows. The desktop contains objects, called *icons,* that you use to start applications, copy, move, and delete files, connect to the Internet, and perform other functions. The Classic Windows Desktop is shown in Figure 2.1.

Here are some brief descriptions of the more common desktop items:

Desktop   The basic Windows work area. Here you'll find icons for common programs.

Taskbar   Allows you to organize your applications and files and navigate between them.

Quick Launch and Address Toolbars   Two of the Windows tool bars, which provides convenient access to programs you use often.

Icons   Small pictures that represent files, folders, programs, and other objects that you work with.

Start button   Displays a menu of commands for starting programs, changing system settings, locating files, searching the Internet, updating the system, and obtaining help.

Mouse pointer   Indicates the current position of your mouse; also used to select text and choose commands.

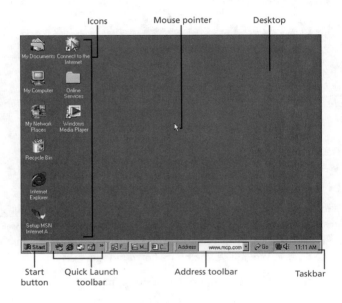

FIGURE 2.1   The Classic Windows Desktop.

Web Integration and the Active Desktop

Windows offers an alternative to the Classic Windows Desktop called the Active Desktop, as shown in Figure 2.2. The Active Desktop combines the aspects of the Classic Desktop with some of the features of a Web browser, making it an ideal choice for people who spend a lot of time on the Internet searching for up-to-date news, weather, and other information.

Channels can be automatically
updated on your system
as they change

Active Desktop Items
display specific content
such as the weather

Channel bar

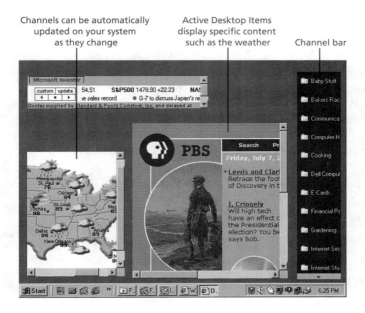

FIGURE 2.2   The Active Desktop displays Web pages in addition to
the Classic Desktop content.

Web Browser   A program used to view Web pages
on the World Wide Web. Web pages often contain
graphics, text, animations, and other special elements,
and a Web browser is designed to display these elements properly. Popular Web browsers include
Microsoft Internet Explorer and Netscape Navigator.

Channel   A Web page that's displayed on your desktop in a channel window and updated automatically
as you wish. When you select a channel for display on
the desktop, it appears in a *channel window* that's
automatically updated as needed.

Channel bar   Allows you to access Web data quickly.

Active Desktop Item   A window that displays specific
information (such as the time, current weather, or
stock prices) that's automatically updated as needed.

With the Active Desktop, you can have up-to-date Web content at your fingertips without the hassle of constantly logging onto the Internet, starting your Web browser, and selecting a Web page to view. For example, you might want to display current stock prices, news, weather, or even updates from your company's local intranet on your desktop so you can quickly review them from time to time. You'll learn how to change to the Active Desktop, subscribe to channels, and display Active Desktop Items in Lesson 27, "Displaying Internet Content on the Desktop."

 Compatible Options   If you use the Active Desktop, you may want to make Windows more Web-like by turning on the Single Click option. See Lesson 10, "Accessing Your Drives, Folders, and Files," for help. In addition, Windows comes with special toolbars you can use to quickly view Web pages that you choose not to display on the desktop.

Using the Taskbar

At the bottom of the desktop is the taskbar. In addition to the **Start** button, the taskbar contains many other elements, as shown in Figure 2.3.

FIGURE 2.3   The Windows taskbar.

- **Start button**   With the **Start** button, you can select commands to open programs, customize Windows, locate files, and search the Internet.

- **Active programs and open windows**   Your currently running programs and any open windows, such as folder windows,

appear as buttons on the taskbar. To switch to an open program
or window, simply click its button. The currently active window
appears on the taskbar as a pushed-in button.

- **Windows Toolbars** Windows contains several toolbars that
  provide quick access to popular programs and functions, such as
  Web addressing. These toolbars include Links, Address,
  Desktop, and Quick Launch. In addition, you can create your
  own toolbars. See the "Using the Windows Toolbars" section
  later in this lesson for help.

- **Status area** On the right side of the taskbar, icons will appear
  occasionally to update you on the status of various things, such
  as the current time (as shown in Figure 2.3), your Internet connection, whether you have new email messages in your inbox,
  and so on. To see what a status icon is telling you, move the
  mouse pointer over it and a message appears.

Moving and Hiding the Taskbar

Initially, the taskbar appears at the bottom of the desktop. However, you
can move it to the top, left, or right side of the desktop by simply clicking
it, holding down the mouse button, and dragging it.

You can also hide the taskbar and cause it to reappear only when needed.
Hiding the taskbar gives you more room on your desktop to view your
programs. To hide the taskbar, follow these steps:

1. Click the **Start** button. The **Start** menu appears.

2. Select **Settings**. A cascading menu appears.

3. Select **Taskbar and Start Menu**. The Taskbar and Start Menu
   Properties dialog box appears, as shown in Figure 2.4. (You can
   also right-click the taskbar and select **Properties** to display this.)

4. Click the **Auto hide** option to turn it on.

5. Click **OK**. The taskbar disappears. To make it reappear, move
   the mouse pointer toward the taskbar's former location.

FIGURE 2.4   The Taskbar and Start Menu Properties dialog box.

To learn other ways to customize the taskbar, see Lesson 9, "Customizing Other Attributes of Windows."

Using the Windows Toolbars

Windows comes with several toolbars that you can use to access the Internet and your programs more quickly. You've probably noticed the Quick Launch toolbar already. It's placed on the taskbar when Windows is set up. These toolbars initially appear on the taskbar, but you can drag them to the desktop when needed for more convenient access.

Here are the Windows toolbars:

- **Links**   This toolbar provides access to Web sites you've created links to in Internet Explorer.

- **Address**   When you type an Internet address here and then click **Go**, Internet Explorer opens to display it.

- **Desktop**   Displays the icons that appear on your desktop. This allows you to access those programs when the desktop is covered with open windows or Active Desktop content.

- **Quick Launch**   Provides easy access to the programs you use most, such as Internet Explorer, Outlook Express, your desktop, and the Active Channel Viewer.

Add to a Toolbar   You can add your own program icons to the Quick Launch toolbar by dragging shortcut icons onto the toolbar. You'll learn how to create shortcuts in Lesson 7, "Customizing Windows."

You can create your own toolbars as well.

To display a Windows toolbar, follow these steps:

1. Right-click an open space on the taskbar and select **Toolbars** from the shortcut menu that appears.

2. Click the toolbar you want to display. The toolbar appears on the taskbar.

To use a Windows toolbar, simply click one of its buttons. If not all the buttons are displayed, a button with double right-arrows appears at its right edge. Click this button and a menu of additional toolbar buttons appears. Select the button you want from this menu. If the toolbar has a text box (such as the text box on the Address toolbar), click inside the text box and type in your information (in this case, the address of the Web page you want to display), and then press **Enter**.

To remove a toolbar from the taskbar, right-click the taskbar, select **Toolbars**, and select the toolbar you want to remove.

You can adjust the amount of space the toolbar takes up on the taskbar by dragging its *handle*—the ridges that appear on its left edge—left or right. Or, you can drag the toolbar off the taskbar and onto the desktop. Simply click anywhere on the toolbar, press and hold down the left mouse button, drag the toolbar onto the desktop, and release the mouse button when the toolbar is in position. Once the toolbar appears on the desktop, you can resize it just like any other window. See Lesson 3, "Working with Windows," for help.

Tidy Up Your Toolbars   Another way to make a Windows toolbar smaller is to remove its title, such as "Address". To remove the title from a Windows toolbar, right-click the toolbar and select **Show Title** to turn that option off. In addition, some toolbars display the name of each item along with an icon. Sometimes, only the icon is necessary to identify a particular button. In such a case, right-click the toolbar and select **Show Text** to turn that option off as well.

Creating a Toolbar

You might want to create your own Windows toolbar to provide quick access to a favorite folder or Web site. Follow these steps:

1. Right-click the taskbar and select **Toolbars.**

2. Select **New Toolbar** from the shortcut menu. The New Toolbar dialog box appears.

3. Select the folder whose contents you want to display as a toolbar, or type the address of a Web page (such as http://www.cnn.com). Then click **OK**.

If you select a folder, a toolbar appears with icons representing the contents of that folder. You can then click the icon for a document, for example, and open that document with its associated program. If you enter the address of a Web page in the New Toolbar dialog box, that address appears on the toolbar. To see the contents of that Web page, drag the toolbar off the taskbar and onto the desktop. The Web page appears in a small window with a title bar but no Internet Explorer toolbars.

Keep in mind that the toolbars you create are only temporary. If you remove a toolbar you've created from the taskbar, you'll need to create it again to get it back. However, if you keep the toolbar displayed on the taskbar, it will remain there even if you restart your PC.

Your Favorite Programs Toolbar   If you want to create a custom toolbar with icons for your favorite programs, just create a new folder and fill it with shortcut
icons to the programs you use most often. Then create
a toolbar that points to that folder. You'll learn how
to create shortcut icons in Lesson 7. As described in
the previous section, you can also add icons for your
favorite programs to the Quick Launch toolbar instead
of creating your own toolbar.

Displaying the Desktop Quickly

As you begin to feel comfortable using Windows, you may find that you
have several windows open at one time. In addition, these windows are
often maximized to make their contents easier to see. It can be a hassle to
display the desktop (where you can access a desktop icon or view Active
Desktop content) because you must minimize all your maximized windows one by one. Instead, click the **Display Desktop** icon on the **Quick
Launch** toolbar to quickly display the desktop.

In this lesson, you learned the differences between the Classic Desktop
and the Active Desktop. You also learned how to use the taskbar and the
Windows toolbars. In the next lesson, you'll learn how to resize, minimize, maximize, and otherwise control open windows.

LESSON 3

Working with Windows

In this lesson, you'll learn how to open, close, resize, move, arrange, and scroll through the contents of windows.

What's a Window?

A *window* is a container for data, such as files, folders, programs, icons, and so on. Depending on your preference, a window can occupy a particular region of the screen or the entire screen. Figure 3.1 shows the parts of a typical window.

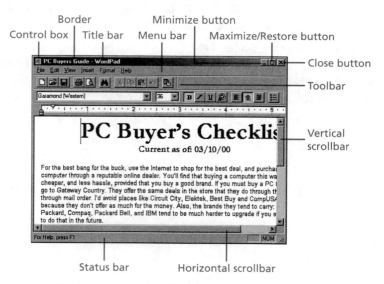

FIGURE 3.1   The parts of a typical window.

Here are some brief descriptions of these elements:

Control box   Provides a menu with commands for controlling the window's size, closing the window, and moving the window. Generally, the control box contains the identifying icon for the program that uses this window. For example, in Figure 3.1, the icon for WordPad serves as the control box. On an Active Desktop Item (a window that contains Web content), the control box looks like a down arrow.

Border   The frame that surrounds the window. You can resize a window by stretching its border.

Title bar   Displays the title of the window, which includes the name of the program (if applicable) and the name of its active file.

Minimize button   Click this button to remove the window from the screen temporarily.

Maximize/Restore button   Click the **Maximize** button and the window fills the screen; click the **Restore** button to return the window to its former size.

Close button   Click this button to close a window and exit its associated program.

Vertical scrollbar   Use this scrollbar to view data hidden above or below the displayed data.

Horizontal scrollbar   Use this scrollbar to view data hidden to the left or right of the displayed data.

Menu bar   Contains the main categories of commands you give to an application. When you click one of these main categories, such as File or Edit, its list of associated commands drops down and you can select a command or pull up a submenu from that list. You'll learn how to use menus in Lesson 4, "Using Toolbars and Menus."

Toolbar   Most applications use toolbars; they contain buttons that you click to perform common commands such as printing, opening, and saving a document.

Status bar   Like toolbars, most applications include a status bar at the bottom of the window. It alerts you to changes in the program and provides other useful information.

Opening a Window

Generally, windows open themselves when you launch an application or open a document within that application.

When you launch an application from the **Start** menu or an Explorer listing, or by double-clicking its icon on the desktop, the application responds by opening its own main window. For an application such as WordPad, which comes with Windows, the window that pops up will be empty, ready for you to enter data into it and save that data as a document file. But for more sophisticated applications that can display multiple documents at a time, such as Microsoft Word, an empty document window might be contained within the application's main window.

 Single-Click Option   Double-clicking typically means "Open up!" But if you're using the *single-click* option, you can open a window with one click on a filename, folder, or icon. See Lesson 10, "Accessing Your Drives, Folders, and Files," for help.

Switching Between Windows

Before you work with the contents of a window, that window must be active. For example, to use a particular program, you must activate the window in which it's contained. Regardless of how many windows you have open at a time, you can only have one *active* window. The active window appears with a brighter title bar than the other open windows (it's blue under the default Windows settings).

To activate a window—in other words, to switch from one window to another—you can perform any of the following:

- Click any part of the open window.

- Press **Alt+Tab** to scroll through a list of open windows. When the list appears, press and hold down the **Alt** key as you press **Tab** until the icon for the window you want to view is highlighted. Then release the **Alt+Tab**.

- Click the window's button on the taskbar.

Sizing a Window with Maximize, Minimize, and Restore

A window can be maximized (made to fill the screen) or minimized (removed from the screen temporarily). To maximize a window, click its **Maximize** button (see Figure 3.1). When the window is already maximized, this button changes to the **Restore** button. Click this button to restore the window to its former size, revealing part of the desktop. You might want a window to be maximized when you're concentrating on its application specifically. On the other hand, when you're working with more than one application at the same time—and with Windows, you can—you might want to see all of their windows simultaneously. In that case, you'll want to leave them at their restored size. To quickly maximize a window, double-click on its title bar. Then, to restore a window to its original size, double-click the title bar again.

The **Minimize** button removes the window from the desktop without terminating (closing) its program. To restore the window so you can start using the program again, click that program's button on the taskbar.

 Don't Minimize the Usefulness of This Tip   To quickly minimize a window, double-click its button on the taskbar. This technique lets you minimize a window even if it's not currently visible.

Resizing an Active Desktop Item Window

The sizing buttons on an Active Desktop Item window are a bit different than an ordinary window, as shown in Figure 3.2.

 Active Desktop Item   A special window on the Active Desktop that displays the same kind of information all the time, such as the weather, the time, or stock prices, all updated through your Internet link. This is different from a channel window, which displays varying Internet content from a specific channel provider (such as Time, CNN Interactive, MSNBC, and so on). A channel window acts like any ordinary Windows window, and can be resized accordingly. To learn more about Active Desktop Items and channel windows, see Lesson 27, "Displaying Internet Content on the Desktop."

FIGURE 3.2   Sizing buttons on an Active Desktop Item window.

Here's a brief description of each button and its purpose:

	Cover Desktop	Maximizes the Active Desktop Item window. It covers the desktop completely, with the desktop icons—if displayed—overlaying the Active Desktop Item window.
	Split Desktop with Icons	Displays the Active Desktop Item window on the right side of the desktop, and the desktop icons on the left.
	Restore	Restores the window to its previous size.
	Close	Closes the Active Desktop Item window.

To access the sizing buttons for an Active Desktop Item window, you must display its title bar. Move the mouse pointer slowly towards the top of the window and rest it there for a moment. The title bar appears.

Minimizing All Windows

To minimize all your windows at once so that only the desktop is visible, do the following:

1. Right-click an *empty* portion of the taskbar (where there are no minimized application buttons).

2. From the pop-up menu that appears, select **Minimize All Windows**.

To restore your windows, right-click the taskbar again and select **Undo Minimize All**.

If you're currently displaying the Quick Launch toolbar on your taskbar, you can also use it to minimize all your open windows. Simply click the **Show Desktop** button.

My Web Windows Are Still There!   Using the Minimize All Windows command doesn't affect the Active Desktop Items you might be displaying on your Active Desktop. (However, channel windows are minimized with the other windows.) To remove Active Channel Items temporarily, switch back to the Classic Desktop. Right-click the desktop, select **Active Desktop**, and then select **Show Web Content** to turn the option off. Repeat these steps to return to the Active Desktop whenever you like.

Sizing a Window's Borders

While a window is not maximized, you can change its size by dragging its border. When you stretch or shrink a window, you can move one side or corner at a time. Here's how to resize any kind of window—an ordinary window, a channel window, or an Active Desktop Item window:

1. Move the mouse pointer to one edge or corner of the window. The pointer changes to a black two-headed arrow.

No Arrow?   If you don't see a two-headed arrow when you move the mouse pointer to a window's border, the window's size probably can't be changed.

2. While the pointer is a two-headed arrow, click and hold down the left mouse button.

3. Drag the mouse pointer in the direction you want to stretch or shrink the window. As you're dragging, an outline representing the window's new size appears.

4. When the window is the size you want, release the mouse button.

See What You're Doing If you prefer, you can display the resized window and its contents while dragging, instead of viewing a mere outline. Just right-click the desktop, select **Active Desktop, Customize My Desktop,** click the **Effects** tab, and select **Show window contents while dragging.**

 Can't Resize a Window? Many applications' windows have minimum applicable sizes. So if the window doesn't budge but the pointer continues to move, the window is as small as it can be.

Using Scrollbars

You can use scrollbars to display the contents of a file that extends beyond the window's current viewing area. Figure 3.3 shows a window with both horizontal and vertical scrollbars.

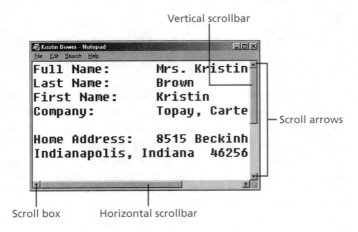

FIGURE 3.3 A window with both scrollbars active.

Here's how you use scrollbars:

- To move by a small amount, click the arrow at either end of the scrollbar that points in the direction you want to move.

- To move by a larger amount, click the open space on either side of the scroll box.

- To move quickly through a document, drag the scroll box along the scrollbar. Many Windows programs move the contents of the window as you move the scroll box; others wait until you release the button to execute the move. Some programs provide a screen tip that displays the page number of the document as you drag the scroll box. This lets you quickly scroll to the exact page you want.

 Be a Third Wheel   If your mouse has a scrolling wheel (such as the IntelliMouse), you can scroll more easily. To scroll by a small amount, rotate the wheel up or down. This enables you to scroll without moving the mouse to the scrollbar. To scroll quickly, click the wheel and move the mouse up or down. Click the wheel again to quit automatic scrolling.

Moving a Window

The title bar displays the name of the program being used by the window, as well as the name of the current active document. (An exception here is the title bar for an Active Desktop Item—as seen in Figure 3.2—which doesn't display a title at all.) The title bar also functions as a handle of sorts. To move a window onscreen, click and drag the window's title bar. When you move a window, its outline follows the mouse pointer.

You can also move Active Desktop Items, such as the one shown in Figure 3.2. Just remember to display the title bar first by moving the mouse pointer toward the top of the Active Desktop Item window. When the title bar appears, click it and drag the window wherever you want.

Special Effect   If you want to display the contents of the window as you drag it, right-click the desktop, select **Active Desktop, Customize My Desktop,** click the **Effects** tab, and turn on the **Show window contents while dragging** option.

 Can't Move a Maximized Window?   You can't move a window that's been maximized. There's no place for it to go.

Arranging Windows on the Desktop

When you have three or four windows open simultaneously, and all of them are pertinent to the job you're working on, stretching and shrinking all of them so that they fit precisely might not be convenient. Thankfully, Windows has a few ways for you to automatically arrange several windows *without* the drag-and-drop maneuver.

Cascading Windows

All the windows in a *cascaded* set overlap one another so that the upper and left borders are always visible—not unlike the way you'd fan out a hand of gin rummy. Figure 3.4 shows a set of four cascaded windows.

Here's how you can make Windows automatically cascade all the open windows on the desktop:

1. Right-click an empty portion of the taskbar.

2. From the shortcut menu that appears, select **Cascade Windows**.

By the way, the **Cascade Windows** command doesn't affect Active Desktop Items.

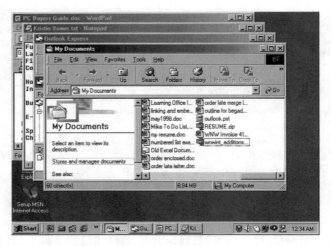

FIGURE 3.4   A set of cascaded windows.

Tiling Windows

By comparison, each window in a *tiled* set (whether the tiling is horizontal or vertical) doesn't overlap in any way—and that's the idea. Figure 3.5 shows the same four windows as Figure 3.4, this time tiled horizontally.

All tiled windows are of equal size. If you have a large number of windows open, tiling can result in rather small windows.

To tile your open windows, right-click an empty portion of the taskbar and select either **Tile Windows Horizontally** or **Tile Windows Vertically**. The Tile commands don't affect Active Desktop Items.

Closing a Window

When you're finished with a window, you should close it. This frees up system resources for other activities. By the way, closing a program's window is the same thing as exiting the program.

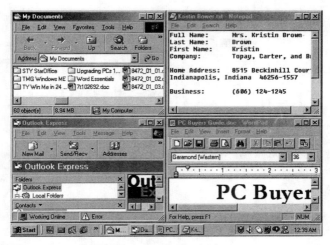

FIGURE 3.5   A set of horizontally tiled windows.

Some windows will immediately close themselves when you click the **Close** button. Other windows—especially programs with open files—might ask if you want to save your information before closing the window. You can also close a window from the Windows taskbar; just right-click on the program's button and select **Close**.

To close an Active Desktop Item, click its **Close** button (see Figure 3.2). Closing an Active Desktop Item temporarily removes it from the Active Desktop. To get the window back, right-click the desktop and select **Active Desktop** from the shortcut menu. Then select the Active Desktop Item you want to display from those listed at the bottom of the cascading menu.

In this lesson, you learned the various parts of a window. You also learned how to move, resize, minimize, maximize, and close a window. In addition, you learned how to operate scrollbars and arrange the windows that programs use on the Windows Desktop. In the next lesson, you'll learn how to use toolbars and select menu commands.

LESSON 4
Using Toolbars and Menus

In this lesson, you'll learn how to use the toolbars that come with many Windows programs. You'll also learn how to select commands from menus.

Using Toolbars

A *toolbar* is a collection of buttons that represent commands. When you click a toolbar button, the associated command is executed. Not every Windows program uses a toolbar, but many do.

 What About Windows Toolbars? In this lesson, you'll learn how to use the toolbars included with many Windows programs, such as Explorer and My Computer. If you want to learn how to use the toolbars that appear on the Windows taskbar, see Lesson 2, "Navigating the Windows Desktop."

Because toolbars offer access to the most common commands, many programs have toolbars that contain the same buttons. Figure 4.1 shows My Computer and some of its toolbars.

The **Delete** button is a common type of toolbar button. You select the files you want to remove and then click the **Delete** button to delete them. Notice the order of events here: You select the object of your command *first*, and *then* you click the button whose command you want to carry out—not the other way around.

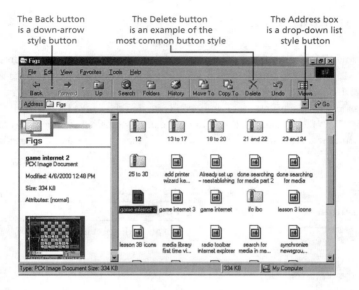

The Back button is a down-arrow style button

The Delete button is an example of the most common button style

The Address box is a drop-down list style button

FIGURE 4.1   My Computer uses common toolbars.

The **Back** button in My Computer is another type of button. The down-arrow to the right of the icon indicates the presence of a drop-down list. If you simply click the **Back** button, the My Computer window moves back to the previous directory (or Web page). But if you click the down-arrow portion of the **Back** button, a menu drops down, showing the most recent directories (or Web pages) in My Computer's history buffer. You then choose the directory (or Web page) you want to move back to by clicking it in the list.

The **Address** box is an example of the third type of toolbar button: a *drop-down list box*. Like the **Back** button, the **Address** box drops down when you click the down-arrow button, revealing a menu—in this case, the hierarchy folder. You choose the directory you want My Computer to move to by clicking it.

Most toolbars you will use are made up of some combination of these three types of buttons.

Common Toolbars

Many Windows programs, such as Windows Explorer, My Computer, and Internet Explorer, use the same set of toolbars: Standard Buttons, Address Bar, Links, and Radio. The purposes of the buttons on these toolbars are explained in Tables 4.1, 4.2, and 4.3. (The Radio toolbar is described in Lesson 25, "Using Internet Explorer") Note that the Links toolbar displays Web pages, and the Radio toolbar controls music downloaded from the Internet. Without an Internet connection, these two toolbars are useless.

TABLE 4.1   The Standard Buttons Toolbar

Button	Name	Purpose
← Back ▾	Back	Displays the previous folder.
→ ▾	Forward	Returns to the original folder.
⬆	Up	Moves up in the folder hierarchy.
🔍 Search	Search	Displays the Search pane so you can locate a missing file, folder, Web page, or email address.
📁 Folders	Folders	Displays the Folder list.
🕒 History	History	Displays a listing of Web pages or folders you've recently visited so you can display them again.
📂	Move To	Moves the selected files to the folder you choose.
📋	Copy To	Copies the selected files to the folder you select.
✕	Delete	Removes the selected file or folder.

Button	Name	Purpose
	Undo	Undoes the last action.
	Views	Lets you choose the way files and folders are displayed.

TABLE 4.2   The Address Toolbar

Button	Name	Purpose
	Address box	Lets you enter or select the address of the folder you want to view.
	Go	Displays the contents of the folder listed in the Address box.

TABLE 4.3   The Links Toolbar

Button	Name	Purpose
	Best of the Web	Displays links to some of the best pages on the Web in categories such as Work & Money, Computing, and Entertainment. You can also search the Internet from this page.
	Channel Guide	Displays a listing of audio and video files you can play using Windows Media Player.

continues

TABLE **4.3**   continued

Button	Name	Purpose
Customize Links	Customize Links	Displays a page that shows you how to customize the Links bar.
Free HotMail	Free HotMail	Displays the HotMail home page, where you can sign up for free Internet email.
Internet Start	Internet Start	Displays the MSN home page.
Microsoft	Microsoft	Displays the Microsoft home page.
Windows Media	Windows Media	Displays the Windows Media home page.
Windows Update	Windows Update	Displays the Windows Update home page, where you can select updates to Windows Me.
Windows	Windows	Displays the Windows home page, where you can learn about other versions of Windows.
Is Your Operating System Genuine	Is your operating system genuine	Displays information on software piracy.

Moving Toolbars

Not all toolbars in Windows can be moved from place to place. You can tell if a toolbar *can* be moved by a single ridge near the left edge (or the top edge if it's a vertical toolbar). You might want to move a toolbar into the work area to make it easier to work with a particular bit of text or a graphic image.

Here are some general methods for moving toolbars:

- To move a toolbar into the work area, click an empty space on the toolbar and drag the toolbar wherever you like. Typically, the toolbar will take on a more rectangular shape, which you can adjust as you might adjust the size of a window.

- To move a toolbar so that it appears *underneath* another toolbar at the top of the window, drag it on top of the toolbar under which you want it to appear and release the mouse button.

- To adjust the boundaries between two toolbars that are horizontally adjacent to each other (for example, the Address and the Links toolbars in Explorer, as shown in Figure 4.1), position the pointer between the two toolbars so that it changes to a black two-headed arrow. Then drag the border in either direction.

- To swap positions between two toolbars sharing the same line (such as the Address and Links toolbars in Explorer, as the Address and Links toolbars do in Figure 4.1), click the ridge of one of the toolbars. Then drag that ridge past the ridge of the other toolbar.

Using Menus

The menu bar is a Windows program's chief device for presenting you with its available commands. Typically, a menu bar is placed just under the title bar in a window (see Figure 4.2). However, some newer programs let you move the menu bar to a different position onscreen, as you might move a toolbar (Explorer is one such example).

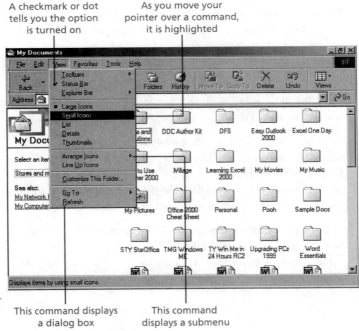

FIGURE 4.2   A typical menu.

When you open one of the menus on a menu bar, it drops down a list of related commands from which you can choose. Here's what typically happens when you choose a command:

- Most commands are executed by the program immediately after you select them. **Cut** and **Paste** are classic examples. Once you select them, the program carries them out without delay and without asking you anything else.

- If a command has a right-pointing arrow, a submenu (also called a cascading menu) with additional choices will appear. For example, in Explorer, if you open the **File** menu and select **New**, a submenu appears. The submenu in this case lists various objects such as folder, shortcut, bitmap image, and so on that answer the question "Create a new *what?*"

- If a command is followed by an ellipsis (...), that command requires more information from you before it can be executed. Thus, when you select such a command, a dialog box appears with several options from which you can choose. For example, the **File, Open** command displays a dialog box from which you can select the file you want to open.

- If a command is preceded by a dot or a check mark, that command is currently active (turned on). To turn the command off, choose it again (to remove its check mark) or select a similar command (to move the dot in front of that command instead).

 Personalized menus You encountered personalized menus in Lesson 1 when you learned about the Start menu, which displays only the most recently used commands. A personalized menu expands to display less frequently used commands when the mouse pointer is rested on its expand button (double down-arrows at the bottom of the unexpanded menu). Many Windows applications use personalized menus, such as Windows Explorer, My Computer, Internet Explorer, and Microsoft Office.

Choosing Menu Commands

To select a menu command with the mouse, click one of the menus so that it drops down, slide the mouse pointer down the menu to highlight the command you want, and then click it. (You'll notice that when you highlight a command, its description appears on the status bar.) If a submenu is involved, it will pop up to the right of that command (or to its left if there's no room to the right). At that point, just slide the mouse pointer onto the submenu (which will keep the submenu open) and click the command you want.

If you don't see the command you need, or if you change your mind, you can click anywhere *outside* the menu area to dismiss the menu altogether. Or you can move the pointer to another menu category, without clicking, to make its menu drop down instead.

To use the keyboard to select a menu command, press and hold down the **Alt** key as you press the underlined letter of the menu command. For example, to open the **File** menu, press **Alt+F**. Once the menu is opened, press the underlined letter of the command you want. For example, to select the **Open** command from the **File** menu, press the letter **O**. You can also use the up- and down-arrow keys on the keyboard to move the highlight line to the command you want and then press **Enter** to select the command.

Using Shortcut Keys

Many commands provide another method for you to select them with the keyboard—without having to open the menu first. For example, the common commands **Cut**, **Copy**, and **Paste** have shortcut key combinations that you can press to select them: **Ctrl+X** for **Cut**, **Ctrl+C** for **Copy**, and **Ctrl+V** for **Paste**. To issue the **Copy** command using its shortcut keys, press and hold down the **Ctrl** key as you press the letter **C**. Shortcut keys are listed next to their corresponding command on menus. For a complete listing of the shortcut keys associated with the program you're using, consult that program's Help system, under the term "shortcut keys" or "keyboard shortcuts."

Using Shortcut Menus

As an alternative to using the menu bar or toolbars, you can issue commands to many Windows programs using the right-click method, which brings up a *shortcut menu* or *context menu*. With this method, you point to the onscreen item that will serve as the object of your command—for instance, a highlighted sentence, a row of cells in a worksheet, or a selected group of files. Then you right-click. If the program supports shortcut menus, one will pop up onscreen near the pointer, as shown in Figure 4.3. From there, you can click a menu command to issue that command to the program or click outside the menu area to dismiss the menu.

Figure **4.3**   You can access common commands with a shortcut menu.

A shortcut menu is also called a context menu because the commands that are displayed are related to whatever the mouse was pointing to when you right-clicked.

Default Command   On the shortcut menu shown in Figure 4.3, the **Open** command is bold. This means that **Open** is the default command—the command that will be executed if you double-click this object (in this case, a file in My Computer).

Shortcut menus are available outside applications as well. For example, right-clicking the desktop brings up a shortcut menu from which you can select commands that arrange your icons, switch you between the Active and Classic Desktops, and change the desktop's properties.

In this lesson, you learned how commands are issued to Windows programs. You studied the operation and arrangement of toolbars onscreen. You then examined the crucial role played by the menu bar in all Windows applications, and you were introduced to the shortcut menu, which provides a convenient alternative to the menu bar. In the next lesson, you'll learn how to select options from dialog boxes.

LESSON 5

Using Dialog Boxes

In this lesson, you'll learn how to select options using all types of dialog box elements, such as text boxes, list boxes, option buttons, and check boxes.

When a Dialog Box Appears

Typically, a dialog box appears after you select a menu command marked with an ellipsis (…). This tells you that the command you've selected requires more information from you before the program can execute it. The dialog box allows you to tell the program which options to use with the command.

Selecting Dialog Box Options

Windows uses a handful of standardized elements that work the same way for any dialog box you encounter. To move through the objects in the dialog box, press the **Tab** key. To back up to the previous element, press **Shift+Tab**. Here's a listing of the elements and how to use them:

- **Text box** A box into which you type text, such as the name of a file, a font size, or a password to access the Windows desktop. To replace existing text, drag over it to highlight it and then type what you want to replace it. Figure 5.1 shows a dialog box from WordPad that contains a text box.

- **List box** A rectangle that lists several choices, just like a menu. If there are more entries in the list than can be shown at once, a scroll bar appears along the right and/or bottom edge. To select more than one item at a time from a list box that allows

you to make multiple choices (such as a file list), hold down the
Ctrl key and click each item. You can also hold down the **Shift**
key and click the first and last item to select those two items and
all the ones between them. A list box is shown in Figure 5.1.

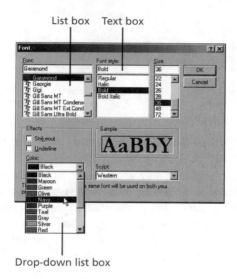

Drop-down list box

FIGURE **5.1**   A text box and two types of list boxes.

- **Drop-down list box**   A variation of a standard list box; the list
  is revealed when you click the down arrow. To select something
  from the list, click it. You can't change or add to the items in a
  list. Figure 5.1 shows a drop-down list box.

- **Combo box**   A hybrid of the text box and the list box. The top
  line of a combo box works like a regular text box, featuring a
  blinking cursor. You can type a choice into this box or choose
  one from the list below the text line. A combo box supports only
  one choice at a time.

- **Check box**   A small square in which a check mark is placed,
  indicating an active option. Check boxes may be grouped
  together, in which case you can choose more than one option.
  Figure 5.2 shows a group of check boxes.

Tabs create several "pages" within a dialog

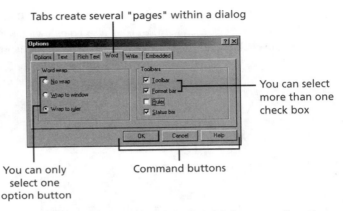

You can select more than one check box

You can only select one option button

Command buttons

FIGURE 5.2   A tabbed dialog box featuring check boxes and option buttons.

- **Option buttons**   Also known as *radio buttons,* option buttons represent a multiple-choice situation. Just as with check boxes, you click the dot or the label beside an option button to make that choice. Unlike check boxes, you can choose only one option in the set. Figure 5.2 shows a dialog box with a set of option buttons.

- **Command button**   This is the most common button in a dialog box. For example, the **OK** and **Cancel** buttons are common command buttons. After making selections in a dialog box, click **OK** to issue the command with the options you've selected, or click **Cancel** to cancel the command. Most dialog boxes have a *default* command button, which is generally the **OK** button. Press **Enter** at any time while the dialog box is active to activate the default command button. Press **Esc** to dismiss the dialog box without issuing the command. Some dialog boxes contain command buttons that display additional dialog boxes! When this happens, make your selection(s) and click **OK** to return to the main dialog box.

Keyboard Shortcut If a dialog box contains a label with a certain letter underlined—such as **No wrap**—holding down the **Alt** key while pressing the underlined letter on the keyboard immediately activates that control. For example, in Figure 5.2, holding down the **Alt** key and pressing **N** places a box around the **No wrap** option and turns it on.

Tabbed Dialog Boxes

Many dialog boxes have *tabs* that compartmentalize the information into multiple pages. A tabbed dialog box looks a little like a file drawer, where you thumb through the tabs sticking up in order to find the folder you want. A tabbed dialog box is shown in Figure 5.2.

To change pages in a dialog box, click one of the tabs. Press **Ctrl+Tab** to move to the next tabbed page in the sequence, or press **Shift+Ctrl+Tab** to move to the previous one.

In this lesson, you learned how to make selections in a dialog box using the most common elements: text boxes, list boxes, drop-down list boxes, check boxes, option buttons, and command buttons. In the next lesson, you'll learn how to access help.

LESSON 6

Getting Windows Help and Support

In this lesson, you'll learn all about the new Windows Me Help and Support system, including the Index, Search, Tours and tutorials, Assisted support, and What's This features.

Getting Help in Windows

Help is always close at hand in Windows. When you press **F1**, the Help system is activated. You can also activate Help by clicking the **Start** button and selecting the **Help** command.

The new Windows Me Help and Support system is HTML-based, which means that it works and acts like pages on the Web. Like Web pages, related Help pages are accessed through underlined *hyperlinks*. So if you're familiar with browsing the Internet for information, you'll feel comfortable using Help and Support. If not, you'll be relieved to know that it's simple and easy to use.

 Hyperlink   A bit of underlined text (typically blue) that, when clicked, displays a related page of information. Move the mouse pointer over a hyperlink and it changes to a hand; click the hyperlink to activate it and display the page. Hyperlinks may also appear as icons, but they work the same as text links.

Help and Support consists of several parts:

- **Home**   The main Help and Support page. By clicking a link displayed on this page, you can move deeper into Help and eventually display a Help topic.

- **Index**   Similar to the index in the back of a book.

- **Search**   Lets you search Help and Support for a particular word or phrase.

- **Assisted support**   Connects you to Microsoft's technical support Web site.

- **Tours and tutorials**   Displays a list of special online tutorials that walk you through a specific task.

In this lesson, you'll learn how to use all of these features.

Finding Help from the Home Page

When you start Help and Support, it displays its home page (starting page). The Help and Support window displays information in two panes, as shown in Figure 6.1. The left pane displays help topics. The right pane initially displays some basic information on using Help and Support, but after you select a help topic from the left pane, the right pane displays information on that help topic.

To display a topic of interest beginning from the home page, do one of the following:

- Click a topic on the left, such as **Personalizing Your Computer**.

- Click a recently viewed topic from the **Recently viewed help topics** list on the right.

- Search for a topic to display. See "Using the Search Feature," later in this lesson for help.

If you click a topic on the left, a list of additional topics appears. Keep clicking topics until you find the one you want to display. Displayable topics appear with either a question mark, Internet Explorer icon, or movie camera icon. If you click a topic marked with a question mark icon, the topic appears in the right pane (see Figure 6.2). If you click a Web topic with an Internet Explorer icon, Internet Explorer appears. A page on Microsoft's support Web site is then displayed. If you click a movie camera icon, the tour window opens to display the tour. You'll learn more about tours and tutorials later in this lesson.

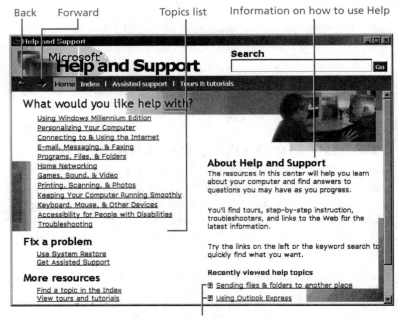

FIGURE 6.1   Welcome to Windows Help and Support.

 Internet Connection Needed   To view an topic marked with an Internet Explorer icon, you must be connected to the Internet.

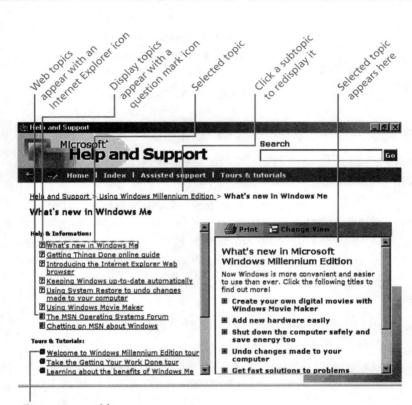

Tours appear with
a movie camera icon

FIGURE 6.2   Select a displayable topic and it appears on the right.

As you browse deeper and deeper into Help and Support, you'll notice
that the topics and subtopics you've opened appear in a line at the top of
the window (see Figure 6.2). To return to a previous subtopic, just click it.

You might see one of the following within the topic text:

- **Green underlined term**   Click one of these terms and a defini-
  tion appears in a small window. Click outside this window to
  close it.

- **Related topics**   When you click **Related topics**, which often
  appears at the end of a topic, a small window appears with a list

of related topics. Click one of these topics to display it. (If there's only one related topic, it's displayed immediately after you click **Related topics**.)

- **Troubleshooter link**   Click **XXXXX Troubleshooter** for a series of pages that help you resolve a particular problem with your system.

At the top of the topic pane, two buttons appear:

Print   Prints the displayed topic.

Change view   Reduces the Help and Support window so that only the topic pane appears. Click this button again to redisplay the entire Help and Support window.

At the top of the Help and Support window, you'll find these buttons as well:

Back   Returns you to a previously viewed Help page.

Forward   After you've clicked **Back**, click this button to return to your original Help page.

The **Index**, **Assisted support**, and **Tours & tutorials** buttons that appear to the right of the **Back** and **Forward** buttons will be discussed in detail later in this lesson. Click the Home button to redisplay the home page (starting page) at any time.

I Can't See!   If the left or right pane is too small to clearly see the information listed, you can adjust the size of either pane by dragging the border that separates them left or right.

Using the Index Feature

Help's Index feature is similar to an index you might find at the back of a book. You simply type in the word you're looking for and associated topics appear in a list, as shown in Figure 6.3. Select a topic from this list and it's displayed in the right pane.

Select a topic from those listed   Type a word or phrase here   Selected topic displayed here

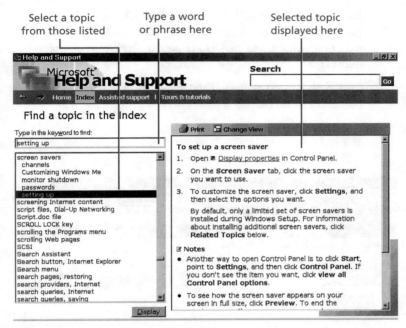

FIGURE 6.3   Use the Index to locate a specific word or phrase.

Follow these steps to use the Index feature:

1. From any page within Help and Support, click **Index**.

2. Type a word or phrase in the **Type in the keyword to find** text box. As you type, Help searches the Index for a match, so you might not have to type the entire word.

3. Double-click the topic in the list that you'd like to display. The topic appears in the right pane. (A dialog box of selections may appear. If so, select the subtopic you want and click **Display**.)

Using the Search Feature

Unlike Index, which searches the topics list for a match, Search looks for a match to your word or phrase within the contents of the topic itself. Follow these steps to use Search:

1. From anywhere within Help and Support, click within the
   Search box at the top of the screen, type the word or phrase you
   want to search for, and click **Go** or press **Enter**. A list of topics
   is displayed.

2. Click a topic listed on the left and it appears in the right pane, as
   shown in Figure 6.4.

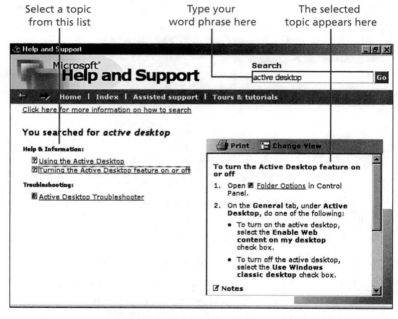

FIGURE 6.4   Search allows you to search the text within Help topics.

Displaying a Tour or Tutorial

Tours provide quick overviews of Windows topics, such as entertainment
and multimedia. Tutorials provide more detailed information. To use a
tour or tutorial, follow these steps:

1. From anywhere in Help and Support, click the **Tour & tutorials** button.

2. Select a tour or tutorial from those listed. You can also click a tour listed in the topics list. A tour window appears, as shown in Figure 6.5. (You must use at least 800 × 600 resolution to display a tour)

Click a button to view other topics

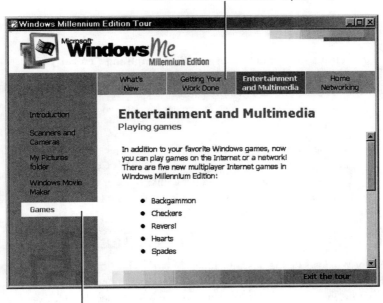

Click a tab to view a related tour

FIGURE **6.5**   Taking a tour of a Windows feature.

3. Scroll down to view the tour. To display other tours within the same topic, click a tab on the right. When you're through, click **Exit the tour**.

If you select the **Windows Millenuium Edition Preview**, a movie appears instead of the tour window. after the movie stops, click **Exit**.

Getting Assisted Support

Help and Support allows you to find answers to common questions about Windows on the Internet. Like many Web sites, the content of Microsoft's Help site may change frequently, so the specific steps in this section and the selections available at the time you access the site may vary.

To locate answers to common Windows questions, follow these steps:

1. Connect to the Internet.

2. From anywhere within Help and Support, click the **Assisted Support** button.

3. Select a support link, such as **MSN Computing Central Forum**. Depending on the support link you select, you may see a list of additional links from which to choose. Select one, and Internet Explorer will display the appropriate page on Microsoft's Web site.

4. Browse the Web page for the answer to your question. For example, if you selected a message board on MSN's Computing Central Forum, browse through the links or enter a search phrase to display messages with information pertaining to your problem.

Using the What's This? Feature

Many Windows dialog boxes include a **What's This?** button (shown in Figure 6.6). After you click it, you can click any option within that dialog box to view a description of it. This lets you quickly decide which options within a dialog box you want to use.

Follow these steps to use the What's This? feature:

1. Click the **What's This?** button. The mouse pointer changes to an arrow with a question mark.

2. Click any option within the dialog box. A description of that option appears.

3. After reading the description, click anywhere outside the description box to remove it from the screen and to turn off the What's This? feature.

What's This? button

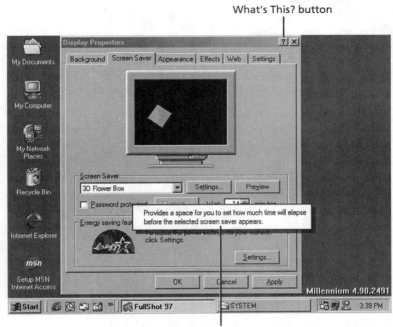

When you click an option with
the What's This? pointer, a description appears

FIGURE **6.6**   The What's This? feature helps you identify which dialog box options you want to use.

Quick Description   To display a description of a dialog box option more quickly, just right-click the option and select **What's This?** from the shortcut menu that appears.

In this lesson, you learned how to use the Windows Help and Support system, including its home page, Index, Search, Tours and tutorials, and Assisted support. You also learned how to use the What's This? feature. In the next lesson, you'll learn how to customize Windows to suit your needs.

LESSON 7
Customizing Windows

In this lesson, you'll learn various ways to customize Windows to fit your needs.

Arranging Icons on the Desktop

The icons on your Windows Desktop provide quick access to the programs you use most often. However, if the icons are placed on the desktop haphazardly, it becomes difficult for you to find the icon you want when you need it.

You can drag each icon into place manually, of course. But to quickly arrange the icons on the desktop in neat rows, follow these steps:

1. Right-click the desktop and select **Arrange Icons** from the shortcut menu.

2. Select a command from the cascading menu that appears:

   by Name   Arranges the icons alphabetically.

   by Type   Arranges the icons by their type (their filename extension).

   by Size   Arranges the icons by the size of their files.

   by Date   Arranges icons by their file date (the date they were created or changed).

   Auto Arrange   Arranges icons automatically. If you add an icon to the desktop, it's automatically arranged with the other icons in neat rows.

You can also arrange your icons in neat rows by right-clicking the desktop and selecting **Line Up Icons**.

 Icons and the Active Desktop You can completely remove icons from the Active Desktop and avoid trying to see them through your channel and Active Desktop Item windows. If you use the Active Desktop and you choose to hide your desktop icons, you can still access them when needed by displaying the Desktop toolbar on the Windows taskbar. To hide your desktop icons, right-click the desktop and select **Active Desktop, Show Desktop Icons** to turn the option off. Hiding your Active Desktop icons has no effect on the Classic Desktop; when you switch back to the Classic Desktop, your desktop icons will reappear.

Adding Shortcuts to the Desktop

Your desktop already contains many icons for programs that Microsoft felt you would use often. Some of these icons are merely *shortcuts* to a program and not the actual program icons themselves. For example, you might see shortcut icons to Media Player and Internet Explorer on your desktop. When you double-click a shortcut icon (or single-click, if you use the Single-Click option), the program associated with it opens. So by placing shortcut icons for Internet Explorer and Media Player on your desktop, Microsoft has made it easier for you to start those programs. You can usually identify a shortcut icon by its bent arrow, as shown in Figure 7.1.

The bent arrow identifies
this icon as a shortcut icon

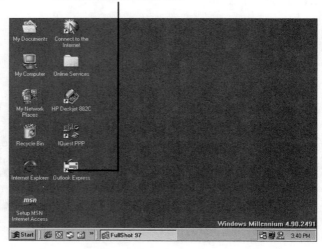

FIGURE 7.1   Shortcuts provide quick access to your favorite programs.

Shortcuts   A shortcut is an icon that points (redirects Windows) to the EXE (executable) file associated with a particular program. You can safely create and remove shortcuts when needed without affecting the actual files on the hard disk that run your applications.

To create a shortcut icon on your desktop, follow these steps:

1. Open Windows Explorer or My Computer and select the program file to which you want to create a shortcut. (If you need
   help using Windows Explorer or My Computer, see Lesson 11,
   "Viewing Drives, Folders, and Files.") The program file you
   need will be found in that program's main folder. Look for a file
   that ends in .exe or is identified with a special icon that looks
   like the program's logo.

2. If needed, resize the Windows Explorer or My Computer window so you can see a portion of the desktop as well.

3. Right-click the file and drag it onto the desktop. A shortcut
   menu appears.

4. Select **Create Shortcut(s) Here**, as shown in Figure 7.2. The
   shortcut icon appears on the desktop. You can move the icon by
   dragging it or rearrange your icons as you like using the tech-
   niques you learned earlier in this lesson.

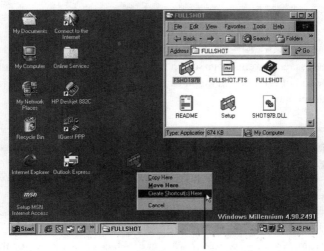

Drag your program's
file to the Desktop

FIGURE 7.2 Add shortcuts to favorite programs to the desktop.

Adding Icons to Quick Launch Toolbar   You can add your favorite programs to the Quick Launch toolbar by creating shortcut icons within the `\Windows\Application Data\Microsoft\Internet Explorer\Quick Launch` folder. Open Windows Explorer (because it will be easier to use in this instance). Then right-click the program's file, drag it to the Quick Launch folder on the Windows Explorer's Folder List, and select **Create Shortcut(s) Here** from the menu that appears. You can also drag shortcut icons directly onto the Quick Launch toolbar if you like.

 Add to the Start Menu   You can also add shortcuts to the Start menu rather than the desktop. See Lesson 9, "Customizing Other Attributes of Windows," for more information.

Adding a Screen Saver

A screen saver prevents your screen from displaying a static image for a long period of time, which might cause a permanent burn-in of that image on your monitor.

 Screen Saver Not Needed?   Newer monitors automatically turn themselves off after a certain period of inactivity. If you have such a monitor, a screen saver isn't needed—although you can still use one.

To coordinate your screen saver with other Windows elements, see the section, "Using Themes for a Coordinated Look," in Lesson 8. To simply select a screen saver, follow these steps:

1. Right-click the desktop and select **Properties**. (You can also double-click the Monitor icon in the Status area of the taskbar.) The Display Properties dialog box appears.

2. Click the **Screen Saver** tab. The Screen Saver page appears, as shown in Figure 7.3.

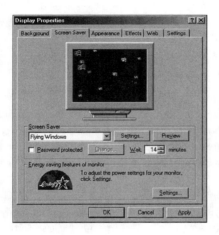

FIGURE 7.3   Windows offers several screen savers.

3. Select the screen saver you want to use from the **Screen Saver** list. A preview appears at the top of the dialog box. (If you want to use the new My Pictures screen saver, see the next section for more help.)

4. In the **Wait** text box, enter the number of minutes of inactivity before Windows initiates the screen saver.

5. If you want to protect your PC from unauthorized use when you're away from your desk, select the **Password protected** option, click the **Change** button, enter a password, and click **OK**. You'll have to enter this password to gain access to your system whenever the screen saver is initialized.

6. Click the **Settings** button next to the **Screen Saver** list box to access the available options for the screen saver you selected. Make your changes and click **OK**.

7. Click **OK** when you're through.

When you come back to your desk after the screen saver has been activated, simply move the mouse or press a key to return to work.

Using the My Pictures Screen Saver to Display Your Own Images

Windows Me comes with a new screen saver called the My Pictures screen saver, which you can use to display your own images in a kind of personal slide show. You can scan in pictures of your loved ones, import images from a digital camera, or download graphics from the Internet to use with this screen saver. You're limited only by your imagination.

 Almost No Limits   Windows supports only bitmap (BMP) and JPEG (JPG) images for use with the My Pictures Screen Saver.

To begin, collect the images you want to use in the screen saver and place them all in a single folder. You can use the My Pictures folder within the My Documents folder, or you can create another folder if you like. Then follow these steps to set up the My Picture screen saver:

1. Right-click the desktop and select **Properties**. (You can also double-click the Monitor icon in the Status area of the taskbar.) The Display Properties dialog box appears.

2. Click the **Screen Saver** tab. The Screen Saver page appears, as shown in Figure 7.3.

3. Select **My Pictures Screen Saver** from the **Screen Saver** list.

4. In the **Wait** text box, enter the number of minutes of inactivity before Windows initiates the screen saver.

5. If you want to protect your PC from unauthorized use when you're away from your desk, select the **Password protected** option, click the **Change** button, enter a password, and click **OK**. You'll have to enter this password to gain access to your system whenever the screen saver is initialized.

6. Click **Settings**. The My Picture Screen Saver Options dialog box appears, as shown in Figure 7.4.

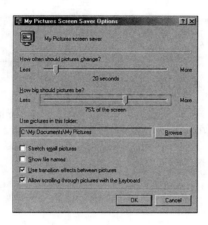

FIGURE 7.4   Select how you want the My Pictures Screen Saver to display your images.

7. To change the frequency with which images are displayed, drag the **How often should pictures change?** slider left (to display each image longer) or right (to change images more frequently).

8. To set the maximum size of any image, drag the **How big should pictures be?** slider left (to shrink large images to a smaller size) or right (to allow large images to fill the screen if needed).

9. By default, the images in the My Pictures folder are used for the screen saver. To use another folder instead, click **Browse**, select the folder you want to use, and click **OK.**

10. Select any additional options you desire:

   Stretch small pictures tells Windows to stretch images as needed to fill the maximum allowable screen area set in step 8.

   Show file names displays the filename for each image at the top of that image as it appears onscreen.

   Use transition effects between pictures adds transition effects (such as fade-in or pop-in) between images as they change.

   Allow scrolling through pictures with the keyboard allows you to skip pictures using the left and right arrow keys without turning off the screen saver.

11. Click **OK** to return to the Display Properties dialog box, and then click **OK** again.

Modifying Your Power Management Settings

If your monitor is compatible with Power Management, you can save energy when your PC isn't in use by letting Windows put your monitor (and the hard disks) into "suspended animation." This feature is especially useful on a laptop, where power is at a premium, but it's also useful for desktop systems.

To set up Power Management, follow these steps:

1. Click the **Settings** button at the bottom of the Screen Saver dialog box. The Power Schemes dialog box appears, as shown in Figure 7.5. (Power Management options vary from computer to computer.)

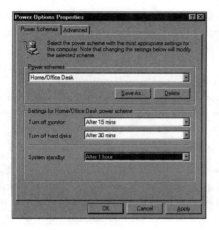

FIGURE **7.5**　To save energy, set up Power Management.

2. Select the scheme that best suits your situation from the **Power
   schemes** list box. (In most cases, this will be the Home/Office
   Desk scheme.)

3. Change the other options as needed:

   Turn off monitor tells Windows how long to wait before powering
   down the monitor.

   Turn off hard disks tells Windows how long to wait before powering down the hard disks.

   System standby tells Windows how long to wait before going into
   standby mode. Standby provides minimum power to RAM and the
   CPU. You can leave programs open, have the system go into
   standby, and come back out of standby quickly to redisplay your
   programs and desktop. However, a power outage while in standby
   mode will result in the loss of data that has not been saved. To
   restore the computer after it has gone into standby, simply press any
   key or move the mouse.

System hibernates tells Windows how long to wait before going into hibernation. Hibernation saves the most power, since it actually shuts down the computer. Like standby mode, you can leave programs open, let the system go into hibernation, and then redisplay program windows and the desktop when you return to your computer. Unlike standby mode, all data is saved, so even if a power outage occurs while you're gone, you can't lose anything. To restore the computer after it has gone into hibernation, press any key or move the mouse.

4. If it exists, click the **Hibernate** tab and select the **Enable hibernate support** to turn on hibernation. (Some computers display this check box on the **Power Schemes** tab, so you may not see a **Hibernate** tab. Also, some computers simply don't support this option.)

 Standby and Hibernate You can have your computer go into standby after a short period of inactivity, then go into hibernation if the computer is left idle for a longer period of time by setting a short standby period such as 15 minutes, and a longer hibernation period such as 1 hour, on the **Power Schemes** tab.

5. Click the **Advanced** tab and select additional options as desired, such as requiring a password to turn the power back on and displaying a Power Management icon on the taskbar to provide quick access to the Power Management options. (Options vary by computer.)

6. Click **OK** to save your selections.

You can force the computer to go into standby or hibernation mode at any time with the **Shut Down** command on the **Start** menu. See Lesson 1, "Introducing Windows," for more information.

Changing the Screen Resolution

Resolution settings are identified by the number of pixels (or dots) used horizontally and vertically. For example, 640×480 resolution uses 640 pixels horizontally and 480 pixels vertically. Typically, that's the lowest resolution you can use. In addition to the number of pixels, you can control the range of colors your monitor uses. More colors means better display of certain graphics, but this option takes up more video memory.

When you use a higher resolution, such as 1024×768, the images might become clearer but your icons and text will become smaller. With more pixels onscreen, the relative size of each pixel is smaller. To compensate for this, you should turn on the **Large Fonts** option—just click the **Advanced** button on the Settings tab of the Display Properties dialog box. (To increase the size of the icons, use the Effects tab, as explained in Lesson 8, "Changing the Appearance of Windows".)

To change your screen resolution, follow these steps:

1. Right-click the desktop and select **Properties**. (You can also double-click the Monitor icon in the Status area of the taskbar.) The Display Properties dialog box appears.

2. Click the **Settings** tab, shown in Figure 7.6. If you're using more than one monitor, select the monitor whose settings you want to change.

3. To change to a higher resolution, drag the **Screen area** slider toward **More**. To switch to a lower resolution, drag the slider toward **Less**.

4. Select the number of colors you want to use from the **Colors** drop-down list box.

5. If you're using two monitors and you'd like to use them in synch to display a single image of your desktop, select the second monitor in step 2 and then select the **Extend my Windows desktop onto this monitor** option.

6. Click **OK** when you're done.

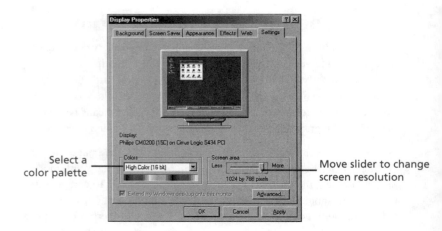

Select a color palette ——— Move slider to change screen resolution

FIGURE **7.6**   Changing the resolution affects how items are displayed onscreen.

To change from one resolution to another without changing anything else, just click the **Monitor** icon in the **Status** area, and select the resolution you want to use.

In this lesson, you learned how to customize Windows by arranging icons, adding shortcuts, selecting a screen saver, setting up the special My Pictures Screen Saver, adjusting your Power Management settings, and selecting a different screen resolution. In the next lesson, you'll learn how to change the appearance of the desktop, window colors, and icons.

LESSON 8

Changing the Appearance of Windows

In this lesson, you'll learn various ways to change the way Windows looks.

Changing the Background of the Desktop

Initially, the desktop is solid blue. Instead of a plain color, you can use a graphic as wallpaper to cover the background. You can choose a Windows graphic or use one of your own, perhaps downloaded from the Internet. Windows accepts .bmp, .gif, and even .jpg images. You can also use an HTML document (a Web page) as your wallpaper. If you want to simply change the color of your desktop background from blue to something else, see the section "Changing the Appearance (Colors) of Windows."

 Bitmap Image A bitmap (.bmp) image is a graphic format in which the image is stored as a series of pixels or dots.

You can also choose a pattern (a series of small dots) to use as your Windows background, but you can't use both a wallpaper graphic and a pattern. You can even edit these patterns to customize the look of your desktop, if you like.

To coordinate your wallpaper with other Windows elements, see the
"Using Themes for a Coordinated Look" section later in this lesson.
Follow these steps to select a graphic or Web page for your Windows
desktop:

1. Right-click the desktop and select **Properties**. (You can also
   double-click the Monitor icon in the Status area of the taskbar
   and click the **Background** tab.) The Display Properties dialog
   box appears, as shown in Figure 8.1.

Select your graphic —

Select how to
display the graphic

FIGURE 8.1   Wallpaper your desktop with a nice graphic.

2. Select a graphic from the **Wallpaper** list. A preview of your
   selection appears at the top of the dialog box. To select your own
   graphic or a Web page, click **Browse** and select it from the list.
   (You must first save the web page you want to use to the hard
   disk, using Internet Explorer's **File>Save As** command.)

Quick Change   If you see a graphic image on the
Internet that you want to use as a background, right-
click the image and select **Set as Wallpaper** from the
menu that appears. To use a Web page as a background, you must save it first.

Active Desktop Required   Graphics identified by a paper icon with a small frame and paintbrush inside it require you to change to Active Desktop in order to use them. See Lesson 27, "Displaying Internet Content on the Desktop," for help changing to the Active Desktop.

3. Select either **Tile, Center,** or **Stretch** from the picture **Display** drop-down list. **Tile** arranges copies of the graphic or Web page across the desktop in neat rows. **Center** places the graphic or Web page in the center of the desktop. **Stretch** stretches the graphic or Web page to fit the entire desktop.

4. To test the graphic or Web page on your desktop, click **Apply**. If you don't like the result, select another graphic and click **Apply** again.

5. When you're satisfied with your selection, click **OK**.

 System Too Slow?   You might notice a slight degradation in performance when you use a graphic or a pattern as a background. This is because it uses more of your system resources than a simple color.

Follow these steps to select a pattern:

1. Right-click the desktop and select **Properties**. (You can also double-click the Monitor icon in the Status area of the taskbar and click the **Background** tab.) The Display Properties dialog box appears (See Figure 8.1).

2. If you were using a graphic for your background, select **(None)** from the **Wallpaper** list.

3. Click **Pattern**. The Pattern dialog box appears, as shown in Figure 8.2.

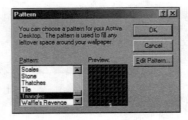

FIGURE 8.2   You can use a pattern as a background for your desktop.

4. Select a pattern from the list. If you want to edit the pattern, click **Edit Pattern**. If not, skip to step 6.

5. Click within the **Pattern** box to change the pattern one pixel at a time. You can give your variation a new name by typing it in the **Name** text box. When you're through, click **Change** to save your changes. Then click **Done**.

 Change Your Mind?   If you start editing a pattern and then change your mind, click **Done** and then choose **No** in the dialog box that appears.

6. In the **Pattern** dialog box, click **OK**.

7. To test the pattern on your desktop, click **Apply**. If you don't like the result, follow steps 3 through 6 to select another pattern and click **Apply** again.

8. When you're satisfied with your selection, click **OK**.

Changing the Appearance (Colors) of Windows

Windows uses a particular color scheme by default. This color scheme determines the color of the title bars of active and inactive windows, the color of the desktop, the style of the window text, the size and spacing of icons, and so on. You can select a different color scheme entirely or change only the colors of individual elements.

To coordinate your color scheme with other Windows elements, see the "Using Themes for a Coordinated Look" section later in this lesson. To simply change color schemes, follow these steps:

1. Right-click the desktop and select **Properties**. (You can also double-click the Monitor icon in the Status area of the taskbar.) The Display Properties dialog box appears.

2. Click the **Appearance** tab. The Appearance page appears, as shown in Figure 8.3.

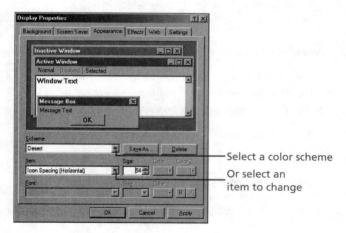

FIGURE 8.3   Windows lets you customize its appearance.

3. Select a color scheme (such as Desert) from the **Scheme** drop-down list. A preview of the scheme appears at the top of the dialog box.

4. You can change the color and style of individual Windows elements, even after selecting a scheme. For example, you can change the color of inactive title bars. Simply select the element you want to change from the **Item** drop-down list and then select the color or style you desire.

5. When you're through making selections, click **OK**.

Adding Special Effects

In addition to changing the background of the desktop and the colors of
various Windows elements, Windows offers various effects that you can
add to liven things up. Many of these effects change how your icons
look—for example, you can exchange the desktop icons for icons that are
more meaningful. You can also display larger and/or more colorful icons,
animate menus and toolbars, and add other special effects.

 More Space Required?   If you want to adjust the
amount of space between icons, use the **Appearance**
tab, as explained in the preceding section.

To change the effect options, follow these steps:

1. Right-click the desktop and select **Properties**. (You can also
    double-click the Monitor icon in the Status area of the taskbar.)
    The Display Properties dialog box appears.

2. Click the **Effects** tab. The Effects page appears, as shown in
    Figure 8.4.

FIGURE 8.4   Visual options are available on the Effects tab.

3. To change one of the desktop icons, click it and then click
   Change Icon. Windows opens a file of default icons from which
   you can choose. Select one and click **OK**. If you have another
   icon file you want to use instead, click **Browse** to select the file
   first. To coordinate your desktop icons with other Windows elements, see the next section, "Using Themes for a Coordinated
   Look."

4. Select other icon options if you want:

   Use transition effects for menus and tooltips   Animates your
   menus and tooltips when you open or close them.

   Smooth edges of screen fonts   Helps to make tiny fonts more
   readable.

   Use large icons   Displays desktop icons in a larger size.

   Show icons using all possible colors   This option uses more
   video memory, but it also makes icons prettier.

   Show window contents while dragging   Displays the contents
   of a window (rather than just an outline) when you drag that
   window to move it.

5. Click **OK** to save your selections.

If you exchange a desktop icon for something else and then later change
your mind, just return to the **Effects** tab, select the icon you want to
restore, and click **Default Icon**.

Using Themes for a Coordinated Look

To give your Windows environment a more special look, you can select a
theme, such as baseball. When you do, several Windows elements are
changed all at once. For example, the desktop wallpaper sports a baseball
graphic, the desktop icons have baseball images, Windows event sounds
(such as a warning sound) are baseball-related, the screen saver has a
baseball theme, and so on. When selecting a theme, you control which
parts of Windows it affects—such as only the wallpaper and sounds.

No Themes? Initially, Windows doesn't install any themes on your system. However, they're easy to add by following the steps under the "Adding or Removing Windows Components" section in Appendix A.

After installing your themes, follow these steps to select the one you want:

1. Click **Start** and select **Settings**, **Control Panel**.

2. If needed, click **View all Control Panel options** to display the **Desktop Themes** icon. Double-click the icon and the Desktop Themes dialog box appears, as shown in Figure 8.5.

Select a theme

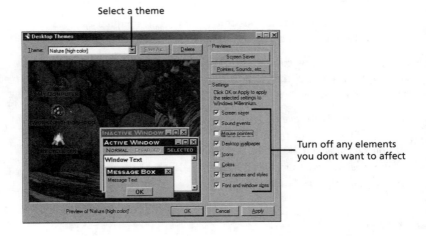

Turn off any elements you dont want to affect

FIGURE 8.5 Use a theme to coordinate various Windows elements.

3. If you want to save your current Windows setup so you can return to it easily, click **Save As**, type a file name, and click **Save**.

4. Select a theme from the **Theme** drop-down list.

High Color   In order to use some of the themes, your screen resolution settings must be set to high color, not just 256 colors. To change to high color (assuming your monitor and graphics card will support it), see Lesson 7, "Customizing Windows."

5. Click the **Settings** options you don't want to affect (this removes their check marks).

6. To preview the screen saver, click **Screen Saver**. To preview other elements, click **Pointers**, **Sounds**, **etc**. When you're through, choose **OK**.

In this lesson, you learned how to change the background, change window colors, change how icons are displayed, and use a theme to create a coordinated look. In the next lesson, you'll learn additional ways to customize Windows.

LESSON 9

Customizing Other Attributes of Windows

In this lesson, you'll learn various ways to customize the taskbar, Start menu, sounds, mouse settings, and Windows Update.

Changing the Taskbar

The taskbar and its Start menu are your Windows lifeline, providing access to your programs, Windows settings, often-used documents, and help. Follow these steps to change how the taskbar appears:

1. Click the **Start** button and select **Settings**, **Taskbar and Start Menu**. The Taskbar and Start Menu Properties dialog box appears, as shown in Figure 9.1.

2. Select the options you desire:

> **Always on top** Makes the taskbar appear on top of any window so you can always see it.

> **Auto hide** Causes the taskbar to disappear. To make it reappear, move the mouse pointer toward its former location. For example, move the pointer towards the bottom of the screen and the taskbar reappears.

> **Show small icons in Start menu** The main Start menu uses large icons, which can make it quite wide. (Submenus of the Start menu use small icons.) Choose this option to display small icons on the main Start menu as well.

Show clock   Displays the current time on the taskbar.

Use personalized Menus   Causes the Start menu to list only the commands you use most often. To expand a menu and display hidden commands, click its expand button (the down arrow at the bottom of the menu) or simply rest the mouse pointer on the menu for a moment until it expands on its own.

The display changes to
reflect the options you select

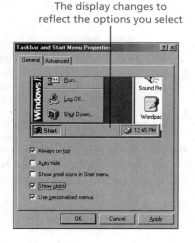

FIGURE 9.1   It's easy to customize the taskbar to suit your needs.

3. Click **OK** to apply your selections.

Reorganizing the Start Menu

When you install a new program, it automatically adds a start-up command to your Start menu. However, you might prefer to reorganize the commands for your programs into groups that you find more logical. You may also want to add your DOS programs because they don't automatically add their commands to your Start menu. To add a command to your Start menu, follow these steps:

1. Click the **Start** button and select **Settings, Taskbar and Start Menu**. The Taskbar and Start Menu Properties dialog box appears (see Figure 9.1).

2. Click the **Advanced** tab. To add a new command to the Start menu, click **Add**.

3. Type the path to the program you want to add, or click **Browse** and select it from the file list. Click **Next**.

4. Select the menu under which you want your command to appear. You can create a new menu by clicking **New Folder** and typing a name. Click **Next**.

5. Type a name for the command as you want it to appear on the menu. Click **Finish**.

To remove a command from the Start menu, follow these steps (if you want to remove a program from the hard disk, see Lesson 18, "Installing and Uninstalling Applications"):

1. Click the **Start** button and select **Settings, Taskbar and Start Menu**. The Taskbar and Start Menu Properties dialog box appears (see Figure 9.1).

2. Click the **Advanced** tab. Click **Remove**. The Remove Shortcuts/Folders dialog box appears.

3. Select the command you want to get rid of and click **Remove**. Remove additional commands, or just click **Close** to return to the Taskbar and Start Menu Properties dialog box.

To re-sort the commands on the Programs menu so they appear in alphabetical order, click the **Re-sort** button on the Taskbar and Start Menu Properties dialog box.

Fast Changes You can add a command to the Start menu by dragging a command file (or even a folder!) from an Explorer window to the **Start** button. When the Start menu opens, drag the command to its place on the menu. To remove a command, drag it off the **Start** menu. To reorganize your Start menu, drag commands to their new locations, one by one. If you add a folder to the Start menu, it becomes a submenu that lists the files it contains. You can then click a file on the submenu to quickly open it.

Clearing the Documents Menu

The Documents menu (from the main Start menu) displays a listing of the last 15 files you've worked on. All you need to do to open a listed document is open the Documents menu and select a file. The file appears in its associated program. If you want, you can clear this menu of documents you no longer expect to work on and Windows can fill it with your favorites. To clear the Documents menu, click the **Start** button and select **Settings**, **Start Menu and Taskbar.** Click the **Advanced** tab, and then click the **Clear** button.

Setting Other Start Menu Options

Windows provides many additional options you can use to modify the Start menu. For example, you can remove the Logoff command if you don't use a network, or the Run command if you don't like to start programs that way. You can also add the Favorites command, which displays the contents of the Favorites folder. There are many other options from which you can choose. Just click the **Start** button and select **Settings**, **Start Menu and Taskbar.** Click the **Advanced** tab, select the options you want from the **Start menu and Taskbar** list, and click **OK**.

Changing the Sounds Associated with System Events

You can replace the sounds that are played for system events (such as when an error is displayed or you exit Windows) with sounds you've created or downloaded from the Internet. You can also replace the default Windows sounds with another sound scheme, such as Jungle. To coordinate your sounds with other Windows elements, see Lesson 8, "Changing the Appearance of Windows." To change selected sounds, follow these steps:

1. Click the **Start** button and select **Settings**, **Control Panel**.

2. If needed, click **View All Control Panel options** to display the **Sounds and Multimedia** icon. Double-click the icon and the Sounds and Multimedia Properties dialog box appears, as shown in Figure 9.2.

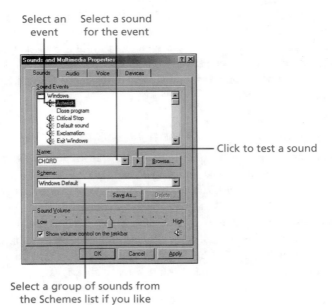

Select an event

Select a sound for the event

Click to test a sound

Select a group of sounds from the Schemes list if you like

FIGURE 9.2   Change how Windows sounds with the Sounds and Multimedia Properties dialog box.

3. From the **Sound Events** list, select the event whose sound you want to change. For example, select Critical Stop.

4. Select a sound file from the **Name** list, or click **Browse** and select your own sound file. To listen to the sound, click the right-arrow button in the **Preview** area.

5. Click **OK**.

Changing the Date and Time

The time that appears on the taskbar is based on the clock setting for your computer. If it's off, you need to adjust the computer clock:

1. Double-click the clock icon on the right end of the taskbar. (If the clock isn't displayed on the taskbar, see the "Setting Other Start Menu Options" section earlier in this lesson for help.)

2. To change the system date, click on a new date. (If needed, you can select a new month or year from the drop-down list boxes.)

3. To change the system time, use the spinner that appears under the clock.

4. Click **OK**.

Adjusting the Volume

Sounds are an integral part of the Windows experience. They warn you of problems, tell you when you've received new mail, and so on. Many Web sites play a sound when a particular page is displayed. You can also download radio broadcasts from the Internet or play the newest CD-ROMs in your CD-ROM drive. However, none of these events will be very pleasant for you if the volume on your speakers is too high or too low. To adjust your speaker volume, follow these steps:

1. Double-click the **Sound** icon on the taskbar. (If it doesn't appear on the taskbar, display it by selecting that option in the Sounds and Multimedia Properties dialog box, shown in Figure 9.2.) The Volume Control dialog box appears, as shown in Figure 9.3.

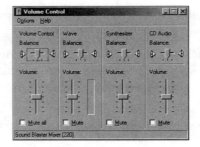

FIGURE 9.3   The Volume Control dialog box.

2. Drag the **Volume Control** slider up to make system sounds louder or down to make them softer.

3. To adjust the balance between your right and left speakers, drag the **Balance** slider right or left.

4. Adjust the other sliders as needed and close the dialog box by clicking its **Close** button. For example, you might want to adjust the CD Audio volume to change the sound level on your CD headphones.

You can display additional sliders for other options applicable to your sound card. Select **Options, Properties**, select the sliders you want to display in the Volume Control box, and choose **OK**. You can also use the Properties dialog box to display sliders that allow you to adjust recording levels (nice if you plan on recording your own sounds).

Quick Control   To quickly adjust just the system volume, click the **Volume** icon on the taskbar. A miniature slider appears. Drag the slider up or down, or click **Mute** as needed. You can also adjust the system volume from within My Computer, Windows Explorer, Media Player, or Internet Explorer by dragging the **Volume Control** slider or the Radio toolbar or clicking the **Mute** button to mute all system sounds.

I Can't Hear Anything!   The check mark under each slider controls that component's capability to play sound through the system speakers. For example, to prevent your microphone from playing any sounds it might be picking up, display the check mark under the **Mic** slider by clicking the **Mute** option. To turn off your system sound completely, click the **Mute All** button under the **Volume Control** slider. To mute the speakers but play sound through your CD headphones, click the **Mute** button under the **CD Audio** slider.

Modifying Mouse Settings

If you find that you're having trouble getting the mouse to click or double-click properly, you might try adjusting its sensitivity. You can also increase the size of the mouse pointer if you find that you're having trouble locating the mouse onscreen (especially on laptops). To change these and other mouse settings, follow these steps:

1. Click the **Start** button and select **Settings**, **Control Panel**.

2. If needed, click **view all Control Panel options** to display the **Mouse** icon. Double-click the icon and the Mouse Properties dialog box appears.

3. On the **Buttons** tab, select from these options:

    Left-handed   Switches the functions of your mouse buttons.

    Double-click speed   Adjusts the speed at which your mouse recognizes a double-click. If you find it hard to click twice fast, move the slider toward **Slow**. To test the setting, double-click within the test area. If a jack-in-the-box appears when you double-click, the setting is fine.

    ClickLock   Allows you to drag objects (such as files or icons) without having to hold the mouse button down the whole time. Click an object you want to drag, hold the mouse button down momentarily, and then release and drag. To drop the object in position, click the mouse button again.

4. Click the **Pointers** tab. Here you can select a different set of mouse pointers from the **Scheme** list box. For example, you might want to select **Animated hourglasses** or **3D Pointers** to jazz things up. Or you might want to select **Windows Standard (large)** or **Windows Standard (extra large)** if you're having trouble seeing the mouse pointer.

Coordinate! If you want to coordinate the style of your mouse pointers with other Windows elements, see Lesson 8.

5. Click the **Pointer Options** tab. Choose from various options:

   Pointer speed   To adjust how fast the mouse moves across the screen, drag the slider.

   Snap To   Moves the mouse pointer to the default button of a dialog box when it appears.

   Visibility   If you use a laptop and you find that the mouse pointer is getting lost, turn on this option and use the slider to adjust its speed.

   Hide pointer while typing   If the mouse pointer distracts you while you're typing, turn on this option.

   Show location of pointer when you press the Ctrl key   Tired of hunting for the dumb mouse pointer? This option should help.

6. Click **OK** when you're done selecting options.

Changing How AutoUpdate Works

The Windows AutoUpdate feature keeps your system up-to-date with the latest program changes and fixes by downloading them from the Internet. By default, AutoUpdate works automatically; each time you connect to the Internet, AutoUpdate checks your system for needed updates and downloads them without bothering you. Although this system makes it easy and painless to keep current with the latest changes in technology, you might prefer to change AutoUpdate so that it cannot make changes to your system without you knowing. Here's what to do:

1. Click the **Start** button and select **Settings**, **Control Panel**.

2. If needed, click **View All Control Panel options** to display the **Automatic Updates** icon. Double-click the icon and the Automatic Updates dialog box appears.

3. Select the option you desire:

   Automatically download updates   Downloads updates in the background whenever you're connected to the Internet, without asking you for confirmation. However, you'll be notified by an icon on the Status bar after updates are downloaded, and you can then install only the updates you want. (For help in stalling an update, see Lesson 18, "Installing and Uninstalling Applications."

   Notify me before downloading   Still performs the system update check whenever you're online, but notifies you of needed updates so you can cancel any you don't want to download. Windows will notify you again when the selected updates are downloaded and ready to be installed. (For help installing updates, see Lesson 18.)

Missing an Update?   If you choose not to cownload a particular update and then change your mind, you can download it manually as described later in this section.

Turn off automatic updating   Deactivates AutoUpdate. If you want to update your system, you'll need to do it manually.

4. Updates you may have been offered but didn't select are hidden and aren't offered again. If you cancelled (declined) any updates previously, you can display them along with newer updates the next time AutoUpdate checks your system by clicking **Restore Hidden Items**.

5. Click **OK**.

If you turn off AutoUpdate, you'll need to perform periodic updates to your system manually. (You can also use this option to update your system manually at any time.) Connect to the Internet, click **Start**, and select **Windows Update**. You'll be taken to Microsoft's Windows Update Web site. Click **Product Updates**. Your system is analyzed and you get a list of updates you might want to apply. Select the updates you want and click **Download** to copy them to your system. Then follow the onscreen instructions to install these updates to your system.

In this lesson, you learned how to customize Windows to suit your tastes. In the next lesson, you'll learn how to view your files, folders, and drives using My Computer and Explorer.

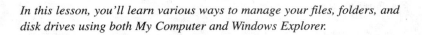

LESSON 10

Accessing Your Drives, Folders, and Files

In this lesson, you'll learn various ways to manage your files, folders, and disk drives using both My Computer and Windows Explorer.

Understanding Drives, Folders, and Files

Your computer comes with at least two disk drives: the hard disk drive and the floppy diskette drive. The hard disk drive provides large-capacity storage for your programs and the data files you create. Windows itself is also stored on the hard disk drive. The floppy diskette drive lets you transfer data from one computer to another easily.

The drives are assigned letters so that the computer can tell them apart. Typically, the hard disk is drive C: and the floppy diskette drive is A:. Your PC might have more than one hard disk, or the hard disk might be divided into separate partitions. If so, the additional drives are labeled D:, E:, and so on. If your PC has more than one diskette drive, it's labeled B:. If your PC has a CD-ROM drive and/or a Zip drive, they're assigned the first available drive letters, such as D: or E:.

Typically, a new folder is created for each program you install on the hard disk. You can create additional folders to organize your data into manageable units, just as you might organize your work papers into various folders within your file cabinet.

Files are placed into each folder, just as you might place individual pieces of paper into a file folder. There are two basic file types: *program files* (files that are used to run an application, such as Word) and *data files* (files created by an application, such as letters, reports, and memos). You can mix both types within a folder if you want.

Filenames under Windows can contain up to 255 characters, with a three-character extension. Although there are some characters you can't use (/, \, ;, *, ?, >, <, and |), this still gives you a fair amount of freedom in assigning names to your files that will help you later identify their purpose, such as "Sales for 4th Quarter 2000." Note that filenames can include letters, numbers, *and also spaces.*

Extension   A file's extension identifies its purpose. For example, a filename that ends with the extension .txt contains only text. A filename that ends in .exe is a program file, and a filename that ends in .bmp is a bitmap graphic file. There are many other file types, but you don't need to learn them because Windows specifies the type of file in the Type column in both My Computer and Explorer. Also, each file type is identified by a special icon.

Naming Your Files   If you still use old DOS programs, you'll need to restrict their filenames to eight characters or less (no spaces). Those older programs don't recognize the longer filenames used by Windows. You should also restrict the names of the folders you use with DOS programs to eight characters or less.

Using My Computer

Windows offers two programs that allow you to view your files, folders, and drives: My Computer and Windows Explorer. They're remarkably similar, as you'll soon see. My Computer is shown in Figure 10.1.

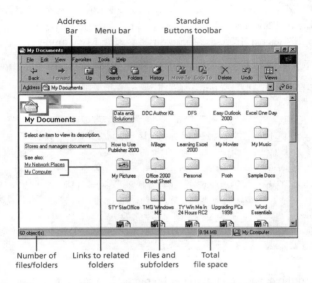

FIGURE 10.1 You can view your files, folders, and drives with My Computer.

You should notice several things: First, folders (identified by a folder icon) typically appear first in the listing, followed by files, which are usually listed alphabetically. Files are identified by icons that show which program can be used to view and edit them. With some folders, such as the My Documents folder shown here, you may see links to related folders. Click either of the links to display that folder. You can change the order in which files appear and the manner in which they're displayed. See Lesson 11, "Viewing Drives, Folders, and Files," for help.

You should also notice the information that appears on the status bar. When you open a folder, the number of files and subfolders it contains is listed, along with the total space used by the files in that folder (files in subfolders are not included). In addition, pay attention to the information that appears to the left of the file listing. Here, you'll often find links to related folders and a description of the current folder—provided folders are being displayed using Web view and not Classic view, as explained later in this lesson. Here are some tips on using My Computer:

- To start My Computer, double-click its icon on the desktop.

- To display the contents of a drive or folder, double-click it.

 Bytes   The size of a file is measured in *bytes*. One byte is equal to the amount of space it takes to store one character, such as the letter K. A *kilobyte* is roughly one thousand bytes (1,024 bytes to be exact). A *megabyte* is roughly one million bytes (1,048,576 bytes), and a *gigabyte* is roughly one billion bytes (1,073,741,824 bytes).

- To move back up the folder hierarchy to a previous folder, click the **Up** button on the Standard Buttons toolbar.

- You can also move from folder to folder or to a different drive by selecting it from the **Address** drop-down list box.

- To view a related folder, click its link.

- To return to a previously viewed folder, click the **Back** button on the Standard Buttons toolbar as many times as needed. Or, click the arrow on the **Back** button and select it from the list.

- To return to a previously viewed folder after moving back, click the **Forward** button as needed. Or, click the arrow on the **Forward** button and select it from the list.

- To refresh the display (for example, if you switch diskettes in a drive and you want to display the contents of the new diskette), press **F5** or open the **View** menu and select **Refresh**.

- You can browse the Web by typing the address of the page you want to view in the **Address** list box. Internet Explorer displays the page you requested.

 Single-clicking   You can single-click to open folders and select files by turning on the Single-Click option, as explained later in this lesson.

 No Display?   Some folders are designed to hide their contents because you shouldn't mess with any of the files they contain. For example, the Windows folder contains files critical to your computer's operation, so it doesn't display its contents when you open it. If you must display files in such a folder, click the **View the entire contents of this folder** link.

My Computer doesn't normally include a folder hierarchy list (called the Folders list) in a separate panel on the left, as Explorer does. This is the main difference between the two programs. The presence of this list might make it easier for you to quickly jump from folder to folder as you browse (in which case you might prefer to use Explorer), or it might confuse or annoy you (in which case you might prefer to use My Computer). In any case, you can display the Folder list in My Computer by clicking the **Folders** button on the Standard Buttons toolbar.

Using Windows Explorer

Windows Explorer isn't much different from My Computer, as you can see from Figure 10.2. The only real difference is the addition of the Folders list that you can use to jump from one drive or folder to another. However, you can easily hide or redisplay the Folder list in both Windows Explorer and My Computer by clicking the **Folders** button on the Standard Buttons toolbar, so you may prefer to use My Computer all the time since it is easier to access.

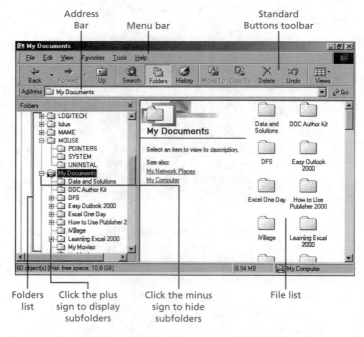

FIGURE 10.2   Explorer is another program you can use to view files, folders, and drives.

You may also notice that the Windows status bar displays the total free space left on a disk, along with the total number of files/folders and total file space, when you select any folder from the Folders list. Provided you display the Folders list in My Computer, you'll see this information as well. Here are the only differences you need to keep in mind:

- To start Explorer, open the **Start** menu and select **Programs, Accessories, Windows Explorer**.

Faster Exploration   If your computer's keyboard contains a key with the Windows logo on it, you can use that key to start Windows Explorer. Just press and hold the **Windows logo** key and then press **E**.

- Display the contents of a folder or a drive by clicking it in the Folders list.

- If a folder in the Folders list is preceded by a plus sign, it contains subfolders. To display them, click the plus sign. To hide them again, click the minus sign that appears.

Turning on Classic View

In Web view, shown in Figures 10.1 and 10.2, the file list appears on the right, while the folder name, links to related folders, and other important information appears on the left. Still, you might want to try Classic view sometime. Unlike Web view, in which the contents your folders are displayed as Web pages, Classic view removes the folder's name and related folder links from the left side of the window, as shown in Figure 10.3. This leaves more room to display a folder's contents. It's especially helpful to change to Classic view if you like to display the Folder list, which takes up a lot of room itself. To display your folders using Classic view, follow these steps:

1. Select **Tools, Folder Options**.

2. Choose **Use Windows classic folders** from the **Web View** pane and click **OK**. All folders in both My Computer and Explorer are displayed in Classic View.

Files displayed in classic view

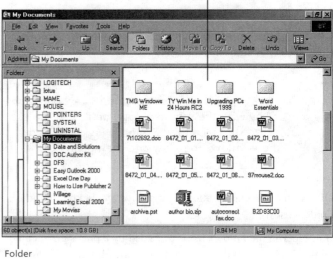

Folder
list

FIGURE 10.3   In Classic view, there's more room to display the contents of a folder.

Painless Panes   When the Folder list is displayed, you can change its width by dragging the border between it and the file pane left or right. If you make the Folder list wider, the information area seen in Web view (where the folder name, links, and other information appear) may disappear temporarily in order to use the room that's left to display files. This way you can change to a sort of Classic view on a temporary basis without actually turning the Classic view option on.

Turning on the Single-Click Option

When you turn on the Single-Click option, the purpose of clicking and double-clicking is changed. Instead of clicking to select a file, you simply point to it. And instead of double-clicking to open a file, you click it once. This change affects not just Explorer, but My Computer and the desktop as well.

To turn on single-clicking:

1. Select **Tools, Folder Options.**

2. Choose **Single-click to open an item (point to select)** from the **Click items as follows** pane.

3. Choose how you want selected items to be highlighted (under-lined), and then choose **OK**:

   Underline icon titles consistent with my browser   Underlines all files, folders, and icons, whether selected or not. This helps to remind you that single-clicking is turned on.

   Underline icon titles only when I point at them   Files, folders, and icons are highlighted (underlined) only when you point at them.

Here are some tips on using single-clicking:

- To open a subfolder, click it just as you'd click a link within a Web page.

- To select a file, simply point to it. A description of the file appears on the status bar.

In this lesson, you were introduced to both My Computer and Explorer. You also learned the difference between Web View and Classic View and how to turn on the Single-Click option. In the next lesson, you'll learn how to use Explorer to view your files and folders and how to customize the display.

LESSON 11

Viewing Drives, Folders, and Files

In this lesson, you'll learn various ways to view and sort the files in My Computer and Explorer.

Changing the Display in My Computer and Windows Explorer

As you learned in the preceding lesson, My Computer and Windows Explorer are remarkably similar. So much so, you can consider them the same program. In fact, when you make a change in one program, you'll see the same change in the other program. So it should come as no surprise that all the tasks you'll learn in this and subsequent lessons can be performed in either program. For the sake of simplicity, the figures show only My Computer because it's easier to start (just double-click its icon on the desktop). When you want to display the Folder list in My Computer, (which makes copying and moving files easier), just click the **Folders** button. To remove the Folders list from Explorer or My Computer, click the **Folders** button again.

Large Icons display

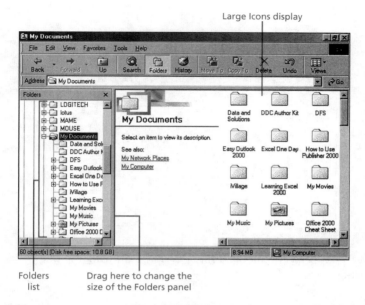

Folders   Drag here to change the
list   size of the Folders panel

FIGURE **11.1**   The Folders list provides quick access to your folders.

If you want to display the Folders list but you'd like it to take up less
room, resize the Folders panel by dragging the bar that separates it from
the file list. Just keep in mind that if you make the Folders list too wide,
the file/folder information area (which normally appears in Web view)
may disappear. If that happens, simply resize the Folders list to make it
smaller.

Changing the File List Display

In Figure 11.1, files are displayed using large icons. This is how My
Computer and Explorer normally display files, but it's just one of many
ways you can list them. To change the file list display, click the arrow on
the **Views** button and select the view option you want: **Large Icons**,
Small Icons, **List**, **Details** (which provides the file's name, size, type, and
date of last modification, as shown in Figure 11.2), or **Thumbnails** (in
which a small preview of a file is displayed instead of a simple icon).
You'll learn more about Thumbnails view later in this lesson.

Files listed in
Detail View

Drag between the
columns to widen them

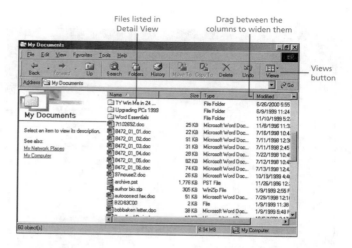

Views
button

FIGURE 11.2   The Details view provides more information about your files.

More Room   If you choose the Details view, you can change the size of the columns by dragging their borders. For example, to make the Name column wider, move the mouse pointer to the right edge of the Name column header. When the pointer changes to a two-headed arrow, drag the border to the right and release the mouse button when the column is the size you want.

Customized Details   In Details view, you can customize the columns by choosing **View, Choose Columns,** selecting the columns you want to view, and clicking **OK**. You can also change the order of the columns in the list and their default width.

Normally, file extensions such as .doc, .txt, .bat, and so on don't appear in the file list. If you want to see the extensions to help you better identify your files and the programs they belong to, select **Tools, Folder Options,** click the **View** tab, and deselect the **Hide file extensions for known file types** option. To display hidden system files (such as win.ini, autoexec.bat, and so on), select the **Show hidden files and folders** option as well. Then click **OK**.

Controlling the Order in Which Files Are Displayed

As shown in Figures 11.1 and 11.2, files are normally displayed in alphabetical order, with folders appearing at the top of the file list. To change the order of files in the list, follow these steps:

1. Open the **View** menu and select **Arrange Icons**.

2. Select the option you want: **by Name, by Type, by Size,** or **by Date**. If you're using the Large Icons or Small Icons view, you can select the **Auto Arrange** option to automatically arrange the icons in neat rows. (To arrange the icons one time, select the **Line Up Icons** command on the **View** menu.)

Fast Arrangement   If you're using the Details view, as shown in Figure 11.2, you can quickly sort the file list by any column by clicking that column's header. For example, click the **Modified** header to sort the files by date. The column by which files are currently being sorted appears with a small triangle on its header.

Replacing the Folders List

The Folders list can be replaced with other Explorer Bars, such as the History list shown in Figure 11.3.

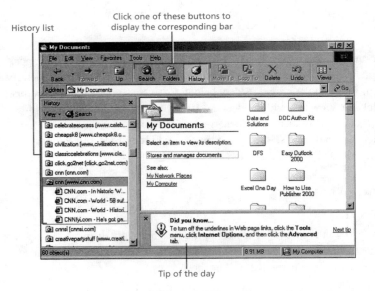

Click one of these buttons to display the corresponding bar

History list

Tip of the day

FIGURE 11.3   The History list displays pages (folders or Web pages) you've viewed recently.

Here's a description of each Explorer bar:

Search   Displays a bar that lets you search your computer, network, or the Internet. You'll learn how to perform searches in Lesson 15, "Creating, Deleting, Renaming, and Finding Files and Folders."

Favorites   Displays a list of your favorite Web sites, as well as a few special folders such as My Documents. You add to this list just as you would within Internet Explorer. See Lesson 26, "Searching for Web Pages and Saving Your Favorites," for help.

History   Displays a list of pages (folders and Web sites) you've visited recently. To display a page, open its folder by clicking it, and then click the page you want to view. Whether the page is a Web page or a file folder, its contents are displayed in the file list window. The History list is displayed in Figure 11.3.

Web Pages in Explorer?   Both My Computer and Explorer can be used as Web browsers of sorts. With the help of the Explorer Bar panels such as Search, Favorites, and History, you can quickly display your favorite Web pages without having to start Internet Explorer.

Tip of the Day   This pane may be displayed *whether or not the Search, Favorites, History, or Folders lists are displayed,* as shown in Figure 11.3. Scroll through tips on how to use My Computer or Explorer by clicking Next tip.

To display the Explorer Bar panels in either My Computer or Explorer, open the **View** menu and select **Explorer Bar**. Then select the panel you want to display. To display the Folders, History, or Search bars more quickly, you can click the appropriate button on the Standard Buttons toolbar.

Viewing Graphic Files

Although Windows 98 provided a simple way of viewing your graphic files from within My Computer and Explorer, Windows Me goes much, much further. So if you have a scanner or digital camera, or if you simply like to collect graphic images from the Web (or create your own graphics using Paint or some other graphics creator), you'll welcome these new changes.

Using Image Preview to View a Graphic

If you use Web view and select a graphic file, it's automatically previewed
on the left of the file list window, along with other file information such
as the file size and date of last modification. This is one method you can
use to quickly locate the image you need. However, if you store your
graphics in the My Pictures folder, you get a bit more than just an image
and some file information. Instead, the graphic is displayed in a small
Image Preview window that provides you with control over the view, as
shown in Figure 11.4.

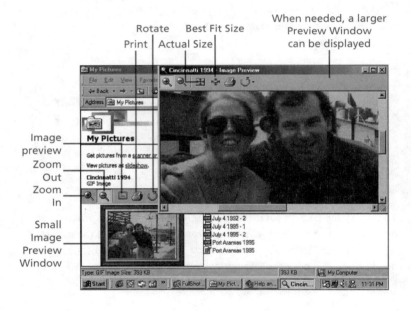

FIGURE 11.4   Image Preview gives you more options for previewing
graphics.

Here are the tools in the Image Preview window:

> **Zoom In**   Enlarges the image.

> **Zoom Out**   Displays more of the image.

Image Preview   Displays the graphic in a larger Image Preview window.

Print   Prints the image.

Rotate   Rotates the image clockwise or counterclockwise.

Actual Size   Displays the picture at its actual size. This button appears only in the larger Image Preview window.

Best Fit Size   Fits the picture to the window. This button appears only in the larger Image Preview window.

Turn On Image Preview   If you want, you can turn on Image Preview for folders other than the My Pictures folder. See "Customizing Web View Folders" later in this lesson.

View Graphic Files as a Full-Screen Show

The Image Preview page displayed in the My Pictures folder provides some additional options for viewing your graphic images. One option allows you to display your graphics, full-screen, in a kind of slide show:

1. Change to the My Pictures folder, or any other folder where Image Preview has been turned on.

2. Click the **slideshow** link, which appears just above the small Image Preview window. The selected image appears. Additional images appear about every ten seconds or so.

You can control the slide show by moving the mouse or pressing any key to display the Slide Show toolbar, shown in Figure 11.5. To stop the slide show at any time, press **Esc** or click **Close the window**.

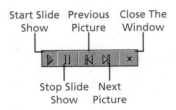

Start Slide   Previous   Close The
Show   Picture   Window

Stop Slide   Next
Show   Picture

FIGURE 11.5   The Slide Show toolbar.

Accessing an Image on Your Scanner or Digital Camera

The Image Preview page provides another useful link. If you use a scanner or digital camera to capture digital images, you can quickly import an image to your computer by following these steps:

1. Change to the My Pictures folder or any other folder where Image Preview has been turned on.

2. Click the **scanner or camera** link, which appears just above the Image Preview window. The Scanner and Camera wizard appears. (You can also choose **Start**, **Programs**, **Accessories**, **Scanner and Camera Wizard** to start the wizard.)

3. If needed, select the device (scanner or digital camera) from which you wish to import the image and click **Next**.

4. Select the options you want. For example, if you're importing a scanner image, you can change from color to grayscale if you like. You can also adjust the quality of the imported image. If you're importing images from a digital camera, select the images you want to import. Click **Next**.

5. Type a name for the file(s), select a folder where you want to store it, and select a file type (or in the case of digital images, enter a file extension, such as .JPG.) If you're importing digital images, you can delete these images from the camera after importing them by selecting **Delete copied pictures from camera.** Click **Finish** when you're through.

6. If you're importing images from a digital camera, check the manual to see if there is any switch (such as a Connect switch) you must change before unplugging the camera from your computer.

Grab That Image In some programs that handle graphic images, such as Paint, you can grab an image directly from your scanner or digital camera, without having to leave the program itself. Just look for a **From Scanner or Camera** command on the program's **File** menu. Then follow the steps in the wizard that appears.

The New Thumbnails View

When you're trying to locate an image, or if you simply want to review the kinds of images you've stored in a particular folder, you may want to switch to Thumbnails view. As shown in Figure 11.6, Thumbnails view displays each graphic in the file list as a miniature "thumbnail" of the image.

Other Files as Well Thumbnails view can be used to display the contents of other files as well, such as Word documents, Excel worksheets, and so on. However, the thumbnails are so small that this view may not be as useful as it is with graphic files.

As explained earlier, to change to Thumbnail view, click the arrow on the **Views** button and select **Thumbnail**.

Slow Down! Changing to Thumbnail view does slow down the file listing because it takes a while to display each thumbnail.

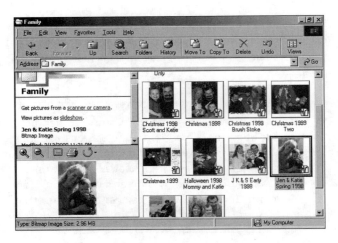

FIGURE **11.6**   Graphic images can be displayed as small thumbnails.

Using Kodak Imaging to View a Graphic

Kodak Imaging is a graphic viewer that you can use to view and manipulate your graphic images. You can think of it as a more powerful version of Image Preview (the viewer that displays graphic images within My Computer or Explorer). With Kodak Imaging, you can view, zoom, annotate, rotate, and print multiple images (.tiff) at one time. You can also view a fax image.

To preview an image, follow these steps:

1. Click **Start**, and then select **Programs**, **Accessories**, **Imaging**. The Kodak Imaging window appears.

2. Click the **Open** button on the toolbar.

3. Select the image you want to view, and then click **Open**. The image appears in the Image Preview window, as shown in Figure 11.7.

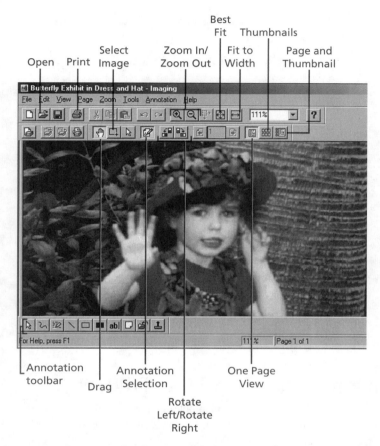

FIGURE 11.7   You can view graphic images with Imaging Preview.

4. Here are some descriptions of the more useful toolbar buttons:

Open   Opens an image for previewing.

Print   Prints the displayed image.

Zoom In   Zooms in on the displayed image.

Zoom Out   After zooming in, this zooms the image back out.

Best Fit   Zooms the image to fit the window.

Fit to Width   Zooms the image to fit the width of the window.

Drag   Lets you move the image within the window by dragging.

Select Image   Lets you select an area of the image.

Annotation Selection   Selects an annotation for copying, moving, deleting, and so on.

Annotation Toolbar   Displays/hides the Annotation toolbar.

Rotate Left   Rotates the image to the left.

Rotate Right   Rotates the image to the right.

One-Page View   Displays one page of the document.

Thumbnail View   Shows multiple pages of the document at once, in small thumbnail-sized windows.

Page and Thumbnail View   Combines the One-Page and Thumbnail views.

Customizing Web View Folders

When you select Web view in My Computer or Explorer, the contents of your folders are displayed as Web pages, with icons representing each file or subfolder. You can customize these Web pages to control how files are organized and displayed within them. You can change the background of a folder by adding a graphic, and change the color of text and the background of the file list. You can also add comments to help explain the folder's contents and intended use. Various templates are provided so you can change to a different file arrangement easily. Or, you can always design your own Web page from scratch. For example, the My Pictures folder displays its graphics using the special Image Preview window. You can add Image Preview to any folder by selecting the Image Preview template.

To create a Web page for a folder, follow these steps:

1. Choose **View, Customize this Folder**. Click **Next**.

2. Choose the option(s) you want and click **Next**:

   Choose or edit an HTML template for this folder Here, you can select a template (such as the Image Preview template) or edit the page using your Web page editor (such as FrontPage or Netscape Composer).

   Modify background picture and filename appearance Add a colorful background to the file list and/or change the colors used in the file list (text and background).

   Add folder comment Add a comment or description for this folder. The comment appears when the folder is selected in the file list—*not when the folder itself is displayed*. You can also add any other HTML command into the text box that appears.

 HTML Short for *Hypertext Markup Language*, HTML is the language used to create Web pages.

---

3. Follow the Wizard's instructions to enter the information needed for the selections you made in step 2. Then click **Finish**.

You can remove your customization of this folder by selecting the **Remove customization** option in the Customize this Folder Wizard dialog box. Then you'll be able to select which aspects of the customization you want to remove, such as the template, background, colors, and folder comment.

In this lesson, you learned how to change the appearance of files in My Computer and Explorer. You learned how to sort files, view graphics, and display files in Web pages. In the next lesson, you'll learn how to set up a home network and access its resources.

LESSON 12

Accessing Resources on Your Home Network

In this lesson, you'll learn how to access files and folders on your home network.

What Is a Network?

A *network* is a collection of interconnected computers. Your computer might be part of a network, especially if you work for a large corporation. A network has *servers* and *clients*. A server shares a resource, such as a hard disk, a printer, or an application. A server can also provide a service, such as email handling. A client uses those resources.

On the network, your computer plays the role of the client, accessing the shared resources you need. On an office network, a special computer is dedicated to the role of server: sharing files, programs, printers, and providing email services. On a home network, a dedicated server is not needed, since with Windows, your PC can *also* play the role of a server, sharing the folders and files you designate with your family members. A network in which there is no dedicated server is called a peer-to-peer network, and it's the only type of network you can create using Windows Me.

System Administrator The system administrator is the person who oversees the network's setup and operation. This person adds and deletes users from the network, controls their access, performs network system updates, and troubleshoots problems.

Installing a Home Network

Not only is home networking getting more and more affordable, but with Windows Me, it's also relatively easy to set up. So, if you own more than one computer and you want them all to share resources such as printers, scanners, Zip drives, hard disks, and even modems, follow these steps:

1. Install a NIC (Network Interface Card) adapter card in each PC that you want to include in the network.

 Easy as Pie If you want more help on deciding what type of network equipment to buy, check out the section on home networking in Windows Help. You'll find details on various types of networking equipment and illustrated plans for setting up different kinds of networks in your home. In most cases, your simplest option will be to buy a networking kit (and extra NICs as needed) to create a simple home network.

2. Using **Add/Remove Hardware** in the Control Panel, set up the NIC for each computer.

 Two Cards If you plan on using Internet sharing (a process that allows you to share a single Internet connection through the network) *and* you plan on connecting to the Internet via DSL or cable modem, you'll need a second NIC in the Internet sharing host PC that's connected to the DSL or cable modem.

3. Connect each NIC to the network hub using twisted pair (CAT 5) wire.

4. Make sure that all the computers on the network are on. On the Windows Me computer, double-click the **My Network Places** icon on the desktop.

5. Double-click the **Home Networking Wizard** icon. The Home Networking Wizard dialog box appears.

6. Click **Next** to continue.

7. If you've already run Home Networking on this computer, you can skip to the part where you create a floppy disk by selecting **I want to create a floppy disk to set up Home Networking on other computers**. Skip to step 13. Otherwise, select **I want to edit my Home Networking settings on this computer**. Click **Next**.

8. Select how you want to connect to the Internet and click **Next** to continue (see Figure 12.1).

   To connect directly via a modem on this computer, select **A direct connection to my ISP using the following device** and choose the appropriate device from those listed. If you use a modem to connect to the Internet, select "Dial-Up Adapter" from the list. If you use a cable modem, DSL, or ISDN connection, select your network interface card from the list.

   To enable Internet Connection Sharing so that this computer can connect to the Internet using a device attached to another computer on the network, select **A connection to another computer on my home network that provides direct access to my Internet service provider (ISP)**. Skip to step 9.

   If you don't plan on accessing the Internet on this computer at all, select **No, this computer does not use the Internet**. Skip to step 9.

9. Type a name for your computer in the **Computer name** text box. This name may include spaces, but it's limited to 15 characters.

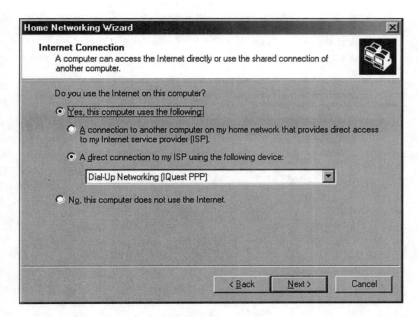

FIGURE **12.1** Choose the method you want to use to connect to the Internet.

Automatic Updates If you choose to let Windows automatically connect to the Internet when needed, AutoUpdate will do so as well. If you don't want Windows to automatically update your computer with new features, turn off this option by following the steps in Lesson 9, "Customizing Other Attributes of Windows."

10. All the computers on your home network must use the same workgroup name. The default workgroup is MSHOME. You can change the name of your workgroup by selecting **Use the workgroup name** and typing a name in the text box. Click **Next** to continue.

11. Select whether you want to share the My Documents Folder, and/or any printers connected to this computer and click **Next** (see Figure 12.2).

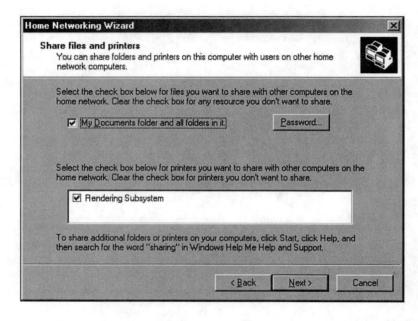

FIGURE 12.2   Select the folders you want to share over the network.

By default, the contents of the My Documents folder are shared. To prevent access to the files in this folder, select **My Documents folders and all folders in it** to turn that option off. If you opt to share the folder, you can require a password to use it by clicking the **Password** button, typing and confirming a password, and clicking **OK**.

Sharing is Nice If you share the My Documents folder, all of its subfolders are shared as well.

A list of printers attached to this computer appears at the bottom of the dialog box. Select any printer(s) you want to share. Click **Next** to continue.

 Share a Few Folders If you want to share selected folders on your computer, follow the steps in the "Sharing Your Resources" section later in this lesson.

12. If you want to add any Windows 95 or 98 computers to your network, create a Home Networking Setup disk by choosing **Yes, create a Home Networking Setup disk**. Click **Next** to continue. (If you select No, then skip to step 15.)

13. If you opted to create a Home Networking Setup disk, insert a disk now and click **Next**. Otherwise, skip this step.

 Don't Lose Important Data! Make sure that the disk you use doesn't contain any important data, because it will be erased.

14. If you created a Home Networking Setup disk, remove it and click **Finish**.

15. You may be prompted to restart the computer. If so, close any programs and click **Yes** to continue. When prompted, type the username and password you want to use to gain access to the network and your computer. (If you like, you can use the same username and password you used before you set up the network.)

16. If you restarted your computer, there's a message telling you that Home Networking has been set up properly. Click **OK**.

If you're setting up other computers on your network, follow the preceding steps for any Windows Me computer. If a computer on the network is running Windows 95/98, follow these steps to add it to the network:

1. Insert the disk you just created into its drive. Then click **Start**, **Run**, type **setup.exe** in the text box, and click **OK**.

Windows 95/98 Only   You can use the Home Networking Wizard described here to set up the other computers on our network, but only if they're using Windows 95 or 98.

2. Click **Next** to begin.

3. Select whether you want to share an Internet connection over the network or use your own. Click **Next** to continue.

4. Type a name for your computer in the **Computer name** text box. If you want, change the name of your workgroup by selecting **Use the workgroup name** and typing a name in the text box. Click **Next** to continue.

5. Select whether you want to share the My Documents folder and/or any printers attached to this computer. As before, you can add a password to the shared folder for better security by clicking **Password**, typing and confirming a password and clicking **OK** and click **Next**.

6. Click **Finish**. The network is now set up on this PC. Repeat this process for each computer you want to add to the network.

Setting Up Multiple Users for One Computer

After you've set up a network on your Windows Me computer, the computer is restarted and you're prompted to type a username and password. Doing so gives you access to the resources of your computer and the network. If more than one person uses this computer, you can set up multiple usernames so that each user can select preferences for the desktop and Start menu and create separate Documents, Favorites, My Documents, and downloaded Web page folders. Follow these steps:

1. Click **Start**, **Settings**, **Control Panel**.

2. If needed, click **view all Control Panel options** and then double-click **Users**. The Enable Multiple-user Settings dialog box appears. Click **Next**.

3. Type a name for the new user in the **User name** text box and click **Next**.

4. Type a password, type it again to confirm, and click **Next**.

5. Select the items you want to vary by user and click **Next** (see Figure 12.3).

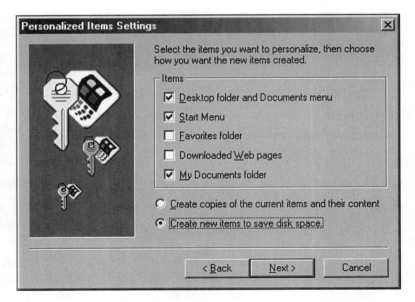

FIGURE **12.3**   Select the items you want to be unique to this user.

6. Click **Finish**.

7. You're asked if you want to log back on as this new user. Choose **Yes** or **No** as you prefer.

Repeat these steps to set up unique usernames/passwords for other users.

To log on as a different user at any time, click **Start**, **Log Off**, and then type a different username/password after the computer restarts. After you log on, the preferences and folders established by that user are displayed. To display a list of users at startup, make Microsoft Family Logon your primary network logon by right-clicking the **My Network Places** icon, choosing **Properties**, selecting **Microsoft Family Logon** from the **Primary Network Logon** list, and clicking **OK**.

Accessing Shared Resources

You access the network's shared resources, such as folders, files, and printers, through My Network Places. Follow these steps:

1. Double-click the **My Network Places** icon on the desktop, or select it in My Computer or Explorer.

2. Shared folders appear. To open a shared folder, double-click it.

If you double-click the **Entire Network** icon, the computers on the network appear. Printers attached to the network appear also. To view the shared folders on a computer, double-click its icon.

 Shared Printers   Before you can use a printer that's shared over a network, you must copy its driver files to your computer. These driver files help your computer talk to that particular printer. To learn how to install a shared printer, see Lesson 20, "Printing in Windows."

Locating a Resource   If you know the name of a file, folder, or computer on the network, you can use the **Search** command to locate it. In My Computer, My Network Places, or Explorer, click **Search**. Type the name of the file, folder, or computer in the text box. Then, if needed, click the appropriate link: **Computers** or **Files or Folders**. Click **Search Now**.

Connecting to the Internet Through a Shared Modem

When you set up the home network, you had the option of sharing the Internet connection of any computer with other computers on the network by using something called Internet Connection Sharing. If you set up Internet Connection Sharing on one of your network computers, follow these steps to access the Internet from any of the other computers on the network:

1. If you didn't opt for automatic connection, connect to the Internet manually on the Internet Connection Sharing computer.

2. From any other computer on the network, start a Web browser or email program and request information in the normal manner.

 It's Not Too Late   If you've already set up your network and you'd like to turn on the Internet Connection Sharing feature, rerun the Home Networking Wizard (as explained earlier in this lesson) and select that option.

Sharing Your Resources

When you used the Home Networking Wizard to set up your home network, you may have opted to share your My Documents and Shared Documents folders and/or your printer. You can share other folders and any new printers if you like. When you share a resource, you determine the level of access you want to provide, and to whom. There are three levels of access:

Read Only   Users can view the contents of a file, but they can't change its data.

Full   Users can view and change the contents of a file.

Depends on Password   A user's access level depends on his or her password.

To share a folder on the network, follow these steps:

1. In My Computer or Explorer, right-click the folder you want to share and select **Sharing**.

2. Click **Shared As** to enable sharing. See Figure 12.4.

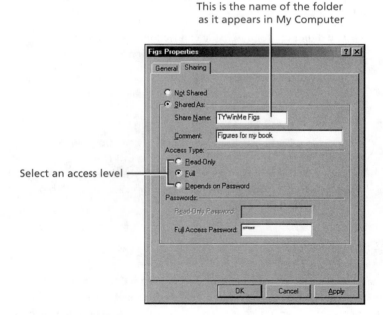

FIGURE 12.4   Selecting users to share with.

3. If you like, change the share name for the folder. (This is the name that appears in a user's My Computer, Explorer, or My Network Places window.) Add a comment as well. (This comment appears when the mouse is placed over the shared folder for a moment.)

4. Select the access level you want to use with this folder.

5. If you selected **Depends on Password** in step 4, type different passwords under **Read-Only** and **Full**. (You can leave the **Read-Only** text box blank if you want to allow all users at least read-only access to the folder.) A person's access level to the folder will depend on the password he or she uses.

    If you selected **Read-Only** or **Full** in step 4, you can place additional security on the folder by typing a password in the appropriate box, although passwords aren't required.

6. Click **OK**.

7. If prompted, retype any passwords you entered and click **OK**. The shared folder appears in My Computer, Explorer, and My Network Places with a shared icon (a hand holding a folder).

Sending Notes Over the Network

Using Win Popup, you can send quick notices over your network to anyone else on the network. You might use this to remind your kids it's time for bed or to challenge your spouse to a rousing game of Descent.

You may need to install Win Popup by following the steps in Appendix A, "Configuring Hardware and Adding/Removing Windows Components." Win Popup must be installed on all the computers on the network with which you want to communicate. It isn't added to the Start menu automatically, so you'll need to do that as well. See Lesson 9 for help. (You'll find Win Popup in the Windows folder.)

To use Win Popup to send messages:

1. Start Win Popup on all the computers. (You might want to add Win Popup to the Start folder so that it's started automatically each time you restart the computer.)

2. Win Popup can remain minimized most of the time. When you want to send a message, click the **Send** button, as shown in Figure 12.5.

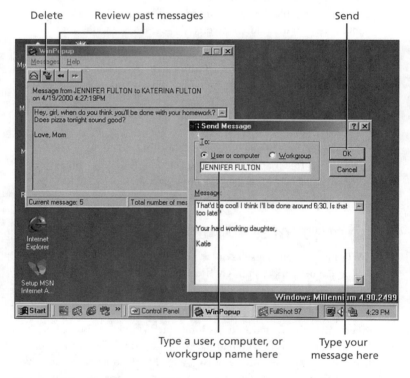

Delete   Review past messages   Send

Type a user, computer, or   Type your
workgroup name here   message here

FIGURE **12.5**   Sending a quick message over a network is easy.

3. Select either **User or computer** or **Workgroup**, enter a name, and type your message. Click **OK** to send.

4. You're told that your message was sent. Click **OK**.

If Win Popup is minimized, you hear a chime when a message comes in. Open the Win Popup window to view the most recent message. To review older messages, click the left-arrow button. To delete the current message, click **Delete**. You can set up Win Popup to automatically open its window when a message is received by choosing **Messages**, **Options**, selecting **Pop up dialog on message receipt**, and clicking **OK**.

In this lesson, you learned how to access resources on the network. You also learned how to share your own resources.

LESSON 13

Selecting, Copying, and Moving Files and Folders

In this lesson, you'll learn how to copy and move files and folders.

Selecting Multiple Files and Folders

Before you can copy or move a file or folder, you must select it. When you select a file or folder, it becomes highlighted. You can select more than one file or folder at a time in order to move or copy multiple files or folders in one step.

To select a file or folder, do either of the following:

- Click the file or folder you want to select.

- If you have the Single-Click option turned on, simply point at the file you want to select. After a second or so, the file is highlighted to indicate it's selected.

Notice that when you select a file or group of files, the total size and number appears in the status bar, as shown in Figure 13.1. If you're using Web view, this information appears to the left of the file list. (To see the amount of free space on a drive, select a drive or folder on that drive from the Folder list.) Although it's not shown in Figure 13.1, if you select a single file, you'll see detailed information about that file—such as the file type, date of last modification, size, and author—to the left of the file list. In addition, you'll usually see a small preview of the file's contents.

To select files or folders listed next to each other, as in Figure 13.1, do one of the following:

- Click the first file or folder in the list, and then press and hold the **Shift** key as you click the last file you want to select.

- If you're using the Single-Click option, point at the first file or folder you want to select and then press and hold the **Shift** key as you point to the last file you want to select.

- To select all files in a folder, press **Ctrl+A** or choose **Edit**, **Select All**.

Noncontiguous files

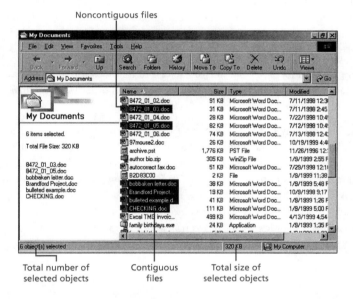

Total number of   Contiguous   Total size of
selected objects   files   selected objects

FIGURE 13.1   You can select multiple files or folders to copy or move.

To select files or folders that are *not* listed next to each other (see Figure 13.1), do one of the following:

- Click the first file or folder you want to select, and then press and hold the **Ctrl** key as you click each additional file or folder.

- If you're using the Single-Click option, point at the first file or folder you want to select, and then press and hold the **Ctrl** key as you point to each additional file or folder.

Copying and Moving Files and Folders

Once the files or folders you want to work with are selected, you can copy or move them as needed. When you copy a file or folder, the original file or folder remains as is and a copy is placed in the location you choose. Thus, two copies of the file or folder exist. You might copy files to another drive (as a backup in case the originals are damaged somehow) or to a disk for transport to another computer.

When you move a file or folder, it's deleted from its original location and then placed in the new location you select. In this scenario, only one copy of the file or folder exists. You might move files in order to reorganize them so they're easier to locate.

The simplest way to copy or move a file or folder is to use *drag-and-drop*. Basically, you drag the objects to their new location and then drop them where you want them. In order to drag-and-drop successfully, you must be able to see, within the My Computer or Explorer window, both the original location of the file or folder *and* the location where you want to copy or move it. (See Figure 13.2.) You can still copy or move your files even if you can't see both locations, but you'll want to use the copy to or cut-and-paste method, as explained later in this section.

For Easy Drag-and-Drop, Use the Folders List
Because the file hierarchy of your computer appears in the Folders list, it's easy to arrange things so that you can see both the original location and the final location of your files. Display the Folders list (by clicking the **Folders** button) when you drag-and-drop files to copy or move them.

Destination Folder

Files to be
copied or moved

Contents of original folder
are displayed here

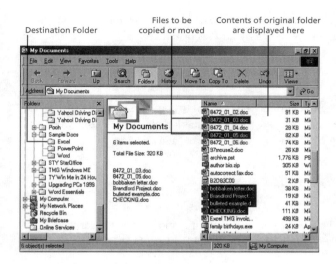

FIGURE **13.2** To make drag-and-drop easier, make sure both the
original folder and the destination folder are visible.

Copying Files and Folders

To copy a file or folder, follow these steps:

1. Select the files or folders you want to copy. (See the earlier section, "Selecting Multiple Files and Folders," for help.)

2. Press and hold down the **Ctrl** key as you drag the files or folders to their new location. Notice that the mouse pointer changes to an arrow with a small plus sign above it.

3. Release the mouse button.

Already There?   If the files already exist in the location you're trying to copy them to, you'll see a warning telling you so. You can overwrite the existing files with the copies by clicking **Yes**.

If neither the original location nor the destination location is visible, you can follow these steps to copy your files or folders:

1. Select the files or folders you want to copy.

2. Click the **Copy to** button on the Standard Buttons toolbar.

3. Select the folder or drive you want to copy to and click **OK**. (You can create a new folder within the selected folder/drive by clicking **New Folder**, typing a name, and clicking **OK**.)

Moving Files and Folders

To move files or folders, follow these steps:

1. Select the files or folders you want to move. (See the earlier section, "Selecting Multiple Files and Folders" for help.)

2. Press and hold down the **Shift** key as you drag the files or folders to their new location.

3. Release the mouse button.

 Drag-and-Drop Methods   If you're moving files within the same drive—for example, from a folder on drive C to another folder on drive C—you don't have to hold down the **Shift** key as you drag. In addition, if you're copying files from one drive to another, you don't need to hold down the **Ctrl** key.

If neither the original location nor the destination location is visible, you can follow these steps to move your files or folders:

1. Select the files or folders you want to move.

2. Click the **Move to** button on the Standard Buttons toolbar.

3. Select the folder or drive you want to move to and click **OK**. (You can create a new folder within the selected folder/drive by clicking **New Folder**, typing a name, and clicking **OK**.)

Oops!   If you copy or move the wrong files or folders, you can undo your mistake by clicking the **Undo** button on the Standard Buttons toolbar.

Using Send To to Copy Files

If you often copy files to a disk or a particular folder, you can use the **Send To** menu option to perform that task more quickly. Follow these steps:

1. Select the files or folders you want to copy.

2. Right-click and select **Send To** from the menu that appears.

3. Select the destination for the files or folders from the **Send To** menu:

   3 1/2 Floppy(A)   Copies the files to a disk drive.

   Compressed Folder   Compresses the selected files and places them in a compressed folder.

   Desktop (create shortcut)   Creates a shortcut icon to the files and places that shortcut on the desktop. You can then open the files by clicking (or double-clicking) them.

   Fax Recipient   Sends the files directly to your fax machine or fax modem for transmission.

   Mail Recipient   Creates a brief email message with the files you selected attached to it.

   My Documents   Copies the files to the My Documents folder.

   Removable Disk   Copies the files to a removable drive, such as a Zip disk.

   Shared Documents   Copies the files to a shared folder.

   Web Publishing Wizard   Sends the files to the Web Publishing Wizard so you can copy them to a Web folder on the Internet or an intranet.

Programs may add commands to your Send To menu, so it may have more options than listed here. You can add your own destinations to the Send To menu as well, such as a favorite folder where you like to keep files. Follow these steps:

1. Select the destination (a folder or a program file) you want to add to the Send To menu.

2. Press and hold down the right mouse button as you drag the folder to the **Send To** folder within the Windows folder on your hard drive.

3. Select **Create Shortcut(s) Here** from the shortcut menu that appears. A shortcut icon to the folder appears within the **Send To** folder. The next time the Send To menu is opened, the shortcut you created will appear on the menu.

In this lesson, you learned how to select, copy, and move files and folders. You also learned how to use the Send To menu option to save time. In the next lesson, you'll learn how to compress and uncompress files.

LESSON 14

Compressing and Uncompressing Files

In this lesson, you'll learn how to compress and uncompress files.

What Is File Compression?

File compression is a method of shrinking a file so that it takes up less space on a disk. If you want to send files to your friends or colleagues by email, first you should shrink those files to their smallest size. By making the files smaller, you'll encounter less problems when transmitting them via email to another destination. You might also want to use file compression to shrink files before copying them to a diskette or a Zip drive for backup storage.

You may have used (or at least heard of) WinZip, a popular file compression program that creates zip files. (Basically, a zip file contains one or more compressed files.) Windows Me now includes its own file compression program, which works in a similar manner, as part of My Computer and Windows Explorer. Compression shrinks a file or group of files through a mathematical process that eliminates unnecessary characters. These files are then placed inside another file, which Windows calls a *compressed folder*.

Compression Depression? The compressed folders feature is not installed by default, so you may have to install it first. See Appendix A, "Configuring Hardware and Adding/Removing Windows Components," for help.

Totally Compatible Compressed folders in Windows are totally compatible with other file compression programs, such as WinZip. The compressed folder—which is really a file—ends with the standard `.zip` file extension, so other users probably won't even notice a difference. Therefore, if you want to share your files with people who use WinZip or some other zip-compatible file compression program, you can.

Compressing Files into a Folder

To compress a file or files, first you must create a compressed folder. Then simply drag the files you want to compress, drop them on the folder, and Windows compresses them for you automatically! Compressed folders are easy to identify by their zipped-folder icon, as shown in Figure 14.1. You should also notice that, because compressed folders are really zip files, *they don't appear in the Folder list*.

To create a compressed folder and add files to it, follow these steps:

1. Change to the folder where you want the compressed folder to appear.

2. Select **File**, **New**, **Compressed Folder**.

3. Type a name for the folder and press **Enter**.

4. Select the files you want to compress and drag them to the compressed folder. The files are compressed and then copied (not moved) to the compressed folder.

Compressed folders
do not appear
in the folders list

Compressed folders
use a special icon

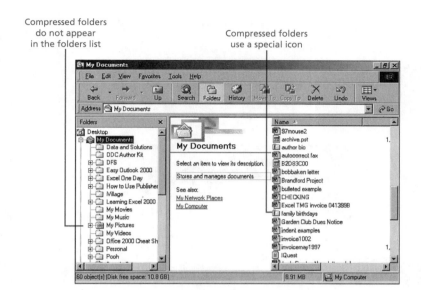

FIGURE **14.1** Compressed folders are easy to identify.

You can add more files to your compressed folder later on by dragging
and dropping them on the folder. To delete a file from a compressed
folder, open the folder, select the file, and press **Delete**. This deletes only
the compressed version of the file, thus making the compressed folder a
bit smaller. The original file is unharmed.

Send Those Files!   After compressing files into a
folder, you can include them with an email message to
share them with your friends and colleagues. Simply
attach the compressed folder file to an outgoing message as described in Lesson 29, "Sending and
Receiving Mail with Outlook Express."

Viewing Files in a Compressed Folder

As mentioned before, the compressed folder appears in the file list with a zip-folder icon. To view the files it contains, double-click the folder to open it. The folder and its contents appear in a new My Computer/ Explorer window, as shown in Figure 14.2.

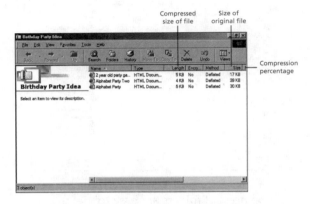

FIGURE 14.2   When opened, a compressed folder looks like an ordinary folder.

 View Details   If you want to view the percentage of compression for each file and other compression details, change to the **Details** view, as shown in Figure 14.2.

You can view the contents of a compressed file without decompressing it first. Just double-click the file you want to view and the program associated with that file opens to display its contents.

Decompress It First! If you want to make changes to a compressed file, you should decompress it first. Also, if you want to open a program file that's stored in a compressed folder, you should decompress it first. You'll learn how to decompress files later in this lesson.

Encrypting a Compressed Folder

If you're going to send your compressed folder over the Internet or post it in a public place such as a network or a shared folder, you may want to control access to the folder with a password. Here's how:

1. After creating the compressed folder and copying the files to it, encrypt the compressed folder by right-clicking it and selecting **Encrypt**.

2. Type a password in the **Password** text box. (Passwords are case sensitive, which means that the password "SECRET" is different than "secret" or "Secret".)

3. Confirm the password by typing it again in the **Confirm Password** text box. Click **OK**.

If someone wants to view the contents of a file within your encrypted compressed folder, they'll need to enter the correct password.

Decrypting a Compressed Folder

To view the contents of any file in an encrypted compressed folder, you must decrypt the folder first. This removes the password protection and allows free access to the compressed files. Follow these steps:

1. Right-click the encrypted compressed folder and select **Decrypt** from the shortcut menu.

2. Type the same password that was used to encrypt the folder in the **Password** text box. The folder is decrypted; you can now view the contents of any file in the folder.

Extracting Files from a Compressed Folder

When files are placed in a compressed folder, they're shrunk so they take up less space. Although you can view the contents of a compressed file, you'll want to decompress (extract) the file before making any permanent changes to it.

To extract selected files from a compressed folder, just drag them from the compressed folder to another folder. If the compressed folder is encrypted, you'll need to type the password in order to proceed. The compressed version of the file remains in the compressed folder; an uncompressed version of the file is then copied to the other folder. If the file was encrypted, the encryption is removed and the file is ready to use. (The copy of the file in the encrypted folder remains encrypted, however.)

Remember, to actually delete a file from a compressed folder, you must select that file and press **Delete**. Also, you can select multiple files and decompress them in a single step if you like.

If you want to extract all the files in a compressed folder, there's a simple way to do that:

1. Right-click the compressed folder and select **Extract All**.

2. Type the path to the folder where you want to place the decompressed files, or click **Browse** and select the folder from a list. If you don't specify anything, Windows creates a folder with the same name as the compressed folder—minus the zip-folder icon, of course.

3. If the compressed folder is encrypted, click **Password** and then type the password in the text box that appears (see Figure 14.3). Click **Next**.

4. If you want, you can choose **Show extracted files** to have Windows open the folder where the decompressed files were copied in a new window.

5. Click **Finish**.

Type a password here

FIGURE 14.3   You can quickly decompress all the files in a folder.

In this lesson, you learned how to compress and uncompress files. In the next lesson, you'll learn how to create, delete, rename, and locate files and folders.

Creating, Deleting, Renaming, and Finding Files and Folders

In this lesson, you'll learn how to create, delete, rename, and find files and folders.

Creating a Folder

Windows provides a My Documents folder for your data files. But instead of dumping all your files into one big folder, you might prefer to organize them by creating subfolders within the My Documents folder. Or you might want to create your own folders somewhere else on your hard drive.

Here's how to create a new folder:

1. Select the drive where you want to place your new folder. To create a subfolder, select the folder where you want your new folder to be placed. For example, select the My Documents folder to create a subfolder for it.

2. Open the **File** menu and select **New**.

3. Select **Folder** from the cascading menu that appears. A folder is created in the current directory.

4. Type a name for the folder and press **Enter**. You can give the folder any name, up to 255 characters long (including spaces).

Deleting a File or Folder

When you delete a file or folder, it's placed in the Recycle Bin. This gives you a chance to retrieve an accidentally deleted file. You'll learn how to use the Recycle Bin in the next section. If you delete a folder, you're also deleting all the files contained in it.

 Insurance Policy Even with the Recycle Bin, it's still possible to lose a file. So you might want to back up your files before you delete them. See Lesson 17, "Performing Disk Management," for help.

To delete files or folders, follow these steps:

1. Select the files or folders you want to delete.

2. Click the **Delete** button on the Standard Buttons toolbar, or press the **Delete** key on the keyboard. The Confirm File Delete dialog box appears.

3. Click **Yes** to delete the files or folders.

 I Didn't Mean to Delete That! If you notice right away that you've made a mistake deleting a file or folder, click the **Undo** button on the Standard Buttons toolbar to restore the file. Otherwise, read the next section to learn how to retrieve your file or folder from the Recycle Bin.

Emptying the Recycle Bin

Once a file or folder is sent to the Recycle Bin, it stays there until you empty the bin. This helps prevent the accidental deletion of files.

To retrieve a file or folder from the Recycle Bin, follow these steps:

1. Open the Recycle Bin by double-clicking its icon on the desktop (see Figure 15.1).

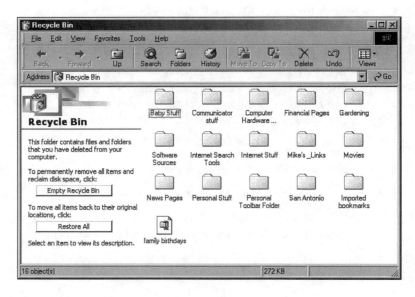

FIGURE **15.1**   Deleted items are moved to the Recycle Bin.

2. Select the items you want to restore and click **Restore**. (To restore everything in the Recycle Bin click **Restore All** without selecting anything.) The items you select are restored to their original locations. (The Restore button, by the way, does not appear until you select a file or folder.)

Not All Files   The Recycle Bin can't be used to restore files that were deleted from a disk or Zip disk. These files aren't saved to the Recycle Bin—only files on the hard disk(s).

Now, because you might have deleted several files or folders in order to make more room on your hard disk, and because all those deleted files and folders were moved to the Recycle Bin but weren't really removed from the hard disk, you'll need to empty the Recycle Bin in order to gain extra hard disk space.

To empty the Recycle Bin, follow these steps:

1. Double-click the **Recycle Bin** icon on the desktop.

2. Click **Empty Recycle Bin**.

3. Click **Yes** to confirm.

If you want to remove only one or two items from the Recycle Bin, you can. Just select them and click the **Delete** button on the Standard Buttons toolbar, or press the **Delete** key on the keyboard.

 Empty It Quickly   You can actually empty the Recycle Bin without opening it. Simply right-click the Recycle Bin icon on the desktop and select **Empty Recycle Bin** from the shortcut menu that appears.

Bypassing the Recycle Bin

You can delete files or folders without sending them to the Recycle Bin. This saves you the step of emptying the bin later to get rid of the files. However, it also removes your "safety net." Here's what to do:

1. Select the file or folder you want to permanently delete.

2. Press and hold down the **Shift** key.

3. Right-click and select **Delete** from the shortcut menu.

4. Click **Yes** to confirm.

You can turn off the Recycle Bin for all your file deletions if you want, although it might be dangerous because you'll have no way to restore accidentally deleted files. To turn off the Recycle Bin, right-click its icon on the desktop and select **Properties** from the shortcut menu. Select the **Do not move files to the Recycle Bin** option and click **OK**.

Renaming Files and Folders

You might want to rename a file or folder if it turns out that the original name you chose doesn't clearly identify its purpose. To rename a file or folder, follow these steps:

1. Click the file or folder you want to rename. (You can rename only one object at a time.)

2. Click the file or folder again. The name is highlighted. (These two clicks must be done slowly so they aren't confused with a double-click.)

3. A cursor appears in the filename. Type a new filename, or simply make changes as needed, and then press **Enter**.

You can also rename a file or folder by selecting it and choosing **File**, **Rename**. Use this method if the click-click method is too difficult for you.

Searching for a File

With the large hard drives in use today, it's easy to lose track of a single file. You can search for your lost files by entering a complete or partial name, the date the file was created, the file type, or the file's size. You can even look for some matching text within the file.

 Recent Documents   To find a file you've used recently, try the Documents menu. Click **Start**, and then select **Documents** to display a list of files that you've used recently.

If you're unsure of the exact spelling of a filename, you can use wildcards. There are two wildcards you can use: an asterisk represents multiple characters, and a question mark represents a single character. Table 15.1 lists some sample uses of wildcards.

TABLE 15.1   Examples of Wildcards

Wildcard Entered	Search Results
sales*.doc	sales95.doc, sales 96.doc, sales.97.doc
sales.*	sales.doc, sales.xls, sales.ppt
sales?.doc	sales1.doc, sales2.doc, sales3.doc
sales??.doc	sales11.doc, sales12.doc
sa*.xls	sailing.xls, sales97.xls, sam.xls
sa*.*	sailing.xls, sales97.doc, sam.ppt

If you type just the word "sales" with no wildcards, Windows searches for all files that contain that word, whether it's at the beginning, middle, or end (Sales Report.doc, June Sales.xls, Bert Salesberg.doc, and so on).

To search for a file or folder, follow these steps:

1. In Explorer or My Computer, click the **Search** button on the Standard Buttons toolbar. The Search bar appears, as shown in Figure 15.2.

 Anywhere, Anytime   You can initiate a search without starting My Computer or Explorer. Just click the **Start** button and select **Search, For Files or Folders**.

Type a filename   Select a drive and
to search for   folder to search on

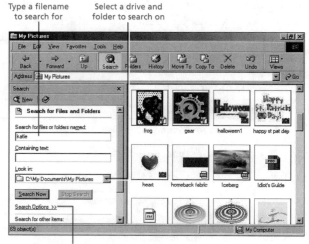

Be sure to check this option to
include subfolders in the search

FIGURE **15.2**   Searching for a lost file.

2. Type the name you want to search for in the **Search for files or folders named** text box. You can use wildcards if you like.

3. If you want to search for a file that contains a particular phrase, type that phrase in the **Containing text** text box.

4. Select the folder or drive you want to search from the **Look in** drop-down list box, or select **Browse** to search for an unlisted folder or drive.

5. If needed, click **Search Options** to set additional conditions for the search:

   Date searches for files that match the date you specify.

   Type searches for files that match the file type you select.

Size searches for files of a particular size.

Advanced Options searches subfolders and/or makes the search case sensitive.

6. When you're through selecting options, click **Search Now**. Windows searches the selected folder or drive, and any subfolders as well (assuming that option is selected, which it is by default). Compressed folders are searched as well if they're contained in the drive/folder(s) you're searching. The results appear in the right pane, as shown in Figure 15.3.

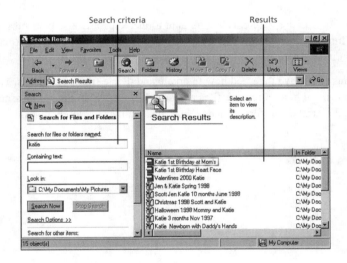

FIGURE 15.3   The results of your search.

 Stop That!   If the search takes too long, you can cancel it by clicking **Stop Search**.

7. If you don't get the results you wanted, you can modify your search criteria and click **Search Now** again. Or, to erase the criteria and start over, click the **New** button at the top of the bar. To remove the Search bar, click its **Close** button or click the **Search** button on the Standard Buttons toolbar.

Once you've located your file, you can open it by double-clicking its icon. You can delete, rename, copy, or move the file as described in this and earlier lessons. To display the folder where the file is located, click the file to select it and then click the folder link that appears at the top of the window.

You can also use the **Search** command to locate people and Web sites on the Internet. See Lesson 26, "Searching for Web Pages and Saving Your Favorites," for help.

In this lesson, you learned how to create and delete files and folders. You also learned how to rename files and search for them. In the next lesson, you'll learn how to format, name, and make copies of floppy disks.

LESSON 16

Formatting, Naming, and Copying Floppy Disks

In this lesson, you'll learn how to maintain your floppy disks. You'll learn how to judge the remaining space on a disk, format a disk, and make a copy of an existing disk.

How to Tell How Much Room Is on a Disk

Even though today's disks contain much more space than old-style disks, they can hold only so much data. So before you decide to use a disk to store a particular set of files, you should see how much room is on it. You can use the same steps to determine the amount of space left on your hard disk.

To see how much room is on a disk, select the drive you want to check from the **Address** drop-down list box or the **Folders** list. In Web view, the total capacity and the amount of free space on the selected drive appears in the information area to the left of the file list, as shown in Figure 16.1. In Classic view, the total amount of space occupied by files appears in the status bar.

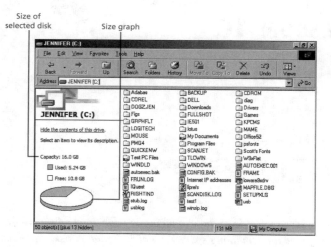

Size of
selected disk   Size graph

FIGURE 16.1   The graph lets you quickly assess the remaining space
on a disk.

Formatting a Floppy Disk

Before you can use a disk for the first time, it must be formatted.
Formatting divides the disk into segments that the computer uses to store
(and later, to locate) data on the disk. Although most disks you buy today
are already formatted, you might want to reformat a disk to erase its contents or to check for errors.

To format a disk, follow these steps:

1. Select **My Computer** from the **Address** drop-down list box or
   the **Folders** list.

2. In the file list, click the icon for the disk you want to format.

Quicker Formatting Another way to format a disk is to right-click it within the Folders list and select **Format** from the shortcut menu that appears. *Do not select the disk from the Folders list or you won't be able to format it.*

3. Open the **File** menu and select **Format**. The Format dialog box appears, as shown in Figure 16.2.

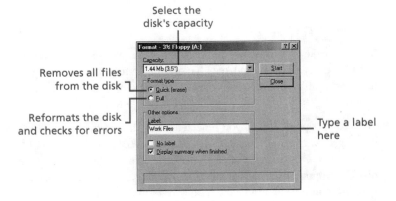

Select the disk's capacity

Removes all files from the disk

Reformats the disk and checks for errors

Type a label here

FIGURE 16.2 To prepare a disk for use, format it.

4. Double-check the capacity and, if needed, select the correct capacity from the drop-down list.

5. Select the type of format you want to perform from the **Format type** list. Usually, a **Quick** format is all that's needed, especially if the disk has been used before. If you're having problems with the disk, select **Full**.

6. Type a label for the disk (up to 11 characters), such as "Work Files". If you don't want to use a label, select that option.

7. Normally, a summary is displayed when the formatting process is over; this allows you to verify that everything went well. If you don't want to display this summary, uncheck the **Display summary when finished** option to turn it off.

8. When you're ready, click **Start** to begin the formatting process. When it's done, a summary is displayed if you selected that option in step 7. After viewing the summary, click **Close**.

9. You can format additional disks by repeating steps 4 through 8. When you're through, click **Close**.

Copying a Disk

You can make an exact copy of a disk whenever you need to. Use the copy for everyday tasks and keep the original in a safe place. This will help ensure that your data won't get lost if some of your disks become damaged.

To make a copy of a disk, you'll need another disk of the exact same size and capacity. *You can't make a copy of one type of disk onto a disk of another size or capacity.* Usually, you'll use a single disk drive to copy disks, swapping disks halfway through the process. However, you can use two different drives, provided that they're of the same type.

Follow these steps:

1. Insert the disk you want to copy into the disk drive.

2. Select **My Computer** from the **Address** drop-down list box or the **Folders** list.

3. In the file list, click the icon for the disk you want to format. *Do not select the disk from the Folders list or you won't be able to copy it.*

4. Open the **File** menu and select **Copy Disk**. The Copy Disk dialog box appears, as shown in Figure 16.3.

FIGURE **16.3**   Make copies of important disks.

5. If needed, select the drive you want to copy from and copy to, and then click **Start**.

6. When prompted, insert the disk you want to copy to and click **OK**.

7. If you have another disk to copy, insert it into its drive and repeat steps 5 and 6. When you're through, click **Close**.

In this lesson, you learned how to determine the amount of space on a disk. You also learned how to format and copy disks. In the next lesson, you'll learn how to perform regular maintenance to protect your computer.

LESSON 17

Performing Disk Management

In this lesson, you'll learn how to perform routine maintenance on your hard disk.

Using the Maintenance Wizard to Improve Performance

With the Maintenance Wizard, you can schedule regular maintenance tasks to be performed on your computer's hard disk. These tasks include the following:

- Defragmenting the hard disk

- Checking the disk for errors using ScanDisk

- Deleting unneeded files with Disk Cleanup

Although you can perform each of these tasks manually, why should you when Windows can perform them at times when the computer's not busy? With Maintenance Wizard, you can choose the Express setup (where you need only specify when you want these tasks to be performed) or Custom setup (which gives you control over which tasks are performed and when/how they're carried out).

To help you make an informed choice, here are brief descriptions of these tasks.

Disk Defragmenter

When a file is stored to a disk, it's broken into chunks and each chunk is stored in the first available sector on the disk. When the disk starts getting full and files are deleted (making certain sectors available), these file chunks are no longer saved in adjacent sectors.

Thus, a file may be scattered (or *fragmented*) throughout the disk, which can slow down its retrieval. To improve the speed of your PC, you should *defragment* your hard disk. Defragmenting reorganizes the parts of each file so that they're once again adjacent to each other on the hard disk, eliminating excess retreival time.

ScanDisk

Sometimes a file isn't stored to disk properly and the computer loses part of it. This can happen when a file is deleted and the references to all the parts of the file aren't removed from the main file directory (File Allocation Table). In any case, it's a good idea to periodically check your hard disk for this type of error and let the computer fix the problems it finds.

Disk Cleanup

You probably know just how quickly a hard disk can be filled with junk. Disk Cleanup removes that junk from the hard disk to make room for more junk (I mean, *important files*). Here's a list of what Windows considers junk (if you disagree, use the Custom setup option in the Maintenance Wizard to select the items you don't want to be removed):

- **Temporary Internet files** When you choose a Web page to view, it takes a while for your Web browser to display it because the background, text, graphics, and sounds must be downloaded to your system. In order to display the page more quickly the next time you return to it, the files needed to display that page are kept on your hard disk temporarily. However, if you don't mind waiting a bit the next time you return to a previously viewed Web page, you can safely rid your system of these files.

- **Offline Web pages**   When you use the Active Desktop to display channels or other Web pages, they're stored on your hard disk so you can view them offline. These pages can be deleted and then downloaded again if you need them.

- **Old ScanDisk files in the root folder**   When ScanDisk encounters a file that wasn't saved properly to the hard disk, it often "fixes" the problem by resaving the remaining portion so you can try to reconstruct the file if needed. In most cases that's impossible, so you might as well delete these files.

- **Temporary files, Temporary Setup Files, Windows Setup temorary files**   A lot of programs save files to your hard disk temporarily, such as installation files and previous versions of updated documents. These programs are supposed to remove their temporary files when they're done with them, but sometimes a problem with the computer prevents that from happening. So why not let Windows remove these unneeded files so you can have more room on the hard disk?

- **Downloaded program files**   Some Web pages contain automated graphics, display windows, and other annoyances that remain on your hard disk long after you leave the page. These, like other saved Web page information, can be safely removed.

- **Temporary PC Health files**   PC Health helps to maintain the integrity of your system by making copies of install files, which you can typically remove after the installation is complete.

- **Application debugging information**   When applications freeze or run into other problems, Windows makes a note of it in case you enlist their technical support staff for help. However, if your programs are running fine, you can safely remove these information-only files.

- **Recycle Bin**   I don't need to tell you that the Recycle Bin is full of junk you no longer need, so why not let Windows take out your trash?

- **Windows uninstall information**   If you're upgrading to Windows Me from a previous version of Windows, Setup automatically saves information it needs to return you to that previous version. If, after using Windows Me for awhile, you decide that there's no reason to return to an older version of Windows, you should remove these files because they take up a lot of room.

Setting Up the Maintenance Wizard

Once you set up the Maintenance Wizard, it will run automatically at scheduled times and perform the tasks you've assigned it. After the Maintenance Wizard is set up, you can make changes to it at any time (see the next section, "Modifying Scheduled Tasks.")

If you want to run Disk Defragmenter, ScanDisk, and Disk Cleanup, all you need to do is decide when that maintenance should happen by using Express setup:

1. Click **Start**, and then select **Programs**, **Accessories**, **System Tools**, **Maintenance Wizard**.

2. Select **Express** and click **Next**.

3. Select the time when you want to have maintenance done, and then click **Next**. (See Figure 17.1.)

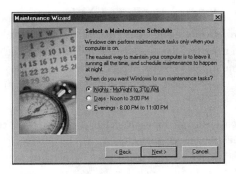

FIGURE **17.1**   Scheduling your maintenance.

4. A summary screen appears. Review the tasks that have been scheduled. If you see a mistake, you can click **Back** to return to a previous screen. If everything's okay, click **Finish**. (If you want the tasks you've selected to be performed *now*, select **When I click Finish, perform each scheduled task for the first time**.)

If you would prefer to review each maintenance task and select only the tasks you want to occur, follow these steps instead:

1. Click **Start**, and then select **Programs, Accessories, System Tools, Maintenance Wizard**.

2. Select **Custom** and click **Next**.

3. Select the time when you want to have maintenance done, and then click **Next**.

4. A listing of the programs that are currently scheduled to run at startup appears. To prevent a program from running at startup, click it to remove the check mark. Click **Next**. (If you don't have any startup programs, skip to step 5.)

5. If you don't want Disk Defragmenter to run automatically, click **No, do not defragment my disk**. Otherwise, if you want to change the time when this occurs, click **Reschedule**. To change the drive you want to defragment (and other options), click **Settings**. When you're ready, click **Next**.

6. If you don't want ScanDisk to run automatically, click **No, do not scan my hard disk for errors**. Otherwise, if you want to change the time when this occurs, click **Reschedule**. To change the drive that you want to scan (among other options), click **Settings**. When you're done, click **Next**.

7. If you don't want Windows to delete unneeded files, click **No, do not delete unnecessary files**. Otherwise, to change the time when this occurs, click **Reschedule**. To select the types of files that are automatically deleted, click **Settings**. When you're done, click **Next**. (See Figure 17.2.)

FIGURE 17.2   Select the types of files you want to delete.

8. A summary screen appears. Review the tasks that have been
scheduled. If you see a mistake, you can click **Back** to return to
a previous screen. If everything's okay, click **Finish**. (If you
want the tasks you selected to be performed *now*, select **When I
click Finish, perform each scheduled task for the first time**.)

Modifying Scheduled Tasks

After the Maintenance Wizard has been set up, you can pretty much for-
get about it and get on with your work. When a scheduled task comes up,
the Maintenance Wizard performs that task without bothering you. If you
decide to change the times when the tasks occur or some of the options
you selected, you can do so easily using the Task Scheduler. You can also
add programs that you want to run periodically to the Task Scheduler,
such as a virus scanner, backup program, or other utility. You can even run
programs just at startup, or just when you log on to a network. Follow
these steps to add a new task:

1. Click **Start**, then select **Programs**, **Accessories**, **System Tools**,
Scheculed Tasks. The Scheduled Tasks window appears, as
shown in Figure 17.3.

To add a new task
double-click here   Scheduled tasks

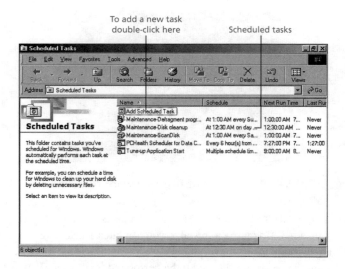

FIGURE 17.3   Programs scheduled to run automatically appear in the Task Scheduler.

2. Double-click **Add Scheduled Task**. The Scheduled Task Wizard appears. Click **Next**.

3. Select the application you want to run from those listed (or click Browse to locate the program yourself), and then click **Next**.

4. Type a name for the task if you like. Then select how often you want this task to run. Click **Next**.

5. Select the time, day, and/or other options that define when the task should start, and then click **Next**.

6. You can select additional options for the task by choosing **Open advanced properties for this task when I click Finish**. For example, you can have Windows "wake up" your computer, perform the task only if the computer is idle, or stop the task after a specific period of time, among other options. Click **Finish**.

7. If you opted to review the properties for the task, make any additional selections as needed and click **OK**.

To delete a scheduled task, select it from the Scheduled Tasks window and press **Delete**. Then click **yes** to confirm. To modify an existing task, double-click the task and make any changes you want. Then click **OK** to save them.

Creating a System Startup Disk

Your data's best protection is fairly simple to create: a Windows startup disk. You can use it to start Windows if you have problems starting it from the hard disk. Needless to say, this startup disk is a required part of any Windows medical kit, and that's why it's created during installation. However, if you've installed any new hardware or upgraded to Windows Me since you bought your computer, you should update your system startup disk as well. Here's how:

1. Click **Start**, and then select **Settings**, **Control Panel**.

2. Click the **Add/Remove Programs** link.

3. Click the **Startup Disk** tab.

4. You can reuse your original startup disk or any disk you want; just place it in the drive and click **Create Disk**.

5. After the startup disk has been created, move it to a safe location and click **OK** to close the dialog box.

Backing Up Your Files

Windows Me no longer includes a backup program because it's unlikely that you'll want to back up a large hard disk using floppy disks. This doesn't mean that you shouldn't make copies of important files—on the contrary, backups are your insurance if something happens to your computer or your files.

When you perform a backup, it's not necessary to back up every file on your hard disk. You should back up your document files (which are usually stored in the My Documents folder) and certain system files, but you don't need to back up program files because they can be reinstalled from their original installation disks.

If backing up to disks is no longer practical, how should you perform this very important task? You have several options:

- **Back up to tape**   If you add a tape backup to your system, you can use its program to back up the files you select.

- **Copy files to a Zip disk**   If you add a Zip drive to your system, you can use My Computer or Windows Explorer to copy important files to a Zip disk as a backup. Just open My Computer/Windows Explorer, display the Folders list, and drag the files you want to back up to the Zip drive icon that appears in the Folders list. Perform this task periodically to update the disk with revised copies of your files.

- **Copy files to drive D**   If your system has a second hard disk, use it as a backup drive. Store your documents on drive C (in the My Documents folder, for example). To back them up, just open My Computer/Windows Explorer, display the Folders list, and drag the files you want to back up to the D drive icon in the Folders list. You can drag entire folders (such as the My Documents folder) if you want. If the folder already exists on drive D, you'll need to tell Windows that it's okay to overlay any existing files. The reason it's a good idea to use drive D as a backup drive is that it's a whole lot less likely to crash than drive C is. When you know you won't be needing a file again, copy it from drive D to some kind of removable media, such as a floppy disk or a Zip disk. Then delete the file from both C and D.

If something happens to one of the original files, you can simply restore the copy from the backup tape, Zip drive, or D drive.

Performing a System Restore

New applications typically make a lot of changes to important system files. Usually this isn't a problem, but occasionally a program will make a change that causes major problems with your system. Luckily, Windows automatically makes copies of these system files prior to running any installation program, creating *restore points* that you can return to in just such a case. Windows also creates restore points prior to any Windows Update/AutoUpdate change, and you can create your own manual restore points prior to making changes you think may be a bit risky. Here's a listing of the types of restore points that System Restore creates automatically:

 Caution   No Restore?.System Restore is enabled on PCs with less than 200MB of free space

- **Initial System Checkpoint**   This restore point is created the first time Windows Me is run after its initial installation.

- **Periodic Checkpoints**   Even if you don't make a change to your computer, restore points are created every 10 hours when your computer is left on, and every 24 hours whether the computer is left on or not. If the computer is off at the time a restore point should be made, one is created the next time you turn the computer on.

- **Program Installations**   If an application uses InstallShield or Windows Installer to run its installation program, a restore point is created prior to installation. If you're installing a program that doesn't invoke InstallShield or Windows Installer, exit its setup, create a manual restore point, and begin installation again.

- **AutoUpdate**   If you allow AutoUpdate to download and install updates automatically, a restore point is created for you. If AutoUpdate is turned off, or if it's set up to download updates but not install them, you'll need to create manual restore points yourself prior to installing the update.

If you discover that your system has become unstable after you've made a system change, added new hardware, or installed a Windows Update or other program, you can restore it to a point prior to the change. You won't lose any documents you've created, email you've received, Web favorites you've saved, or your document usage/Internet history. Even so, you can always undo a System Restore if you find that you don't like it.

Creating a Manual Restore Point

Although Windows creates restore points automatically whenever it feels it's necessary, you may want to create some of your own as well. Follow these steps to create a manual restore point:

1. Click **Start**, and then select **Programs, Accessories, System Tools, System Restore**.

2. Click **Create a restore point** and click **Next**.

3. Type a descriptive name for the restore point and click **Next**.

4. Click **OK**.

Undoing Changes to Your Computer

If your system becomes unstable or difficult to work with after you install some new hardware, program, or Windows Update, you can restore it to a prior condition. You can also use this procedure to fix your computer after accidentally deleting or changing important system files.

 How Many Changes?   You can restore your computer to any point that's been saved by System Restore. Typically, this includes all changes made in the last two to three weeks, although it could be more or less. It all depends on the actual number of changes System Restore has had to record and the amount of space it has been given to record them.

Here's what to do:

1. Click **Start**, and then select **Programs, Accessories, System Tools, System Restore**.

2. Click **Restore my computer to an earlier time** and click **Next**.

3. Click a day on the calendar and then select a restore point created on that day, as shown in Figure 17.4. Click **Next**. (Days on which a restore point was created are displayed in bold).

Select a day   Select a restore point

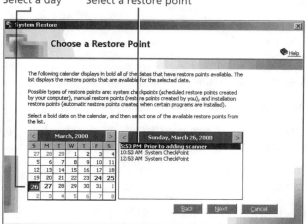

FIGURE 17.4   Select the system configuration date to which you want to return.

4. A warning appears, reminding you to close all programs before proceeding. Do so and click **OK**.

5. In the System Restore dialog box, click **Next**. Don't attempt to run any programs, open, modify, or delete files, or perform any other task until the restoration is complete.

6. Windows restores your old system files and restarts the computer. When the System Restore dialog box reappears, click **OK**.

Not an Uninstaller   Although System Restore restores your important system files to the state they were in prior to the installation of a program, you should still run Add/Remove Programs (as described in Lesson 18, "Installing and Uninstalling Applications") to remove the actual program files themselves.

Undoing a Restoration

If, for whatever reason, you feel like the restoration didn't help and you want to undo it, follow these steps:

1. Click **Start**, and then select **Programs, Accessories, System Tools, System Restore**.

2. Click **Undo my last restoration** and click **Next**.

3. Once again, you're reminded to close all programs before proceeding. Click **OK**.

4. Click **Next**. Windows restores your newer system settings and restarts your computer.

5. When the System Restore dialog box reappears, click **OK**.

In this lesson, you learned how to perform basic maintenance tasks on your hard disk. In the next lesson, you'll learn how to install and later remove your Windows applications.

Lesson 18

Installing and Uninstalling Applications

In this lesson, you'll learn how to install and remove your applications.

Installing Software

Most applications today come with their own installation programs, so installing software is a fairly simple process. But before you start, check these items:

- First, make sure you exit any programs you're running. Most installation programs make changes to your system files, so exiting your programs will prevent any conflicts. In addition, you might need to restart your computer during the installation, so exiting your programs will prevent any possible loss of data.

- If you're upgrading your software to a newer version, be sure to make copies of all your existing data in case something happens to it during the upgrade process. Also, be aware that some programs (but certainly not the majority) require you to uninstall the previous version before upgrading. Most allow you to simply upgrade on top of the existing software, however. Read the installation manual before proceeding.

To install a program, follow these basic steps:

1. Insert the first installation diskette (or the CD-ROM) into its drive.

2. Click **Start**, **Settings**, **Control Panel**.

3. Click the **Add/Remove Programs** link. The Add/Remove Programs dialog box appears.

4. Click **Install**.

5. Click **Next** to begin.

6. Windows searches for installation programs and displays the path for your installation program in the **Command line for installation program** text box. Make any changes if needed, and then click **Finish** to start installation.

7. Windows starts the setup program. Typically, it displays a message that it's preparing the InstallShield Wizard to help with the installation process, as shown in Figure 18.1.

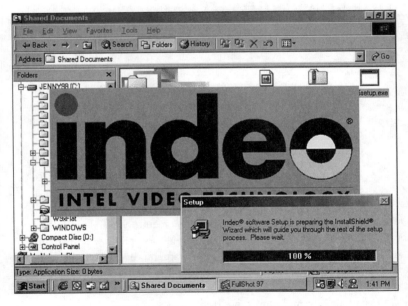

FIGURE 18.1   InstallShield helps with the installation of your program.

Assuming your application uses InstallShield or Windows Installer (which also displays a message) to install its files and run its setup program, System Restore will automatically create a restore point so you can return your system to its state *prior* to the installation of your new application. You'll need such a restore point if you discover later on that your application made some changes to your computer that rendered it difficult (or impossible) to use. If you don't see the InstallShield or Windows Installer message, you should click **Cancel** as soon as possible to stop the installation process. You should then create a manual restore point and begin the installation again. (See Lesson 17, "Performing Disk Management," for help.)

8. After your application's setup program begins, you'll be prompted to make whatever selections are needed. For example, you might be asked to select the options you want to install. If you're upgrading from a prior version, make sure you select the directory where the program was originally installed. Follow the onscreen prompts until the program has been installed successfully.

Many installations offer more than one type of setup. For example, you might be offered the choice of Compact, Typical, or Custom setup. Compact offers you a slimmed-down version of the program (a good choice if you're short on hard disk space), while Typical installs all the basic options. Custom lets you select just the options you want (and avoid those you don't want).

The installation program creates any folders that are needed. After making sure there's enough space, it then copies the contents of the installation diskettes or CD-ROM to your hard disk. It also adds a command for starting the program to your Start menu.

Install a Windows Update

As you learned in Lesson 9, "Customizing Other Attributes of Windows," Windows Update can be set up in one of three ways:

*   To download updates to the operating system automatically.

- To notify you of updates so you can select the ones you wish to download.

- To check for updates only when you issue the Windows Update command manually.

Regardless of the method you use to check for and receive updates, once an update is downloaded, a reminder appears on the taskbar in the status area. To install the update, follow these steps:

1. Click the globe icon that appears on the taskbar. The Updates dialog box, shown in Figure 18.2.

need figure supplied

FIGURE 18.2   Installing a Windows Update is easy.

2. Perform one of the following:

   - To install all of the updates without reviewing them, click **Install**.

   - To review the updates prior to installation, click **Details.** A list-ing of updates appears, with a brief description of each one. Deselect any update you do not want to install, then click **Install** to install the selected updates.

 Missing Updates   If you decide not to install an update and then change your mind, you can restore the update to your system so you can install it. Click **Start**, then select **Settings, Control Panel**. Double-click the **Automatic Updates** icon, and click **Restore Hidden Items**.

   - To skip the update installation for now and to remove the reminder message temporarily, click **Remind Me Later**. Select the amount of time you want to delay the installation, then click **OK**. The reminder icon will reappear after the allotted time so you can install the updates.

3. If you elected to install some updates, Windows will perform the installation automatically, then notify you that it needs to restart the computer. After exiting all programs, click **Restart**.

4. You'll see a message telling you when the installation process is complete. Click **OK**.

Installing DOS Programs

DOS programs are installed the same way as Windows applications, but there are a few things you need to keep in mind:

   - Create a manual restore point before installing any DOS pro-gram. (See Lesson 17)

- In most cases, you'll need to add a command to start the program to your Start menu because the DOS program's setup won't do it for you. (See Lesson 9, "Customizing Other Attributes of Windows.")

- A few DOS programs prefer to start from an actual DOS prompt and not from a command on the Start menu. To display the prompt, choose **Start**, **Programs**, **Accessories**, **MS-DOS Prompt**. Then type the command to start your program and press **Enter**.

- When a DOS program is started, a special area in memory is carved out and some system resources are allocated to the program. Some programs might need to make adjustments to the resource allotment in order to run properly under Windows. To do that, right-click the program's .exe file in My Computer or Explorer, and then select **Properties**. Click the appropriate tab and select the options you want. For example, to change the program's memory requirements, click the **Memory** tab. Click **OK** when you're through.

- DOS programs run in small windows, just like Windows applications. To switch between full-screen view and a window, press **Alt+Enter**.

- Keep in mind that DOS programs don't recognize long filenames, so use only eight characters plus a three-character extension, like this: carsales.wks.

Talking to Someone While Playing a Game

Some computer games allow you to chat with your Internet/intranet/network opponent by talking into your computer's microphone. Your opponent's reply can be heard through your computer's speakers (or your headphones, if they're are connected through the sound card). In order for voice chat (also known as DirectPlay) to work, it must be supported by the game that you're playing, your online opponent's computer, and the host that you use to connect to each other. To enable voice chat for a particular game, follow these steps:

1. Click **Start, Settings, Control Panel**.

2. If needed, click **view all Control Panel options** and double-click the **Gaming Options** icon.

3. In the Gaming Options dialog box, click the **Voice Chat** tab.

4. Only games that support DirectPlay are listed. Select the one you want to use and then click **OK**.

Not Listed?   If your game supports DirectPlay but isn't displayed in the Voice Chat list, the game provides its voice chat controls within the program itself. To enable voice chat for such a game, use its integrated voice chat controls.

5. The Sound Hardware Test Wizard may appear. If so, follow the onscreen steps to test your microphone, speakers, and sound system.

Slow Down!   Needless to say, digitizing your voice and sending it to your opponent over the Internet will cause your game to slow down a bit. If you find that voice chat is slowing down your game too much, you may want to turn it off.

Choose TCP/IP   If your game gives you a choice, be sure to choose Internet TCP/IP Connection for DirectPlay. This enables voice chat over a network (in this case, the Internet).

Uninstalling Software

When you no longer need a particular program, you should remove it from the hard disk to make room for the programs you do use:

1. Click the **Start**, **Settings**, **Control Panel**.

2. Click the **Add/Remove Programs** link. The Add/Remove Programs Properties dialog box appears, as shown in Figure 18.2.

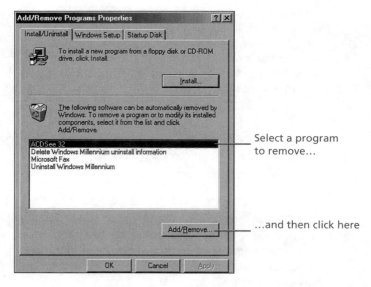

FIGURE 18.3   Removing unwanted programs from the hard disk.

3. Select the program you want to delete and click **Add/Remove**.

4. You're prompted to insert the installation diskette or CD-ROM for the program you're removing. Do so and then click **OK**.

5. Your application's uninstall program starts. Follow the onscreen prompts to remove the program from your hard disk.

Uninstall Windows Me? You'll notice a couple of interesting items in the Add/Remove Programs list, shown in Figure 18.3. One of them, **Delete Windows Millennium uninstall information,** allows you to remove the information needed to return your system to a previous version of Windows. If you've been using Windows Me for a while and you plan to keep it, you should remove this information because it takes up a lot of space. The other item, **Uninstall Windows Millenium,** allows you to uninstall Windows Me and return to your previous version of Windows, provided the uninstall information hasn't been removed. *Do not select this option unless you want to remove Windows Me from your system.*

Uninstalling a Windows Update

Windows Update and AutoUpdate (a version of Windows Update that works automatically) help to keep your system up to date by downloading and installing patches, bug fixes, driver updates, and new programs for Windows Me from Microsoft's Web site. If you install one of these patches, fixes, updates, or programs and you decide later on to remove it, follow these steps:

1. Choose **Start, Programs, Accessories, System Tools, System Information.**

2. Select **Tools, Update Wizard Uninstall.**

3. Select the item you want to remove and click **Remove.**

4. You may be prompted to restart your system. Close any open programs and click **Yes** to continue.

Use Add/Remove Programs Some Windows Updates may be uninstalled using the Add/Remove Programs icon, as described in the "Uninstalling Software" section. You may also be able to remove certain Windows Updates by going to the Windows Update site. Just click **Start** and select **Windows Update**.

Using the CD-ROM Sampler to Preview Microsoft Applications

The Windows Me CD-ROM provides several trial versions of Microsoft applications you can try, and later purchase. They include International Football 2000, Pandora's Box, Pinball Arcade, Return of Arcade, Entertainment Pack, and Motocross Madness. To test-drive any of these sample programs, follow these steps:

1. Insert the Windows Me CD-ROM.

2. Click **Interactive CD Sampler**.

3. A licensing agreement appears. Click **Accept this Agreement**, and then click **Next**.

4. Click **Next** to install the sampler.

5. Click **Finish**. The Interactive Sampler starts automatically.

6. Click any of the category icons such as **Kids** or **Games**. learn more about the various programs Microsoft has to offer. To install one of the trial programs, click **Trial Versions!**

7. Click **OK** to exit the Interactive CD-ROM Sampler and started the Trial Version installation program.

8. Click the trial program you want to install. Follow the onscreen instructions to complete the installation.

9. You're returned to the Trials dialog box. Select another trial program to install, or click **Exit**.

In this lesson, you learned how to install and uninstall a program on your computer. You also learned how to uninstall Windows updates and install the trial programs on the Windows Me CD-ROM. In the next lesson, you'll learn how to use your applications.

LESSON 19

Using Your Applications

In this lesson, you'll learn how to use your applications: how to start them, how to copy and move information, and how to open, close, and save your documents.

Starting an Application

Before you can use an application, you must start it. When a program is installed, a command to start it is usually placed on the **Start** menu. (See Lesson 9, "Customizing Other Attributes of Windows," for help with adding commands for DOS programs.) To access the proper command, click the **Start** button, select **Programs**, and then select the folder where the program's start command is stored. (See Figure 19.1.)

There are several other ways to start programs:

- **With the Run command**   If the program you want to start doesn't have a command on the **Start** menu, click the **Start** button and select **Run**. Click **Browse**, select the path of the executable file (.exe) for the program, and click **OK**.

- **By file association**   When a program is installed, it registers the types of files that can be created with it. You can then use these file associations to start the program with a particular document. For example, if you select a file with a .doc extension within My Computer or Explorer, you can open the document and start Microsoft Word (or WordPad, if you don't have Microsoft Word) at the same time. Simply double-click a file and the associated program starts.

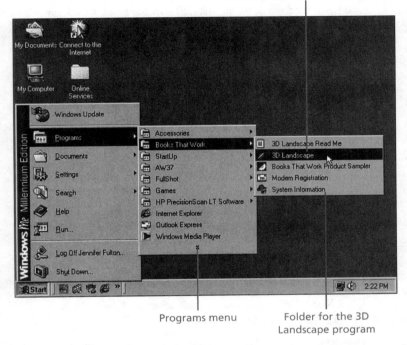

Command to start 3D Landscape

Programs menu

Folder for the 3D Landscape program

FIGURE 19.1   Each program is stored in its own folder.

- **With the Documents menu**   The documents you've worked on most recently are displayed on the **Start**, **Documents** menu. You can use it to start the associated program with the selected document open and ready to work on. In addition, you can access documents you've saved to the My Pictures or My Documents folders.

- **When you start Windows**   You can select certain programs and have Windows start them automatically when you start your computer. Just click a program's startup file in My Computer or Explorer and drag it to the **Start** button. When the menu appears, drag the file to the **Programs**, **StartUp** menu.

- **With a shortcut icon**   You can create an icon for your program and place it on the desktop. Then, to start the program, all you need to do is double-click the icon. To create a shortcut, right-click the program's start file in My Computer or Explorer and then drag the file out onto the desktop. Select **Create Shortcut(s) Here** from the menu that appears.

- **With the Quick Launch toolbar**   You can drag an application's start file (.exe) to the Quick Launch toolbar on the taskbar to create an icon. Click this icon to start the program whenever you want.

Starting an Internet Game

Windows Me comes with many games, some of which are designed to be played against an opponent over the Internet. To play one of these games, follow these steps:

1. Connect to the Internet.

2. Click **Start**, **Programs**, **Games**, and select an Internet game such as Internet Checkers.

3. Click **Play** to begin. You're connected to MSN's gaming server on the Internet.

Total Secrecy   After you start an Internet game, Windows locates another player who matches your skill level. Your identity is kept totally anonymous.

4. Once an opponent is found, the game window appears. In addition, there are some other options available from the game window:

   Chat   You can chat with your opponent by selecting a message from the chat list, such as "Hello" or "Good Game". To turn on chat, click the **on** button in the lower-right corner.

To see whether your opponent has also turned on chat, check their status to the right of the Chat on/off buttons.

Change Skill Level   Choose **Game, Skill Level**, and then choose **Beginner, Intermediate**, or **Advanced**.

Find a New Opponent   Choose **Game, Find New Opponent**.

Leave the Game   To leave the game before it's through, select **Game, Exit**. You'll be asked if you want to leave the game while it's still in progress. If so, click **Yes** to exit.

5. When you're through playing, a dialog box appears. You can play another game with the same opponent by clicking **Play Again**. To play again with someone else, click **New Opponent**. If you're through playing, click **Quit**.

Creating and Opening Documents

After starting your application, you might want to begin a new document or open an existing one.

- To begin a new document, open the program's **File** menu and select **New**. You might need to make additional selections if your program can create more than one type of new document.

- To open an existing document, open the program's **File** menu and select **Open**. The Open dialog box appears. For most programs, it will look something like Figure 19.2. Select the folder where your document is located from the **Look in** drop-down list box, or select a location from the Places bar. Then select your document from those listed and click **Open**.

- If the document you want to open is a recent one, you'll probably find it listed at the bottom of the program's **File** menu.

In a lot of programs, you can open several documents at one time by pressing **Ctrl** and selecting them from the Open dialog box. To switch between documents, open the program's **Window** menu and select the document you want to switch to. In Office 2000, you can also switch between documents by clicking the document's button on the Windows taskbar. (Each Office document has its own button on the taskbar.)

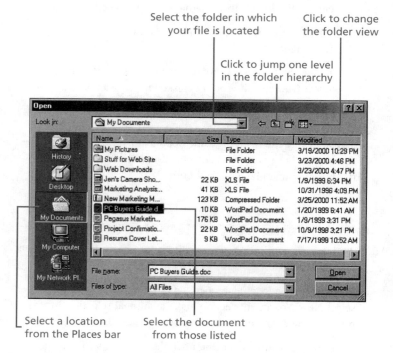

Select the folder in which your file is located

Click to change the folder view

Click to jump one level in the folder hierarchy

Select a location from the Places bar

Select the document from those listed

FIGURE 19.2   You must open a document if you want to make changes to it.

Copying and Moving Information

When you copy or move data, it's first placed on the Clipboard. It's a kind of holding area for the data while the copy or move operation is being carried out. The Clipboard is a part of Windows and not part of any particular program, so you can use it to copy or move data between applications, as well as between documents within an application.

Selecting Text and Graphics

Before beginning a copy or move operation, you must select the item you want to work with. The item you select is highlighted so you can distinguish it from unselected objects.

To select text, drag over it:

1. Click at the beginning of the text you want to select.

2. Press and hold down the mouse button as you drag over the text you want to select. The text is highlighted, as shown in Figure 19.3.

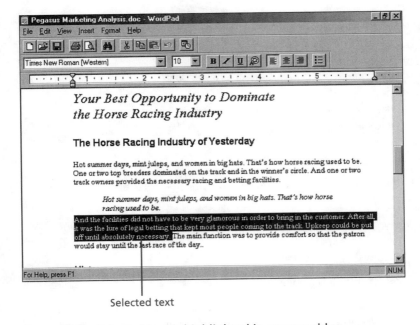

Selected text

FIGURE **19.3** Selected text is highlighted in reverse video.

 Shortcut to Selection Most programs support shortcuts for selecting text. To select a word, double-click it. To select a paragraph, double-click in the left margin.

To select a graphic, just click it. Small boxes, called *handles,* appear around the graphic to show that it's selected, as shown in Figure 19.4.

Handles

FIGURE 19.4   When you select a graphic, handles appear.

Copying Data

To copy data, follow these steps:

1. Select the data you want to copy.

2. Click the **Copy** button on the toolbar (if there is one), or open the **Edit** menu and select **Copy**. You can also press **Ctrl+C**.

3. Click in the spot where you want the data to be copied. You can switch to another document, or even to another program.

4. Click the **Paste** button on the toolbar, or open the **Edit** menu and select **Paste**. You can also press **Ctrl+V**.

Let's do that again!   When data is copied or moved, it's placed on the Clipboard, where it remains until it's replaced by some new item to be copied or moved. This means that if you repeat the **Paste** command, the same data can be copied (or moved) to multiple locations.

Moving Data

To move data, follow these steps:

1. Select the data you want to move.

2. Click the **Cut** button on the toolbar (if there is one), or open the **Edit** menu and select **Cut**. You can also press **Ctrl+X**.

3. Click in the spot where you want the data to be moved. Again, you can switch to another document, or even to another program.

4. Click the **Paste** button on the toolbar, or open the **Edit** menu and select **Paste**. You can also press **Ctrl+V**.

Drag and Drop   You can drag and drop your data to copy or move it. Select the data you want to copy or move, and then drag the data to its new location. *When copying, be sure to press and hold down the Ctrl key as you drag.* Release the mouse button, and the data is copied or moved.

Saving and Closing Documents

After you're through working on a document, you should close it to free up system resources for other applications. Before closing a document, you need to save it so you won't lose any changes you've made.

To save a document, follow these steps:

1. Click the **Save** button on the toolbar (if there is one), or open the **File** menu and select **Save**. If this is the first time you've saved the file, a Save As dialog box appears, such as the one shown in Figure 19.5. This dialog box will *not* appear the next time you save this same file.

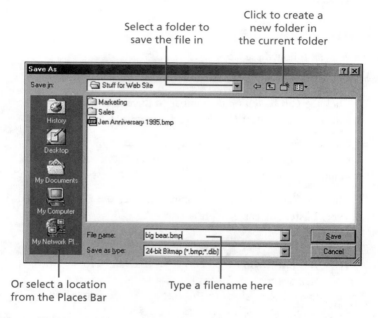

FIGURE **19.5** The Save As dialog box.

2. Select the folder where you want to save your document from the **Save in** drop-down list box, or click a location in the Places bar. To create a new folder for your file, click the **Create New Folder** button, type a folder name, and click **OK**.

3. Type a name for the file in the **File name** text box. The name can contain up to 255 characters (including spaces), followed by a period and a three-character extension. You might not have to type the extension; most programs add the appropriate extension to each filename you type.

The Place to Save   Using one folder can make it easy to keep track of all your documents. By default, Microsoft programs save all documents to the My Documents folder, making them easily accessible from the **Start** menu.

4. Click **Save**.

After you save a document, it remains open so that you can continue working on it. If you make additional changes, save them by clicking the **Save** button or opening the **File** menu and selecting **Save**.

To close a document, open the **File** menu and select **Close**. If the document contains changes that haven't yet been saved, you'll be prompted to save them.

Exiting an Application

Before you exit an application, you should save your open documents. Then, to exit the application, do one of the following:

- **Use the File menu**   Open the program's **File** menu and select **Exit**. If you have any open documents that haven't been saved yet, you'll be asked if you'd like to save them.

- **Use the program's Close button**   You can also click the program's Close button × to exit a program.

- **Use the keyboard shortcut**   If you prefer to use the keyboard, you can press **Alt+F4** to close the program's window and thus exit the program.

In this lesson, you learned how to start and exit your applications, how to open, close, and save documents, and how to copy or move data. In the next lesson, you'll learn how to install a printer and print a document.

LESSON 20
Printing in Windows

In this lesson, you'll learn how to print your Windows documents.

Installing a Printer

When Windows was installed on your computer, it checked for any locally attached (non-networked) printers and set them up automatically. However, if you've purchased a new printer recently, you'll need to install it before you can use it to print your Windows documents. In addition, if you want to use a printer attached to another computer on a network, you'll need to do some installation on your computer first.

To install a new printer that's physically attached to your computer, follow these steps (to install a network printer, see the next section):

1. Click **Start, Settings, Printers**. The Printers folder window appears.

2. Double-click the **Add Printer** icon.

3. The Add Printer Wizard appears. Click **Next**.

4. Select **Local printer**. Click **Next**.

5. Select the manufacturer of your printer from the **Manufacturers** list. Then select your printer from the **Printers** list. If a disk came with your new printer, click **Have Disk**, select the setup file, and click **OK**. Then click **Next**.

6. Select the port you want to use and click **Next**.

7. Enter a name for your printer and select whether you want this printer to act as the default printer for your system. Then click **Next**.

8. Select **Yes** to print a test page, and then click **Finish**. You might be asked to insert your Windows disks or CD-ROM. The icon for your new printer appears in the Printers folder.

Installing a Network Printer

Before you can use a printer that's attached to another computer on your network, you'll need to follow these steps to install its driver files on your computer.

 Driver File A driver is simply a translator. Specifically, a printer driver's job is to translate the information coming from your application into the language the printer speaks so that your document can be properly formatted and printed for the specific printer you choose to use.

 Network-Ready? If you have more than one computer at home, they can share a printer, modem, and even files! You'll be amazed how easy it is (not to mention relatively inexpensive) to create a home network using Windows Me. See Lesson 12, "Accessing Resources on Your Home Network."

1. Click **Start**, **Settings**, **Printers**. The Printers window opens.

2. Double-click the **Add Printer** icon. The Add Printer wizard appears.

3. Click **Next** to begin.

4. Select **Network printer** and click **Next**.

5. Click **Browse** to display a list of available printers.

6. Click the plus sign in front of **Entire Network** to get a list of the various computer groups on your network. (On a home network, typically there's only one group.)

7. Click the plus sign in front of a group to display its list of computers. Then click the plus sign for the computer that's attached to the printer you want to install. A list of shared printer(s) appears, as shown in Figure 20.1.

 Learn to Share   Before you can install a network printer to your computer, the computer it's physically attached to must *share* it first. See Lesson 12.

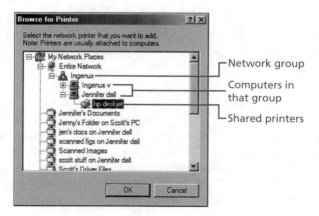

FIGURE 20.1   The shared resources of the selected computer.

8. Select the printer you want to install and then click **OK** to return to the Add Printer Wizard. The network path to that printer now appears in the **Network path or queue name** text box.

9. If you plan on using the network printer to print files from DOS programs, click **Yes**. Otherwise, click **No**. Then click **Next** to continue.

10. Type a name for the printer in the **Printer name** box. This name should be descriptive enough that you can easily distinguish this printer from any others on the network.

11. Choose whether or not to make this printer the default printer for your computer. (You can always change this later if you want. You'll learn more about default printers in the next section.) Click **Next** to continue.

12. To print a test page (recommended, because that's the only way you'll know that everything's set up correctly), click **Yes**. Otherwise, click **No.** Then click **Finish**.

13. Driver files for the printer you selected are copied from the attached computer. When prompted, click **Accept** to accept the license for the printer's software. An icon for the shared printer appears in the Printer window. The printer is now ready to use.

Setting a Default Printer

If you use more than one printer—for example, a local printer and a network printer—you can designate one of them as the default. The default printer is the printer that your applications will use to print your documents, unless you specifically select a different printer from the Print dialog box. (A network printer doesn't need to be set up as the default printer in order for you to use it, as you'll learn in the next section.)

The first printer set up on your computer was automatically established as the default printer. You can designate a different default printer by following these steps:

1. Click **Start**, **Settings**, **Printers**. The Printers window appears.

2. Right-click the icon of the printer that you want to make the default. (The current default printer appears with a small check mark next to its icon.)

3. Select **Set as Default** from the shortcut menu that appears. The default printer appears with a checkmark next to its icon.

Printing from an Application

When you initiate a print command from within an application, the document is prepared and then passed to the print queue, where it waits in line behind any other documents already set to print on that printer. After the document is passed to the print queue, command is then returned to you so that you can continue working in that same application or some other program. In other words, you don't have to wait while your document is being printed. The Windows print queue handles the entire process so you can get back to work.

To print a document from within an application, follow these steps:

1. Open the program's **File** menu and select **Print**. A Print dialog box appears (see Figure 20.2). You can also click the **Print** button on the toolbar (if present), but the Print dialog box won't appear.

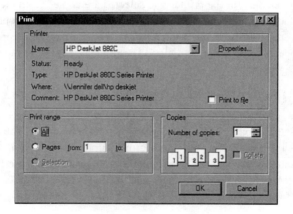

FIGURE 20.2   A typical Print dialog box.

2. The Print dialog box within your particular application might be slightly different, but it will still contain certain elements:

   • From the **Printer** list, select the printer you want to use. Network printers should be listed here; if not, you may have to click a **Network** button to select the printer from a list.

- Select the pages you want to print from the **Print range** area.

- If the option is available, select the number of copies you want to print.

3. After selecting these and other options, click **OK**.

Is What You See What You'll Get? If you'd like to preview your print job before you actually print it, most applications offer a **Print Preview** option on the **File** menu.

Quick Print You can print any document from within My Computer or Explorer by right-clicking the file and selecting **Print**. The program associated with the file will open briefly and send the file to the default printer for printing.

Controlling the Print Job

When you send a document to the printer, it's placed behind any other documents that are already waiting to be printed. You can reassign the order of printing, cancel a print job, or simply pause the printer while you change the paper.

When you view the print queue, as shown in Figure 20.3, each document is listed, along with its print status, owner, size, and the time and date that printing was initiated.

To display the print queue, double-click the **Printer** icon on the taskbar.

Document is currently being printed

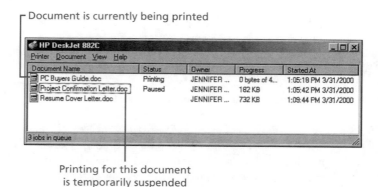

Printing for this document
is temporarily suspended

FIGURE 20.3   Documents waiting to be printed appear in the print queue.

Reordering the Jobs in the Queue

To reorder a document within the queue, simply click it and drag it where you want it. However, you can't place a document in front of a document that's currently printing.

Pausing and Resuming the Queue

You can pause the print queue at any time. This might be necessary if the printer is jammed or some other problem has developed. By pausing the print queue, you can easily correct the problem and then resume printing when you're ready.

Get a Queue   You can't pause a network printer—only printers physically attached to your computer. However, you can pause the printing of a document in the queue by clicking it and selecting **Document, Pause**.

To pause the printing, follow these steps:

1. Double-click the **Printer** icon on the taskbar to open the print queue.

2. Open the **Printer** menu and select **Pause Printing**. A check mark appears next to this command.

To resume printing, open the **Printer** menu and select **Pause Printing** again to remove the check mark.

 Printer Stalled If your printer runs out of paper, Windows will automatically pause the printing process and display a message telling you what's happened. If you don't respond, Windows will automatically retry the printer in five seconds.

Deleting a Print Job

If you notice that you've sent the wrong document to the printer or that you need to make some small change to a document, it's not too late. You can delete a print job from the queue to prevent it from being printed:

1. Double-click the **Printer** icon on the taskbar to open the print queue.

2. Select the document you want to delete from the queue.

3. Open the **Document** menu and select **Cancel Printing**, or press the **Delete** key.

To remove *all* documents from the print queue, open the **Printer** menu and select **Purge Print Documents**.

In this lesson, you learned how to print your Windows documents. In the next lesson, you'll learn how to edit home movies with Movie Maker.

LESSON 21

Editing Video with Movie Maker

In this lesson, you'll learn how to edit your home videos using Movie Maker.

With Movie Maker and a video capture card in your computer, you can edit your home videos and send them with email messages, upload them to a Web site, or view them using Windows Media Player. You can also import digital video, audio, or still image files (such as MPEG movies, MP3 audio, and JPG images) and add them to your imported video, or simply arrange them onscreen to create new videos.

To start Movie Maker, click **Start** and choose **Programs**, **Accessories**, **Windows Movie Maker**. Then import or record your video or graphic images, audio, and narration into a *collection* that can be saved together. Long video sequences can be cut up into *clips* that you can later add together to create your movie. You can take these clips from your various collections and arrange them along a timeline to create a series of video and audio images that are saved as a *project* (movie). When your collection's complete, export it to a file on a Web site, or include it with an email message. The Movie Maker window is shown in Figure 21.1. The first time you start Movie Maker, it invites you to take a tour. Click **Exit** when done.

Clips in current collection   Workspace   Preview window

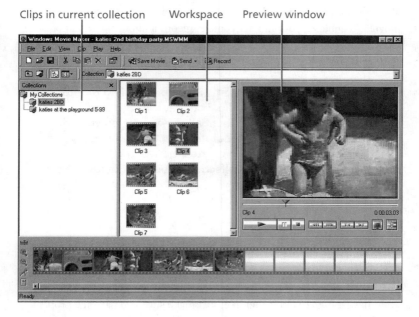

FIGURE 21.1   Movie Maker provides the tools you need to complete your movie.

 Video Output   Using the software that came with your video capture card, you may be able to copy your edited video back onto videotape. When you're shopping for a video capture card, keep in mind that quite a few don't not offer this feature.

Importing and Recording Video and Audio

Before you can edit any video, you must first import or record it. *Recording* is a process that takes raw data (such as a sequence of images from a videotape) and digitizes it for use in Movie Maker. *Importing* is simply taking an already-digitized file and opening it in Movie Maker.

You can combine imported and recorded video to create a completely new movie. To enhance your movie, you can record and/or import audio as well.

 Add to Your Collection   Prior to recording or importing any video or audio, you may want to create a collection file to keep them all in. Organizing your video and audio clips in separate collections will help you to locate them later. To create a new collection file, choose **File, New, Collection**. Type a name for the collection and click **OK**.

Importing Video or Audio Files

You can import video files, such as `.avi`, `.mpeg`, and `.mpg`, and still images, such as `.bmp`, `.jpg`, and `.gif`, for use in Movie Maker. In addition, you can import audio files, such as `.wav`, `.mp3`, and `.aif`. You can grab files from the Web if you like; just make sure you have the proper permissions to use them. Save Web files to the hard disk first, and then import them into Movie Maker.

Follow these steps to import a video, graphic, or audio file:

1. Select the collection into which you want this file to be placed, and then select **File, Import**. (If you don't have a collection for the file, a collection is created for you and given the same name as the imported file.)

2. Select the file you want to import and click **Open**.

 Add a Title   To add a title to your movie, create a title graphic using Paint and then import it into Movie Maker.

Recording Video and Audio

You can record video directly from your video camera, digital camera, Web cam, VCR, cable TV, DVD player, or satellite dish. You can record audio from a stereo, radio, CD, or cassette tape. You can record video and audio together to save time if you like.

Not Recognized   If Windows Me doesn't recognize your video capture device (which it won't, if it's connected to the parallel port), you won't be able to record video with it as described here. Instead, you should use the software that came with the device to convert video into digital format. You can then import the video file into Movie Maker for final editing if you like using the **File**, **Import** command.

Follow these steps to record video or audio:

1. Select the collection into which you want the recorded video or audio to appear, and then click **Record**.

2. Select the type of material you want to record from the **Record** list.

3. If needed, click **Change Device** to select the device you want to record from.

4. Select the quality level you want to achieve from the **Setting** list.

5. To stop recording after a specific period of time, choose the **Record time limit** option and then set the time limit.

6. Set the video or audio source to the point where you want to begin recording, and then click **Record**. (If you're recording from a DVD player, you can use the digital video camera controls that appear to adjust the video source.)

Say Cheese!   To create a .jpg file from a video source, click **Take Photo** in step 6.

7. If you didn't set a time limit, click **Stop** to stop the recording. Stop the video or audio source. (If you're recording from a DVD player, you can use the digital video camera controls that appear to stop the video source.)

8. Type a name for the file and click **Open**.

Editing a Project

Once you've imported or recorded some video, audio, and/or graphic images, you can create and edit your project. Basically, you drag clips from the workspace onto the timeline, arranging them in the order in which you want them to appear in the finished movie.

 Save Your Work   After you begin arranging clips for a project, you should save that project as soon as you can so you won't lose your work. Select **File, Save Project**, type a filename, and then click **Save**.

Follow these steps to add a clip to a project:

1. Select the collection that contains the clip you want to add.

2. Select the clip, drag it to the storyboard/timeline, and drop it where you want it to appear.

You can rearrange your clips on the storyboard/timeline by dragging them to their new locations. To delete a clip, click it and press **Delete**.

Trimming Clips

After arranging your clips, you can trim them to remove unwanted footage by following these steps. You can also trim the amount of time a still image appears onscreen:

1. In the workspace, click the clip you want to trim. If you're using storyboard view, a blue outline appears around the clip.

2. Use the video controls to advance to the beginning of the portion you want to keep, and then choose **Clip, Set Start Trim Point**. (See Figure 21.2.)

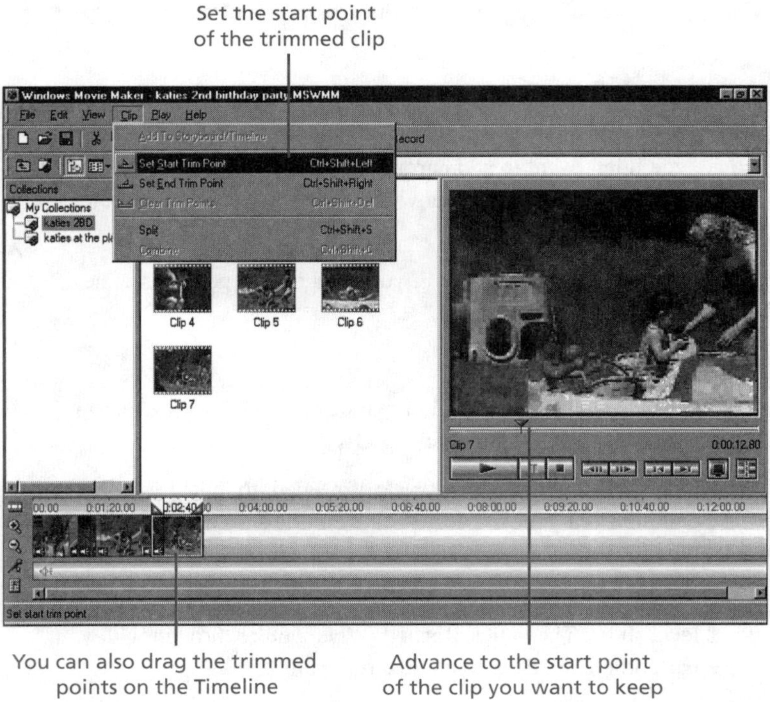

Set the start point
of the trimmed clip

You can also drag the trimmed   Advance to the start point
points on the Timeline   of the clip you want to keep

FIGURE 21.2   Trim clips to include only the footage you want.

Save That Video!   To split a clip into pieces without losing any of it, advance to the point where you want to cut the clip in two, and then click the **Split** button or choose **Clip, Split**.

3. Advance to the end of the portion you want to keep, and then choose **Clip**, **Set End Trim Point**.

If you're using Timeline view, you can drag the trim point on a clip to adjust it. To remove the trim points from a clip (restoring the trimmed video), select the clip and choose **Clip**, **Clear Trim Points**.

Adding Narration

After you've arranged your digital video and still images to create a movie, you might want to add narration. It can be added without affecting any audio you already have. Follow these steps to record narration for a movie:

1. Click the **Timeline** button if you need to change to Timeline view.

2. Click **Record Narration**.

3. If needed, change the audio input device by clicking **Change**, selecting a device, and clicking **OK**.

4. Select **Mute video soundtrack**, if needed, to mute the audio coming from your movie so you won't have to hear it while recording your narration.

5. Change the volume level as needed by dragging the **Record level** slider. Then click **Record**. When you're through with your narration, click **Stop** to end the recording.

6. Type a filename for your narration and click **Save**. The file is saved with a .wav extension and added to your collection automatically.

Creating Transitions

Normally, Movie Maker changes from one clip to another in your project without any fancy flourishes. To soften the change between two clips, you can add a cross-fade transition in which the first clip fades out as the next clip fades in. A cross-fade transition is easy to create by dragging the end trim point of the first clip past the beginning trim point of the second clip, as shown in Figure 21.3. The sound of the first clip will also fade out as the sound of the second clip begins to be heard. Transitions appear as faded images in the timeline.

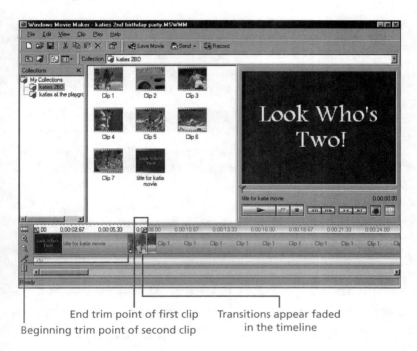

End trim point of first clip   Transitions appear faded
Beginning trim point of second clip   in the timeline

FIGURE 21.3   Drag the end trim point past the beginning trim point of the next clip to create a cross-fade transition.

Previewing the Finished Project

You can preview your project at any time during its creation. To preview a single clip, click it and then click **Play**. To preview the entire project, click in the gray area surrounding the timeline/storyboard and then click **Play**.

If you like, you can view your project full-screen by clicking **Play** and then clicking the **Full Screen** button. Press **Esc** to return to the Movie Maker window.

Saving or Sending Video

Once you're satisfied with your project, you can send it in an email message to your friends and colleagues or post it to the Web. You can also save the movie to your hard disk for private viewing. Follow these steps to save the movie file on your PC:

1. Click **Save Movie**.

2. Select the quality level you want from the **Setting** list. (A higher quality level means a larger file and a longer download for the user.)

3. Type a title for your movie and add a rating if you like. Type a brief description of the movie, and then click **OK**.

4. Type a filename for your movie and click **Save**.

Sending a Movie in an Email Message

You can send your movie in an email message by following these steps:

1. Click the arrow on the **Send** button and select **E-mail**.

2. Select the quality level you want from the **Setting** list. (A higher quality level means a larger file and a longer download for the user.)

3. Type a title and add a rating if you want. Type a description of the movie, then click **OK**.

4. Type a filename (with no spaces) for your movie in the **Enter a file name** box and click **OK**. Movie Maker saves your movie to a Windows Media Player-compatible file.

5. Select your email program from the list and click **OK**.

6. An email message appears. Send your email message by following the steps for your particular email program.

Publishing a Movie on the Web

To publish your movie to a Web site, follow these steps:

1. Log onto the Internet, then click the arrow on the **Send** button and select **Web Server**.

2. Select the quality level you want from the **Setting** list. (A higher quality level means a larger file and a longer download for the user.)

3. Type a title for your movie and add a rating if you like. Type a brief description of the movie, and then click **OK**.

4. Type a filename (with no spaces) for your movie in the **Enter a file name** box and click **OK**. Movie Maker saves your movie to a Windows Media Player-compatible file.

5. Select the Web server where you want to publish your file from the **Host name** list.

 New Host If the Web site where you want to publish your movie isn't listed in the Host name list, you can create a host profile for that Web site by clicking **New**, typing a name for the host, entering the FTP address, typing the Web site address, and clicking **OK**.

6. Type your user/login name and password. Select **Save password** if you like, and then click **OK**.

7. To view the Web site where you published your movie, select
   View Site Now. When you're through, click **Close**.

In this lesson, you learned how to edit your home videos using
MovieMaker. In the next lesson, you'll learn how to play audio and video
with Windows Media Player.

LESSON 22

Using Windows Media Player

In this lesson, you'll learn how to use Windows Media Player to play audio CDs, video clips, and real-time audio over the Internet.

The new Media Player included in Windows Me can play virtually any type of media: audio CDs, digital video, and streaming (real-time) audio and video broadcasts from the Internet. In addition, you can use Media Player to organize your various media files, create your own playlists, and upload music to a portable MP3 player. In this lesson, you'll learn how to do all this and more.

Playing Audio CDs

Media Player lets you play audio CDs from your CD-ROM drive while you work with other applications. Follow these steps:

1. Insert an audio CD into the CD-ROM drive. The Media Player starts, as shown in Figure 22.1.

Exception to the Rule If the audio CD you're attempting to play is an Extended CD or ECD, you may see a directory window instead of the Media Player. This directory will show programs that can be run from the digital portion of this hybrid audio CD/CD-ROM. There should be an icon within this directory that represents the musical portion. To play music, double-click on this icon.

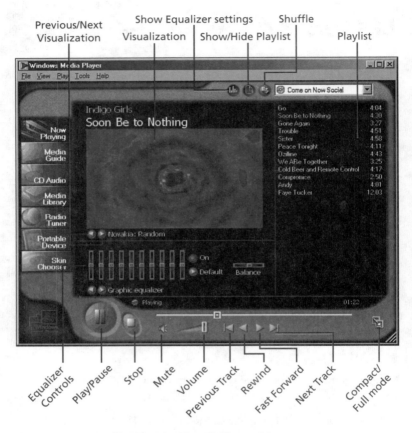

FIGURE 22.1   Media Player's Now Playing tab.

My Player Is Different!   You can customize how Media Player looks by changing its *skin* (interface). Your Media Player may not look exactly like the one shown in Figure 22.1, and it may even contain slightly different controls. You'll learn how to change skins in the upcoming "Applying a New Skin" section.

2. If you're connected to the Internet, Media Player automatically downloads a playlist for the CD. Click the **Show Playlist** button to see it.

 Need Those Names!   If you aren't connected to the Internet when you insert your CD, you can still download the playlist by clicking the **CD Audio** tab and then clicking the **Get Names** button.

3. To pause the playback, click the **Pause** button. Click the **Play** button to resume. Click other buttons as needed:

   Mute   Mutes the player.

   Volume   Adjusts the volume up or down.

   Previous/next visualization   Scrolls through various visualizations of the music being played.

   Show equalizer & settings   Displays controls for adjusting the sound balance.

   Rewind/fast-forward   Skips backward or forward through a track.

   Previous/next track   Skips backward or forward through the playlist.

   Compact/full mode   Displays the player in compact or full mode.

   Show/hide playlist   Displays or hides the playlist.

   Shuffle   Shuffles the playlist so the tracks are played in a random order.

4. If you click the **Shuffle** button to turn on Shuffle mode, the tracks are played randomly. Otherwise, play continues until the end of the CD. To change to a different track, double-click it in the playlist.

Custom Playlists   You can create your own custom playlists with various media as your sources. See the next section for help.

5. The CD stops at the final track. Click **Play** to play it again or **Stop** to stop playback prior to the final track.

Creating Playlists

A playlist is like a schedule or itinerary that determines the order in which Media Player plays songs. Every time you insert a new audio CD, Media Player assumes that its current playlist is the native order of musical tracks on that CD. When you randomize or reorganize that list, you're creating a custom playlist, but only for that particular CD and only for the present time. If you take the extra step of copying musical tracks from your audio CDs onto your computer, you can generate a more complex custom playlist that arranges the tracks in any order, repeats tracks, and even combines them with tracks from another CD or other audio source. The tracks you copy to the hard disk are maintained by Media Player's Media Library. Follow these steps:

1. Click the **Media Library** tab.

2. If this is the first time you've been to Media Library, you see a dialog box asking if you'd like to search your computer for all available media. Media Library needs this list of all media for you to compile your custom playlist, so click **Yes**. Media Player shows the Search Computer for Media dialog box.

3. To begin the search process, click **Start Search**. You may have to wait a few minutes. When the search is completed, click **Close**, and then click it again.

4. To start a new custom playlist, click **New playlist**. Type a name for your playlist and click **OK**. Your new playlist will show up in Media Library under the **My Playlists** category.

Searching Your Network   By default, Media Player won't search the shared directories on your local network for media files. Normally, it will only search your computer's own hard drives and the current contents of your removable drives. To have Media Player search your local network (not the Internet) for available media files, choose **Network Drives** in the Search Computer for Media dialog box. Media Player can search shared drives, but not shared folders.

5. To copy tracks from your currently inserted audio CD to the Media Library, click the **CD Audio** tab to display the playlist for your audio CD (*not* your custom playlist), uncheck the boxes beside the tracks you don't want to save, and click **Copy Music**.

What Do You Mean, "Error"?   Not all audio CDs can be copied in this manner. If Media Player can't copy tracks from your audio CDs, you may need to use other software (generally available over the Internet) to do the job and then import the copied tracks into Media Player later.

6. Repeat these steps with other CDs to save more music to the Media Library.

True Multitasking   If you have a reasonably fast computer and a 32x CD-ROM or higher, you may be able to play your audio CD while you're copying tracks from that same audio CD. For slower computers or CD-ROMs, the sound may become choppy. If your computer is too slow, Media Player won't even try to copy a track while you're listening to your CD.

7. Add other music to your custom playlist by clicking the **Media Library** tab, clicking the **Audio** category, displaying any of the subcategories that lead to the tracks you want (**Album**, **Artist**, or **Genre**), selecting the tracks, clicking **Add to playlist**, and choosing the name of the playlist from the drop-down menu.

8. To see your playlist, click its name under the **My Playlist** category. To change the order of a track in your playlist, select that track and then click on the up- or down-arrow button on Media Player's toolbar. To delete a track from your playlist, select that track, click on the X button, and select **Delete from Playlist**.

Your playlist is always saved automatically. This means you don't have to find a **Save** button or select **Save** from the **File** menu to save your playlist, even when you're in the middle of setting it up.

Playing Videos

With Media Player, you can play various types of video files, including `.avi`, `.mpeg`, `.mov`, and `.asf`.

To play a video, follow these steps:

1. Double-click the **Media Player** icon on the desktop. The Media Player window opens.

2. Choose **File**, **Open**, select the video file you want to play, and click **Open**. The video appears in Media Player, as shown in Figure 22.2.

 Fast Play   Through your Internet connection, you can connect directly to several Web sites and download video files to play. Just click **Media Guide** to display the Windows Media Player Web site, and click various links until you find a video you want to play.

If you're already browsing the Web, click a link to any Media Player-compatible file. Your browser will download the file and start Media Player for you automatically.

Video Settings   Scroll through setting panels

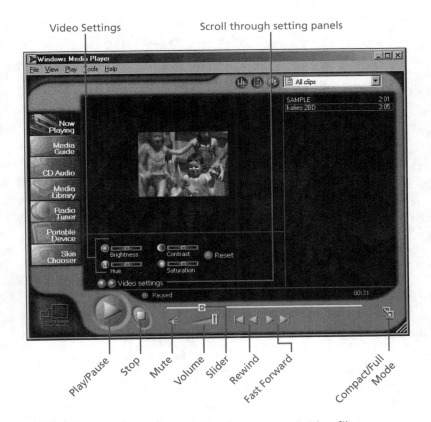

FIGURE 22.2   Media Player plays both sound and video files.

3. Click buttons as needed to adjust the playback. The controls
work as described in the previous section, except for these:

> **Show Equalizer Controls**   Displays controls for adjust-
> ing the video display. (You may need to scroll through the
> various control panels to display the video controls.)

> **Previous** and **Next**   Skips to the previous or next video
> shown in the right column. The current video is high-
> lighted in green.

Quick Slide   To quickly fast-forward or rewind, simply drag the slider forward or backward to the desired position in the file.

If you've used the Media Library to locate all the files on your computer that Media Player can play, video files were included in that search as well. You can see these video files by clicking on the **Media Library** tab, choosing the **Video** category in the left column, and then choosing the **All Clips** subcategory. In the list at the right, double-click the video file you want to play.

Onscreen... Magnify!   To show your video on the full screen (effectively turning your monitor into a TV), press **Alt+Enter**. To bring back your Windows desktop, press **Alt+Enter** again.

Listening to Streaming Audio

Media Player allows you to download and play streaming audio from the Internet. Streaming audio files can be played even before they're fully downloaded. Some audio files can be quite large, so being able to play them while you're downloading means less waiting. To listen to streaming audio with Media Player:

1. Connect to the Internet, then click **Radio Tuner** (see Figure 22.3).

2. Select a list of saved radio stations from the **Presets** list and click one of them, or search for a radio station you like. To search for a station, select the criteria for your search from the first list under **Station Finder**, such as **Format**. Then make additional selections as needed. When a list of matching stations appears, click the **Play** column in front of the station you want to hear. (If the list is more than one page, you may have to click **Next** to display additional pages one at a time.)

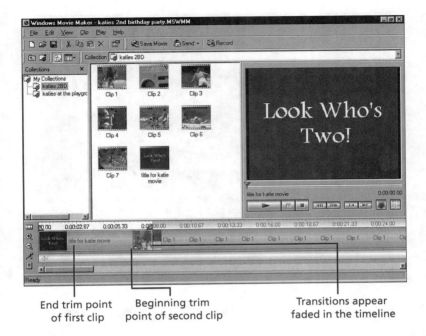

End trim point
of first clip

Beginning trim
point of second clip

Transitions appear
faded in the timeline

FIGURE 22.3 The Radio Tuner allows you to listen to streaming audio.

3. To add a station to the preset list, change to the My Presets list, then select the station and click **Add**. To remove a station from the preset list, select it and click **Delete**.

Applying a New Skin

You can apply a new skin to change the way Media Player looks. As you might assume, a skin changes the cosmetic appearance of Media Player while leaving the essential functions unchanged. Some skins may add additional controls for you to play with, however. To change skins, follow these steps:

1. Click **Skin Chooser**.

2. Select a skin from those listed, and then click **Apply Skin**. Media Player's look changes, as shown in Figure 22.4.

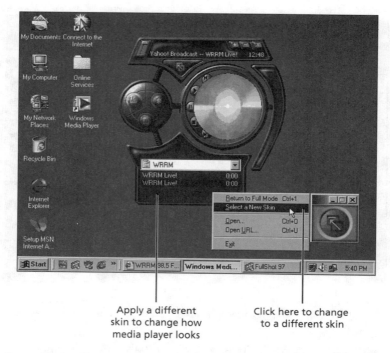

Apply a different
skin to change how
media player looks

Click here to change
to a different skin

FIGURE 22.4   Change the look of Media Player by changing skins.

No Change?   Most of the skins only affect how
Media Player looks when displayed in compact mode,
so you may need to switch from full mode to see your
new skin.

More Skins   To download more skins, click **More
Skins**. You're taken to WindowsMedia.com's Web site.
Click a link to download the associated skin.

In this lesson, you learned how to play audio and video with Windows
Media Player. In the next lesson, you'll learn how to use the WordPad and
Paint accessories.

LESSON 23

Working with WordPad and Paint

In this lesson, you'll learn how to use the WordPad and Paint accessories.

Creating and Editing a Document with WordPad

WordPad is a basic word processing program that you can use to create letters, memos, reports, and other documents. To create a document with WordPad, select **Start**, **Programs**, **Accessories**, **WordPad** and then start typing. To create another new document later, click the **New** button on the toolbar, as shown in Figure 23.1.

Typing Text

When typing text into your document, remember these tips:

- Text is inserted at the *insertion point*. To move the insertion point, simply click in the document at some other point.

- To erase a mistake, press the **Backspace** key. Characters to the left of the insertion point are deleted. If you press the **Delete** key instead, characters to the *right* of the insertion point are deleted. You can also select text and press the **Delete** key to remove it.

- To type over existing text, switch to Overtype mode by pressing the **Insert** key. What you type replaces the existing text, beginning at the insertion point. To switch back to normal (insertion) mode, press the **Insert** key again.

To select text, click at the beginning of the text you want to select and then drag over the text to highlight it. You can select text with the keyboard by pressing and holding down the **Shift** key as you use the arrow keys to highlight text.

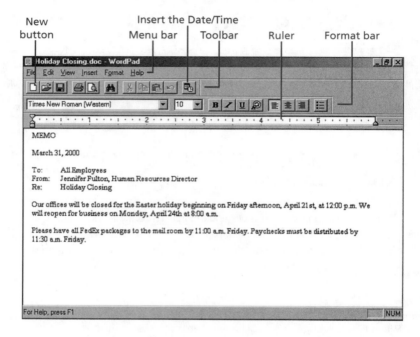

FIGURE 23.1 Creating a new document with WordPad is simple.

Inserting the Date   You can quickly insert the date into a document (rather than typing it) by clicking the **Date/Time** button on the toolbar. Select a format and click **OK**.

Formatting Text

After typing text into your document, you can change its appearance to emphasize your words. Using the Format toolbar, you can change the text's font, font style (its attributes, such as bold and italic), and font size. See Figure 23.2.

 Font   A set of characters that have the same typeface or text style. Times New Roman is the default font used in WordPad. You can change your text to another font as needed.

To change the text's format, follow these steps:

1. Select the text you want to change by dragging over it.

2. Make changes as needed, using the buttons on the Format toolbar:

    *   To change the font, choose another font from the **Font** drop-down list box.

    *   To change the size of the text, select a size from the **Font Size** drop-down list box.

 Point Size   Text size is measured in points. One point is 1/72nd of an inch.

    *   To apply a font style, click the appropriate button: **Bold**, **Italic**, **Underline**, or **Color**.

    *   To change text alignment, click the appropriate button: **Align Left**, **Center**, or **Align Right**.

If you need to change several attributes of your selected text, you might prefer to use the Font dialog box. To display it, open the **Format** menu and select **Font**.

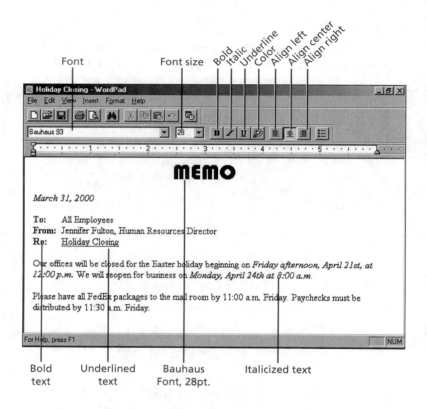

FIGURE 23.2   Formatting lets you change the look of your text.

Creating Graphics with Paint

With the Paint accessory, shown in Figure 23.3, you can create colorful graphic images for use in your documents or as Windows wallpaper. Start Paint by selecting **Start**, **Programs**, **Accessories**, **Paint**.

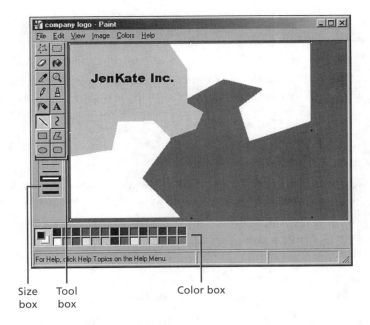

Size   Tool   Color box
box   box

FIGURE **23.3**   Paint is ready for you to create your graphic.

To create your image, use the tools in the Tool Box. Change the color of the objects you draw with the Color Box. (I'll explain more about the use of color in the next section.) Change the width of the lines you draw (and the width of object outline) with the Size box.

 Quick Image   If you have a scanner or digital camera, you can import an image into Paint quickly and easily by choosing **File, From Scanner or Camera**.

Here's how to use each tool:

    Free Form Select   Drag the mouse pointer around the area you want to select.

Select   Click at the upper-left corner of the area you want to select, and then drag down and to the right to select the entire area.

 Eraser/Color Eraser   Drag over any part of the drawing you want to erase (replace with the background color). If you drag using the right mouse button, you'll erase only the selected foreground color and replace it with the background color. (You'll learn how to select these two colors in the next section.)

 Fill with Color   Click any area (a section filled with a single color) of the drawing, and that area is filled with the current foreground color.

 Pick Color   Change the foreground color to any color in the drawing by clicking that color with this tool.

 Magnifier   Click to zoom that area of the drawing. Click the area again to zoom back out.

 Pencil   Drag to draw a freehand line. To draw a straight line, press and hold down the **Shift** key as you drag.

 Brush   Select the size of brush tip you want to use from the **Size** box. Then drag to brush the drawing with the current foreground color.

 Airbrush   Select the amount of spray you want from the **Size** box. Then drag to spray the drawing with the current foreground color.

 Text   Drag to create a text box. Use the Text toolbar to change the font, font size, and style. Then type the text you want.

 Be Careful What You Type   You can't go back and correct your text after you click outside the text box, so be sure it's correct.

Line   Select the line width you want to use from the **Size** box, click where you want to place one end of the line, and drag to draw the line. To create a straight line, press and hold down the **Shift** key as you drag.

Curve   Select the line width you want from the **Size** box. Then click at the point where you want the curve to begin and drag to create a straight line. Then, click where you want the line to curve and drag outward to bend the line. Repeat to add another curve to the line if you wish. (A line can have no more than two curves.)

Rectangle   Select from the **Fill Style** box whether you want a filled or unfilled rectangle. Click to establish the upper-left corner of the rectangle, and then drag downward and to the right until the rectangle is the size you want. To create a square, press and hold down the **Shift** key as you drag.

Polygon   Select from the **Fill Style** box whether you want a filled or unfilled polygon. Click to establish the first corner of the polygon, and then drag to create the first side. Continue dragging to create each side in turn. Double-click when you're through drawing the polygon.

Ellipse   Select from the **Fill Style** box whether you want a filled or unfilled ellipse. Click to establish the upper-left edge of the ellipse, and then drag downward and to the right until the ellipse is the size you need. To create a perfect circle, press and hold down the **Shift** key as you drag.

Rounded Rectangle   Select from the **Fill Style** box whether you want a filled or unfilled rectangle. Click to establish the upper-left corner of the rectangle, and then drag downward and to the right until the rectangle is the size you want. To create a square, press and hold down the **Shift** key as you drag.

Bad Drawing   If you make a mistake while drawing an object, open the **Edit** menu and select **Undo** to remove it.

Selecting Colors

The lower-left corner of the Color Box, shown in Figure 23.4, contains two overlapping squares. The upper square indicates the foreground color, and the lower square determines the background color. In Paint, the foreground color is used for the outline of the object you draw, and the background color is used for the fill (that is, if you choose to draw a filled object). To change the foreground color, click a color in the Color box. To change the background color, right-click a color instead.

Foreground
color

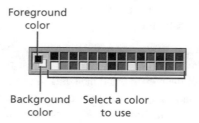

Background   Select a color
color   to use

FIGURE 23.4   Change the color of the objects you draw with the Color Box.

Before drawing an object such as a rounded rectangle, you can choose whether you want it to be filled or unfilled. Simply click the appropriate icon in the **Fill Style** box: **Outline Only, Outline with Fill,** or **Fill Only**.

 Switcheroo   You can create an object that has an outline with the color of the background and a fill with the color of the foreground by using the right mouse button when you draw the object.

In this lesson, you learned how to use WordPad to create text documents, and how to use Paint to create simple graphic images for use in those documents or on the Windows desktop. In the next lesson, you'll learn how to use the other Windows accessories.

LESSON 24
Using Other Accessories

In this lesson, you'll learn how to use the Sound Recorder, Calculator, and Phone Dialer.

Using the Sound Recorder

With Sound Recorder, you can record your own sounds using a simple microphone attached to your sound card. You can even add special effects to sound files!

 Use Media Player Although you can play a single WAV file in Sound Recorder, you may want to use Windows Media Player instead because it can play a long list of WAV files, one at a time. See Lesson 22, "Using Windows Media Player," for help.

To record a sound file, follow these steps:

1. Click **Start** and then select **Programs**, **Accessories**, **Entertainment**, **Sound Recorder**. Sound Recorder opens, as shown in Figure 24.1.

Play | Record
Stop

FIGURE 24.1 Sound Recorder can record WAV files.

2. Open the **File** menu and select **New**.

3. Click **Record** and begin speaking into your microphone.

4. When you're through, click **Stop**.

5. To review what you've recorded, click **Play**. When you're satisfied, open the **File** menu and select **Save** to save the recording to a file. The Save As dialog box appears.

6. Change to the drive and folder where you want to save your file. Type a name for the sound file in the **File name** text box and click **Save**.

Special Effects   You can add an effect to your sound recording by opening the **Effects** menu and selecting an effect from those listed, such as **Add Echo**.

Using the Calculator

Windows comes with a handy calculator you can use to calculate anything you need, from balancing your checkbook to adding up the latest sales figures (see Figure 24.2). Start Calculator by clicking **Start**, **Programs**, **Accessories**, **Calculator**. Using the Calculator is remarkably similar to using a regular pocket calculator. Use the **+** button to add, **-** to subtract,

/ to divide, and * to multiply. To clear the last entry, click **CE** or press the **Delete** key. To clear a calculation completely, click **C** or press the **Esc** key. To compute the final value, click = or press the **Enter** key.

FIGURE **24.2** You can perform simple and complex calculations with the Calculator.

You can store the result of a calculation (or any number) and recall it when needed. To store the displayed value, click **MS**. To recall it, click **MR**. To add the displayed value to the value stored in memory, click **M+**. To clear the memory, click **MC**.

Mad Science? To perform scientific calculations with the Calculator, open the **View** menu and select **Scientific**.

Using Phone Dialer

With Phone Dialer, you can place phone calls using your computer's modem. This saves you the trouble of looking up a number and then dialing it. When needed, Phone Dialer can even dial your long-distance access code or calling card number. It also tracks your calls in a convenient log that you can review when needed.

To use Phone Dialer, follow these steps:

1. Click **Start**, and then select **Programs**, **Accessories**,
   Communications, **Phone Dialer**. Phone Dialer appears, as
   shown in Figure 24.3.

Enter a number to dial here

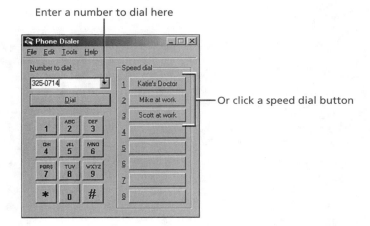

Or click a speed dial button

FIGURE 24.3 Let Phone Dialer dial frequently used numbers for you.

2. Type the number you want to dial into the **Number to dial** text
   box, or click a speed dial button.

Speed dial   To add a phone number to a speed dial
button, click an available button, type the name and
phone number of the person you want to save, and
click **Save**.

3. Click **Dial**. When the caller answers, pick up your phone
   and begin speaking. Your phone line must come out of the wall and
   into the modem, and a second line comes out of the modem and to
   your telephone.

4. When you're through with the call, click **Hang Up**.

Phone Dialer logs each call and its duration. To view the log, open the **Tools** menu and select **Show Log**.

In this lesson, you learned how to various Windows accessories. In the next lesson, you'll learn how to browse the Web with Internet Explorer.

LESSON 25

Using Internet Explorer

In this lesson, you'll learn how to enter addresses into Internet Explorer and move from page to page on the Web.

Internet Basics

The Internet is a vast worldwide network of networks that connects various businesses, government offices, universities, research centers, and so on. Through the Internet, you can access data from these networks, such as scientific research, sales and product information, and travel and weather data. You can connect to the Internet through an Internet service provider (ISP), using a modem (a *dial-up connection*), your cable provider or WebTV (a *coaxial cable connection*), DSL (*digital subscriber line connection*), a dedicated phone line (an *ISDN connection*), or your company's network (a *direct network connection*).

The World Wide Web supports the transmission of graphics, sound, animation, and formatted text—unlike other parts of the Internet, which are strictly text-based. Thus, the Web will probably be the part of the Internet you'll visit most often. To view Web pages—the documents that make up the World Wide Web—you need a Web browser. Windows comes with Internet Explorer, a popular Web browser from Microsoft. However, you might want to use Netscape Communicator instead. Both are compatible with Windows Me.

In this lesson and the next one, you'll learn how to use Internet Explorer. However, don't worry if you've already chosen to use Netscape Communicator; you'll find it remarkably similar. But first, you must enter your Internet connection information into Windows.

Creating Your Internet Connection

Before you can begin using the Internet, you must configure your connecting device, which is probably a modem. (If you need help configuring your modem, see Appendix A, "Configuring Hardware and Adding/Removing Windows Components.") Then you must configure the software that connects you to your Internet service provider (ISP). If you're using a modem, you may choose to go through a local provider or an online service such as AOL, Prodigy, CompuServe, or MSN.

 Network Connection   If you've setup a home network, you can share a single Internet connection over the network if you like. See Lesson 12, "Accessing Resources on Your Home Network," for help.

To configure your computer to connect to an ISP, follow these steps (for help connecting to an online service, see the "Connecting to an Online Service" section):

1. Double-click the **Connect to the Internet** icon on the desktop.

2. The Welcome screen appears. Select the option you desire:

   I want to sign up for a new Internet account   Choose this option if you haven't yet found an ISP. Windows will help you locate a national provider that services your area code.

   I want to transfer my existing Internet account to this computer   Choose this option if you already have an Internet account set up with a national ISP and you want to set up that account for use with this computer.

   I want to set up my Internet connection manually, or I want to connect through a local area network (LAN) Choose this option if you have a local ISP you'd like to use.

   Then click **Next**.

Click **Cancel** if you've upgraded from a previous version of Windows and you want to continue to use your existing Internet connection.

Using Microsoft's Referral Service to Locate an ISP

If you selected **I want to sign up for a new Internet account** in step 2, continue by following these steps:

1. If promped, select from the Mircorsoft Internet Referral Service numbers for your area and ckick Next.

2. A list of national ISPs in your area appears, as shown in Figure 25.1. To find out more about a particular ISP, click on it. To sign up with that ISP, select it from the list and click **Next**.

FIGURE 25.1   Select the ISP you want to use.

3. Enter the information that's needed to sign up with your selected ISP, and then click **Next**.

4. If prompted, select the billing option you prefer and click **Next**.

5. Enter your credit card information and click **Next**.

6. You're connected to the ISP you selected. Follow the onscreen prompts to complete your installation. An Internet icon for the ISP you selected appears on the desktop. Double-click this icon to connect to the Internet.

Setting Up an Existing Account

If you selected **I want to transfer my existing account to this computer**, continue by following these steps:

1. If promped, select from the Mircorsoft Internet Referral Service numbers for your area and ckick Next.

2. A list of national ISPs in your area appears. Select your ISP from the list and click **Next**.

 My ISP Isn't Listed!   If you have an existing account with a national ISP that isn't listed, select that option, click **Next** twice, and follow the steps in the "Manually Entering Information" section of this lesson to enter the information needed to connect to that ISP.

3. You're connected to the ISP you selected. Follow the onscreen prompts to complete your installation. An Internet icon for your ISP appears on the desktop. Double-click this icon to connect to the Internet.

Manually Entering Information

If you selected **I want to set up my Internet connection manually, or I want to connect through a local area network (LAN)**, continue by following these steps:

1. Select whether you want to connect through a modem or your company's network. Click **Next**. If you're connecting through a modem, continue to step 2. Otherwise, follow these additional steps: Select **Automatic discovery of proxy server** and click **Next**. Click **Yes** to set up an email account, **and** then click **Next**. Select **Create a new Internet mail account** and click **Next**. Then skip to step 6.

2. Enter your ISP's phone number. Select whether you need to dial the area code. Click **Next**.

> **Advanced Settings**   Click **Advanced** to specify that you want to use a SLIP connection, log on manually, use a log-in script, and/or connect to a particular IP and DNS address. Your ISP will tell you if you need to set up any of these options.

3. Type the user name and password you use to connect to your ISP. Click **Next**.

4. Type a name for your dialup connection file, such as **Connection to Indy Net**. Click **Next**.

5. Click **Yes** to set up your email account, and then click **Next**. Click **Create a new Internet mail account** and click **Next**.

6. Enter the name you want to appear on your email correspondence. Click **Next**.

7. Enter your email address. Click **Next**.

8. Select your email server type, and then enter the addresses of the incoming and outgoing mail servers. Click **Next**.

9. Enter your email log-in name and password. Click **Next**.

10. If you want to connect to the Internet now, select that option. Click **Finish**. You're through configuring your dial-up connection. An Internet icon for your ISP appears on the desktop. Double-click this icon to connect to the Internet.

Connecting to an Online Service

An online service is a private, members-only service. You can choose from many online services, including America Online, CompuServe, Prodigy, and the Microsoft Network.

Windows provides an easy method for signing up for any of these services. Most of them even let you sign up for a short period of time as a trial. Follow these steps:

1. Double-click the **Online Services** icon on the desktop. (To sign up for MSN, double-click its icon on the desktop instead and skip to step 3.)

2. Double-click the icon for the online service you want to use.

3. Each service has a different setup program. You might be asked to insert the Windows installation disks to continue. Follow the onscreen prompts. An Internet icon for the online service you selected appears on the desktop. Double-click this icon to connect to the Internet.

Disabling Call Waiting

If your call waiting is enabled on the phone line you use to connect to the Internet, you'll want to disable it just prior to connecting so it won't mess up your transmissions. Follow these steps:

1. Click **Start, Settings, Control Panel**.

2. Click **view all Control Panel options** if needed, and double-click the **Modems** icon.

3. Select the modem you dial out on, and click **Dialing Properties**.

4. Select **To disable call waiting, dial**, and then select the code you use to disable call waiting on your particular phone service. Click **OK**.

Starting Internet Explorer

Internet Explorer is a program you can use to view Web sites. To connect
to the Internet and start Internet Explorer, follow these steps:

1. Double-click the **Internet** icon you created in one of the previous sections. The Dial-up Connection screen appears, as shown
   in Figure 25.2.

2. Type your **Password**. To save your password so you don't need
   to enter it again, select **Save Password**. To bypass this dialog
   box and connect automatically to the Internet each time you start
   Internet Explorer, Outlook Express, or Windows Update, select
   Connect automatically. Click **Connect**.

Enter you password here

FIGURE **25.2**   Connecting to the Internet.

3. Double-click the **Internet Explorer** icon on the desktop, or
   click the **Internet Explorer** icon on the **Quick Launch** toolbar.

4. Internet Explorer displays your home page. From here, you can
   enter the address of a page you want to view, or you can search
   for an address. You can also click a link to display a different
   page. You'll learn how to enter an address and click a link later

in this lesson, and you'll learn how to search the Internet in Lesson 26, "Searching for Web Pages and Saving Your Favorites."

 Home Page   When you start Internet Explorer, it takes you to your *home page*. This page is typically associated with the Web browser you've installed, so in this case you're taken to MSN. You can change your home page to any Web page you like.

When you're ready to disconnect from the Internet, simply close Internet Explorer. You'll be asked if you want to disconnect; click **Disconnect Now**. You can keep Internet Explorer open and disconnect by double-clicking the **Internet** icon on the taskbar and selecting **Disconnect**.

Going to a Specific Site

Every page on the Web has a specific address. To view a page, enter its address into Internet Explorer. A typical address looks something like this:

`http://cws.internet.com/menu.html`

Briefly, here's what each part means:

`http:/`	Hypertext Transfer Protocol, the language of the Web
`/cws.internet.com`	The address of a site on the Web
`/menu.html`	The name of a Web page on the CWS site

To enter an address into Internet Explorer, do the following:

1. Type the address into the **Address** text box. (You don't have to type the protocol if it's `http://`. You can type just `cws.internet.com`.)

2. Press **Enter** or click **Go**. The page whose address you typed is displayed. (To stop a page from being displayed, click the **Stop** button.)

My Page Didn't Display! Try checking what you've typed. Make sure you've used / and not \, and then press **Enter** again or click **Refresh**. If that doesn't work, delete the filename from the address and see if you can connect to the site's home page. If everything else fails, you might have to search for the page's correct address. See Lesson 26 for help.

Following a Link

One way to move from page to page is by clicking a *link* (short for *hyperlink*). A link is usually a bit of underlined text, typically blue (although it can be any color), as shown in Figure 25.3.

A link may also be a graphic image. When you move the mouse over a link, whether it's a bit of text or a graphic, the mouse cursor changes to a hand. The address of the link's associated page appears in the Status bar at the bottom of the screen.

To use a link, just click it. You're automatically taken to the Web page for that link. If you later return to the page with the text link you clicked, you'll notice that it's changed color, typically from blue to purple (although, again, it could be any color). This change lets you quickly identify the links you've visited.

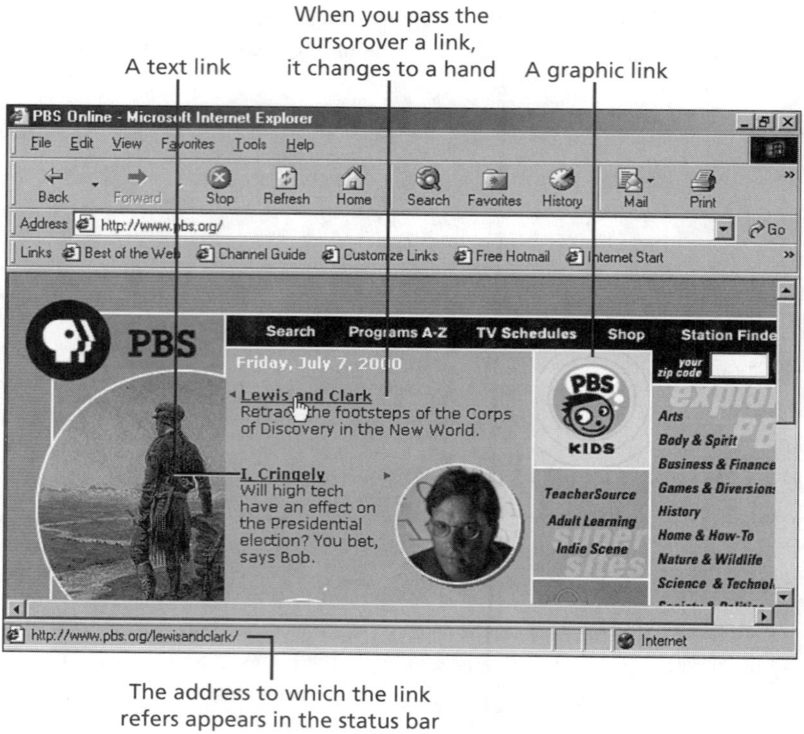

When you pass the
cursorover a link,
A text link   it changes to a hand   A graphic link

The address to which the link
refers appears in the status bar

FIGURE 25.3   A link may be text or a graphic.

Returning to a Previously Viewed Page

As you move from page to page, a history of the pages you've visited is kept. This makes it easy to retrace your steps as needed. Table 25.1 explains some of your options. You'll find these buttons at the tip of the Internet Explorer window.

TABLE 25.1   Navigation Buttons

Action	Button to Click
Move back in the history	Back
Move forward again	Forward
Return to the Home page	Home

 Complete History   You can move back and forth through the history several pages at a time by clicking the down arrow on the **Back** and **Forward** buttons and selecting the page you want.

Using History to Revisit a Page

You can also return a previously viewed page by selecting it from the History list. To display this list, click the **History** button on the Standard Buttons toolbar. This list appears on the left side of the Internet Explorer window, as shown in Figure 25.4.

Initially, pages are listed by site. Click a site, such as PBS (www.pbs.org), and then click a page on that site you want to revisit. Unfortunately, graphics and HTML files you may have opened on your own computer or the network are listed as well, making the History list a bit confusing. You can display history by date, most visited, or visited today by clicking the **View** button and selecting the option you want. To remove the History list, click the **History** button again.

View button   History list

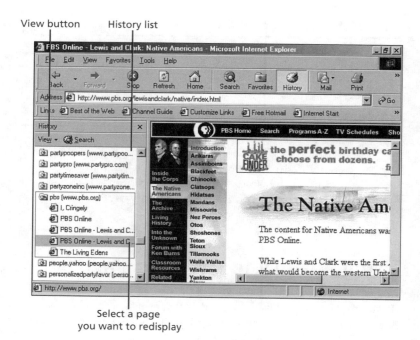

Select a page
you want to redisplay

FIGURE 25.4   Use the History list to revisit a Web page.

Playing Internet Radio Broadcasts

Internet Explorer provides the Radio toolbar, which you can use to listen
to streaming audio over your Internet connection. *Streaming audio* is a
digital audio file that can begin playing on your computer before the
entire file has been received. Since digital audio files are often quite large,
being able to play them before you download them entirely is a particular
advantage. Table 25.2 lists the Radio toolbar's buttons and their purpose.

TABLE 25.2   The Radio Toolbar

Button	Name	Purpose
Stop	Play/Stop	Turns on/off the radio.
Mute	Mute	Turns on/off your computer's speakers.
Volume Control	Volume Control	Adjusts the volume of your computer's speakers.
Radio Stations	Radio Stations	Displays a list of Web sites that play radio music compatible with Windows Media Player.

 Streaming Video   You can also play streaming video files on your computer using Windows Media Player, as described in Lesson 22, "Using Windows Media Player." To begin playing a streaming video file while in Internet Explorer, simply click its link on any Web page. Media Player will start automatically.

To play music while you continue to browse the Internet, select a radio station from the Radio Stations list. Then browse as you like, clicking **Stop** if needed to turn the radio off.

In this lesson, you learned how to use Internet Explorer to explore the Web. In the next lesson, you'll learn how to search for particular Web pages and save your favorites.

LESSON 26

Searching for Web Pages and Saving Your Favorites

In this lesson, you'll learn how to locate specific Web pages and save their locations for future use.

Understanding Web Searches

Search engines are free tools that let you sort through the vast amount of information available on the Internet. If you don't have much luck with one search engine, you can always try another because each one maintains its own list of pages and indexes those pages differently.

Some search engines let you browse their indexes by selecting a series of categories and subcategories until you find the desired Web site. Other search engines let you search for a page using *forms*. You simply enter your search criteria into a form and you get a list of pages that match the criteria. Click a link to one of the listed pages to display it.

 Form A form looks similar to a dialog box. Like a dialog box, you enter the requested information into the form, click a button such as **Search** or **Submit**, and the information in the form is processed.

Here are some tips to remember when you're entering search criteria:

- Try to be as specific as possible. For example, you'll have better luck searching for *Michigan bass fishing* than just *fishing*.

- Don't include common words such as *to*, *the*, *an*, *who*, and so on. The search engine will just ignore them.

- The word *and* is understood. For example, if you type *cigarette tax*, the search engine will look for pages that contain both the word *cigarette* and the word *tax*, although not necessarily in that order or even together.

- To search for two or more words together, enclose them in quotations, as in *"cigarette tax"*.

- You can use the word *OR* when needed. For example, you might search for *Indiana or Ohio*.

- You can combine phrases, as in *Indiana OR Ohio "cigarette tax"*. This will display pages that contain information on either Indiana or Ohio's cigarette tax.

- To make sure that a certain word isn't included in the search results, use the *NOT* operator, as in *Indian NOT American*. This will get you documents on people from India, not American Indians.

- Some search engines let you use wildcards. For example, if you type *stock**, you'll get matches for *stockbroker*, *stockyard*, *stock exchange*, and *stocks*.

- Some search engines let you use parentheses to create more complex search criteria: *("infant car seat" OR "baby seat") AND safety*.

- Some search engines let you enter "search busters," which are words that either must or must not be found within a page for it to be included in the search results. A plus or a minus sign is used to indicate a search buster, as in *+civil*.

Table 26.1 lists search operators (such as *AND* and *OR*) for the most popular search engines. N/A indicates that a search engine doesn't support that particular option.

TABLE 26.1   Search Operators

Operator	AltaVista	Excite	Lycos	Snap	Yahoo!
And	*AND*	*AND*	N/A	*AND*	N/A
Or	*OR*	*OR*	assumed	*OR*	assumed
Not	*NOT*	*NOT*	N/A	*NOT*	N/A
Near	*NEAR*	N/A	N/A	N/A	N/A
Quotes	" "	" "	" "	" "	" "
Parentheses	()	()	N/A	()	N/A
Wildcard	*	N/A	N/A	N/A	*
Must include	+	+	+	+	+
Must not include	–	–	–	–	–

Using Search Engines

Here are some of the most popular search engines:

AltaVista	http://www.altavista.com
Excite	http://www.excite.com
Lycos	http://www.lycos.com
Snap	http://www.snap.com
Yahoo!	http://www.yahoo.com

Internet Explorer provides quick access to these and many other search engines. To use a search engine to locate a Web page, follow these steps:

1. In Internet Explorer, click **Search**.

2. The search page for the search engine being featured today appears in the left panel, as shown in Figure 26.1.

Type your search
criteria here

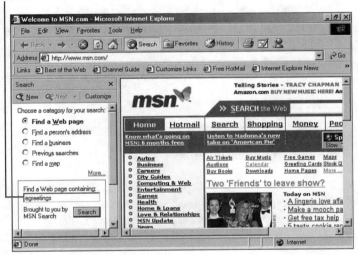

FIGURE **26.1**   Searching the Web.

3. Type your search criteria in the text box and click **Search**.

4. After a list of matching pages is returned, scroll down the list until you find a page you like and click its link. The page appears in the panel on the right, as shown in Figure 26.2. (To view a summary of a page before you click its link, move the mouse pointer over the page's name.)

Click a link to a
page you like

The page appears here

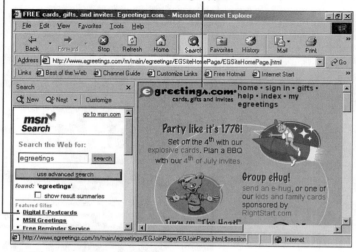

FIGURE 26.2   Your search results.

 Good Match?   Sites are listed in decreasing order according to how closely they fit your search criteria.

5. If you want to search again, you can choose a different search engine by clicking the arrow on the **Next** button and selecting the engine you want to use.

6. To remove the search panel, click the **Search** button again.

Quick Search   You can also start the search by typing *go*, *find*, or *?* followed by your search criteria in the **Address** text box, as in *find Indiana lakes*. Internet Explorer initiates the search using the current search engine.

You can also initiate a search by clicking **Start**, **Search**, **On the Internet**.

Searching Within a Web Page

You can search the text within a Web page just as you search text within a word processing document. Follow these steps:

1. In Internet Explorer, open the **Edit** menu and select **Find (on This Page)**.

2. Type what you want to search for in the **Find what** text box.

3. Select any options you want:

   Match whole word only   Won't search for words that contain the word you typed. For example, if you type *for*, it won't match the word *forward*.

   Match case   Will search only for words that match exactly what you typed. For example, if you type Windows, it won't match the word *windows*.

4. Initially, Find searches the page from the top down. To search in the other direction, select **Up**.

5. Click **Find Next**. If a match is found, it's highlighted on the page. To continue the search, click **Find Next** again. When you're through searching, click **Cancel**.

Searching for People or Businesses

Do you want to locate a long-lost friend or acquaintance? Need the address of a local business. Internet Explorer can help by connecting you with the most popular search engines on the Internet.

To search for someone, follow these steps:

1. In Internet Explorer, click **Search**.

2. When the Search pane appears, click **Find a person's address** to locate a person, or **Find a business** to locate a business address.

3. Select the type of address you want to find from the **Search for** list. For example, select **mailing address** if searching for a person, or **business category** if searching for a business.

4. Type all the information you know about the person or business in the Search pane, such as the person's first name, last name, and city or state.

4. Click **Search**. A list of people or businesses matching your criteria appears.

You can also search for people by clicking **Start**, **Search**, **People**.

Using the Favorites Folder

Once you find a page on the Internet that you like, you can save it in the Favorites folder. That way, you can revisit the page later without having to type in its address.

When you add a page to the Favorites folder, you can subscribe to it at the same time. When you subscribe, you can have Internet Explorer notify you when the contents of the page have changed. You can also instruct Internet Explorer to download the page so you can read its new contents offline.

Adding Favorites

To add a page to the Favorites folder, follow these steps:

1. Go to the page you want to add to the Favorites folder.

2. Click the **Favorites** button on the Standard Buttons toolbar. The Favorites pane appears.

3. Click **Add**. The Add Favorite dialog box appears, as shown in Figure 26.3.

Change the name of the page
if you want

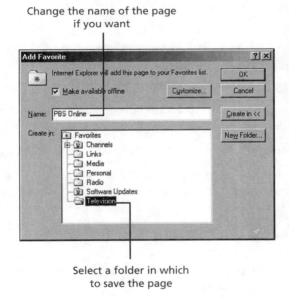

Select a folder in which
to save the page

FIGURE 26.3   Save pages you like to the Favorites folder.

4. Select whether or not you want to make this page available offline. Click **Customize** to change the frequency with which this page is downloaded for offline viewing.

5. If you like, type a new **Name** for the page.

6. Click **Create in** to select the subfolder where you want to add the page. To create a new subfolder, click **New Folder**, type a name for the subfolder, and click **OK**.

7. Click **OK** to add the page to your Favorites.

To visit the page later, click the **Favorites** button on the Standard Buttons toolbar and click the page. If you've placed the page in a subfolder, click the subfolder to reveal its contents and then click the page.

Adding a Favorite to the Links Bar

If you find a page you think you'll visit often, you can add it to the Links bar, located just under the Address bar. Pages that are added to the Links bar appear as buttons. To visit one of the pages, simply click its button.

To add a page to the Links bar, do any of the following:

- Drag the icon that appears in front of the page's address in the **Address** text box onto the Links bar.

- Drag a link that appears on a Web page onto the Links bar.

- If the page has already been added to your Favorites folder, click the **Favorites** button on the Standard Buttons toolbar to display the Favorites list. Drag the page from its location in the list to the Links folder.

To remove a link later on, right-click its button and select **Delete**. You can rename the link by right-clicking its button, selecting **Rename**, and typing the name you want to appear on the button.

In this lesson, you learned how to locate a particular Web page and save its location for future use. In the next lesson, you'll learn how to send and receive electronic mail.

LESSON 27

Displaying Internet Content on the Desktop

In this lesson, you'll learn how to display Web content on your desktop.

Displaying Web Content on Your Desktop

As you learned in Lesson 2, Windows offers you two desktops. Although these two desktops are remarkably similar, by changing from the Classic Desktop to the Active Desktop, you can display live Web content, such as stock and weather information, and access other Web content more easily.

Connecting to the Internet The Active Desktop's main duty is to display Web content, so you must be connected to the Internet—if not all the time, at least when you're selecting the channels and Active Desktop Items you want to display. After that, you can disconnect from the Internet and browse the content you've downloaded. The items on the Active Desktop are updated periodically—sometimes several times a day—but if you're not online at that time, the content is updated the next time you connect to the Internet. For help creating an Internet connection, see Lesson 25, "Using Internet Explorer."

To turn on the Active Desktop, follow these steps:

1. Right-click an open area of the desktop. A shortcut menu appears.

2. Click **Active Desktop**. A cascading menu appears with more options.

3. From the cascading menu, select **Show Web Content**. The Active Desktop is displayed.

That's it! When the Active Desktop option is initially turned on, you won't see much of a change. The channel bar may appear, and with it, you can select favorite Web sites to visit, or channels to display.

Single-Click Option   If you plan on using the Active Desktop a lot, you might want to change to single-clicking. This option lets you point at files and icons to select them, and you just need to click once to open a file or program. See Lesson 10, "Accessing Your Drives, Folders, and Files," for help.

Remove Those Icons   You don't need to have the icons on the desktop appear when you're using the Active Desktop. To remove them, right-click the desktop and select **Active Desktop, Show Desktop Icons**. (This removes the check mark and turns the option off.) If you hide your desktop icons, display the **Desktop** toolbar so you can still access your program icons easily. (By the way, when you switch back to the Classic Desktop, the icons reappear automatically.)

Switching Back to the Classic Desktop

After using the Active Desktop for a while, you might want to switch back to the Classic Desktop. Switching back and forth between the two doesn't remove any customization or channel selections you've made to the Active Desktop.

To switch back to the Classic Desktop, follow these steps:

1. Right-click an open area of the desktop. A shortcut menu appears.

2. Select **Active Desktop**. A cascading menu appears.

3. Select **Show Web Content**. This removes the check mark in front of the command, turning the option off. The Classic Desktop appears.

What Is a Subscription?

To select the content you want to display on your Active Desktop, set up a *subscription*. This allows you to obtain current information from an Internet source automatically. The information is refreshed right on your desktop at intervals you select.

You can display channels or Active Desktop Items on your desktop. A *channel* is a special Web page that can update itself. Forbes.com is an example of a channel to which you might subscribe. You can select any Web page you want and have it act as a channel. When you subscribe to a channel (Web page), it's displayed within an Active Desktop Item window, as shown in Figure 27.1. In any case, what sets a channel apart from other Web data is that its content can be downloaded to your system periodically so you can view it without bothering to start your Web browser and enter the Web site's address. In addition, when the channel's content is downloaded to your computer, you can view it offline anytime you want.

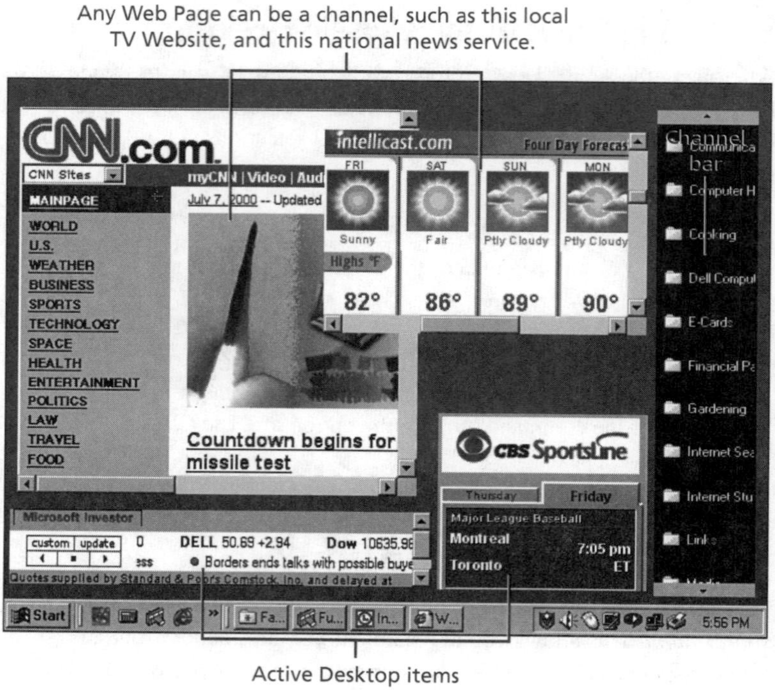

Any Web Page can be a channel, such as this local
TV Website, and this national news service.

Active Desktop items

FIGURE 27.1   Any Web page can be a channel to your desktop.

In addition, Microsoft offers many Active Desktop items, such as stock tick-
ers, sports updates, and weather displays, through its Active Desktop Gallery.
A desktop item is displayed in a small window on the desktop (see Figure
27.1). Finally, you can display your Favorites list on the Active Desktop, and
wait to launch Internet Explorer. To display the Favorites list in the Channel
bar, right-click the desktop, select **Active Desktop** then choose **Internet
Explorer Channel bar**.

Subscribing to a Channel

When you first display the Active Desktop, it contains no active Web content. To select what you want to display, subscribe to either a channel (Web
page) or an Active Desktop Item. You can subscribe to any page on the

Internet and have it act as a channel. You can add as many channels and Active Desktop Items to the Desktop as you wish.

Where are my favorites? If you upgraded from Windows 95 or 98, you may not see the Favorites list on the Channel bar. To display it, delete the old Channel folder, located in the Windows/Favorites folder.

Connect First In order to complete these steps, you must have established your Internet connection already. See Lesson 25 for help.

To subscribe to the Channel bar, follow these steps:

1. If needed, change to the Active Desktop by right-clicking the desktop, selecting **Active Desktop** from the shortcut menu, and selecting **Show Web Content**.

2. Connect to the Internet.

3. Right-click the desktop and choose **Active Desktop**, **New Desktop Item**.

4. Type the address of the Web page to which you want to subscribe in the **Location** textbox and click **OK**.

5. When you add a channel, the Add item to Active Desktop dialog box appears. To update the channel content manually, click **OK**; otherwise click **customize**.

6. If you clicked customize in step 5, click **Next**.

7. Select how often you want to synchronize the page (update its contents):

   • **Only when I choose Synchronize from the Tools menu**
     Updates the channel only when you tell Windows to do so.

- **I would like to create a new schedule** Creates a custom schedule for updating channel information that exactly fits your needs. If you choose this option, after you click **Next** select the schedule you want to use.

Then click **Next**. (See Figure 27.2.)

FIGURE 27.2   Select how or if you want the channel to be updated.

8. If needed, click **Yes** and enter the password required to access the site. Click **Finish**.

9. Click **OK**. Windows downloads the site's information.

To close a channel, click the Close button in the channel window. To redisplay the channel, whether online or off, right-click the desktop, select Active Desktop, then choose the channel window you want to redisplay.

Hide the Bar   You might want to hide the Channel bar to make room for more active content. To hide the Channel bar, right-click the desktop and select **Active Desktop, Internet Explorer Channel Bar**. This removes its check mark and turns it off.

Web Page Background You can use a Web page as your desktop background. If you're connected to the Internet and you click one of its links, the associated page will open in Internet Explorer. See Lesson 8, "Changing the Appearance of Windows," for details.

Subscribing to an Active Desktop Item

In addition to subscribing to a channel, you can select items from Microsoft's Active Desktop Gallery for use on your desktop. Simply follow these steps:

1. If needed, connect to the Internet and change to the Active Desktop by right-clicking the desktop and selecting **Active Desktop, Show Web Content**.

2. Right-click the desktop and select **Active Desktop, New Desktop Item**. The New Active Desktop Item dialog box appears, as shown in Figure 27.3.

FIGURE 27.3 Adding a Gallery item to the desktop.

3. Click **Visit Gallery**.

4. The Gallery appears in an Internet Explorer window. Click a category, such as **News**.

5. Click an item, such as **Microsoft Investor Ticker**, to view its description.

6. A page describing the item you selected appears. Click **Add to Active Desktop**.

7. A confirmation box appears; click **Yes** to continue.

8. The Add Item to Desktop dialog box appears; click **OK** to add the item to your desktop. If you want to change the time when the item is updated, click **Customize** and follow these steps:

   - Click **Next**.

   - Select how often you want to synchronize the page (update its contents), and then click **Next**.

   - Enter any passwords required to access the site and click **Finish**.

You can move an Active Desktop Item. Simply place the mouse pointer over the item's window and a title bar appears. Click this title bar, hold down the mouse button, and drag the window wherever you like. The Active Desktop Item window contains several window buttons to maximize or close it, just like those on an ordinary window. In addition, instead of a Restore button, you'll find a button that resizes the Active Desktop Item window so that it takes up the right two-thirds of the desktop, leaving room for icons or other items on the left. For more help with the Active Desktop Item window, see Lesson 3, "Working with Windows."

Once you have all your Active Desktop Items right where you want them, lock them in place by right-clicking the desktop and selecting **Active Desktop, Lock Desktop Items**. With this option turned on, you won't accidentally drag an item out of place (the window's title bar won't appear when you move the mouse pointer over it.)

To hide an Active Desktop Item temporarily, click its Close button. To redisplay the item, right-click the desktop, select **Active Desktop**, and choose the item you want to redisplay from those listed at the bottom of the menu.

In this lesson, you learned how to subscribe to channels (web pages) and Gallery items. In the next lesson, you'll learn how to adjust the schedules by which active content is updated and how to remove items when needed.

Customizing the Active Desktop

In this lesson, you'll learn how to update your Web content and adjust your subscriptions.

Working Offline

If you have a dial-up (modem) connection to the Internet, you probably won't be connected at all times. Whenever you're not connected, you're considered to be working *offline*. Your subscriptions won't be updated, but you can still view the most recently downloaded content.

To view downloaded content for a channel, display its window on the desktop. Right-click the desktop and select Active Desktop, show web layout if needed. Then select Active Desktop, and choose the channel window you want to display (if the window doesn't appear on the Active Desktop).

When you're offline, some Active Desktop Items will display their most recent content, while others will display a message telling you that they're waiting for updates. To update your active content, follow the steps in the next section.

Synchronizing Subscriptions

If you want to update the subscriptions for your channels (Web pages) and Active Desktop Items before reviewing them, connect to the Internet, right-click the desktop, and select **Active Desktop, Synchronize**. All currently displayed items are updated.

If you want to synchronize any non-displayed items, follow these steps:

1. In Internet Explorer, choose **Tools, Synchronize**. The Items to Synchronize dialog box appears, as shown in Figure 28.1.

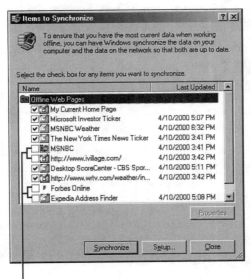

Deselect any items you do
not want to update

FIGURE 28.1 You can update all your subscriptions or just one of them.

2. Click the items you don't want to synchronize (this removes their check marks).

3. Click **Synchronize**.

Changing and Removing Subscriptions

If you want to change the frequency with which a subscription is updated or remove a subscription entirely, follow these steps:

1. In Internet Explorer, choose **Tools, Synchronize**. The Items to Synchronize dialog box appears.

2. Select the item whose frequency you want to change, and then click **Properties**.

3. Perform any of the following:

    - To remove a subscription, click **Make this page available offline** (this removes its check mark).

    - To select a different schedule, click the **Schedule** tab and select the schedule you want to use, or choose **Only when I choose Synchronize from the Tools menu**.

    - To change the amount of data that's downloaded to your system, or to be notified when data at the site has changed, click the **Download** tab and select the options you want.

4. Click **OK**. You're returned to the Items to Synchronize dialog box; repeat these steps to change the schedule for another subscription or click **Close**.

Scheduling Additional Updates

In addition to an item's normal schedule, follow these steps if you want to update particular items when you log on to your computer or after the computer's been idle for a period of time:

1. In Internet Explorer, choose **Tools, Synchronize**. The Items to Synchronize dialog box appears.

2. Click **Setup**. The Synchronization Settings dialog box appears (see Figure 28.2).

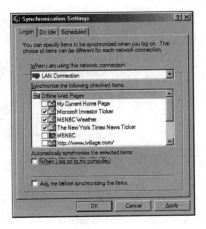

FIGURE 28.2 Change the frequency of active content updates.

3. On the **Logon** tab, select **When I log on to my computer** and choose the items you want to be updated when you log on.

4. If you want to be prompted before any updating occurs, select **Ask me before synchronizing the items**.

5. On the **On Idle** tab, select **Synchronize the selected items while my computer is idle** and select the items you want to update only when your computer has been idle for a period of time.

6. To set the amount of time your computer must be idle before synchronization occurs, click **Advanced**, make your selections, and click **OK**.

7. Click **OK**.

In this lesson, you learned how to adjust how often active content is updated and how to remove items when needed. In the next lesson, you'll learn how to create and send email.

Sending and Receiving Mail with Outlook Express

In this lesson, you'll learn how to send and receive electronic mail messages using Outlook Express.

Windows includes a simple-to-use email program called Outlook Express. With it, you can send electronic messages to your friends, relatives, and colleagues, and they can send messages to you as well. If you use Microsoft Office, you can install and use Outlook instead of using Outlook Express—it contains many more functions, yet it works in a manner similar to that described here.

Entering Email Addresses

To send an email message to someone, you need his email address. It might look like this:

jfulton@indy.net

The first part of the address, jfulton, is the person's *username*—the name by which he's known to the mail server that processes his mail. The second part of the address, indy.net, is the name of that mail server.

Instead of entering the email address manually each time you send a message, you should save the addresses you use often in the Address Book. To enter someone into the Address Book, follow these steps:

1. Start Outlook Express by clicking its button on the Quick Launch toolbar . (See Figure 29.1.)

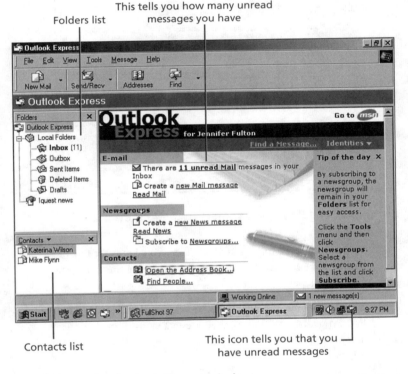

FIGURE 29.1 The Outlook Express window.

2. Click the **Contacts** button and select **New Contact**. The Properties dialog box appears, as shown in Figure 29.2. (If the Contacts list is not displayed, choose **View**, **Layout**, **Contacts**, **OK**.)

3. Enter the contact's name in the **First**, **Middle**, and **Last** text boxes. Enter a title, such as Mr. or Mrs.

Type an email
address
Type a name here   here

FIGURE 29.2   Adding a new contact to the Address Book.

4. Type a nickname for this contact. Then you can enter this nickname in the **To** field of a message to quickly address the message to this person.

5. Select how you want the contact to be displayed on the **Display** list. Typically, you'll display your contacts by name, company name, or nickname, although you can type anything you want in this field.

6. Type the contact's email address in the **E-Mail Addresses** text box and click **Add**. Repeat this step to add additional email addresses.

7. If you know for sure that this person uses an email program that doesn't support HTML formatting, select the **Send E-Mail using plain text only** option.

8. That's all the information you have to enter. If you like, you can use the other tabs to enter additional personal and business information for this contact. When you're through, click **OK**.

By Group   You can place several addresses in a single group and send an email message to everyone in that group. To create a group, click the **Address's** button on the Standard Buttons toolbar, click the **New** button, and select **New Group**. Enter a name for the group and select the addresses you want to add.

When someone sends you an email message, you can quickly add that person to the Address Book. Just right-click the sender's name in the Inbox window (covered later in this lesson) and select **Add to Address Book**. If you reply to a message someone has sent you, his or her email address will be added to the Address Book automatically.

Sending an Email Message

You can send simple text messages with Outlook Express, adding formatting to enhance your words when needed. You can even attach files of any type. The recipient can then detach the files and view them on his computer.

Who Am I?   If you and several family members are sharing one PC and one or more email accounts, you can create *identities* within Outlook to manage all your mail. Each identity can have his or her own contacts, email folders, and settings. Just click the **Identities** button in the Outlook Express folder, and select **Add New Identity**. To switch identities, click the **Identities** button and choose **Switch Identities**. Your identity is used when sending messages, and also when receiving messages from your personal email account.

To send an email message using Outlook Express, follow these steps:

1. Start Outlook and do one of the following:

   - Double-click a name in the **Contacts** list. The message is automatically addressed to that person.

   - If your intended recipient isn't in the **Contacts** list, click the **New mail message** link or the **New Mail** button on the Standard Buttons toolbar. Then type the person's address in the **To** box.

Watch That Case!   Be sure to use the correct mix of upper- and lowercase when entering an email address. For example, JFulton@indy.net is *not* the same as jfulton@indy.net or Jfulton@Indy.net.

Another Way   If your **Contacts** list is too large to browse through, click the **New Mail** button and type the person's nickname in the **To** box, or click the **To** button to display your contacts and select one from those listed.

2. The New Message window appears, as shown in Figure 29.3. If you want to use stationery with this message, choose **Format, Apply Stationery,** then select the stationery you want to use. If you select **More Stationery** from the menu, additional stationery types are displayed.

HTML Users Only!   You can only use stationery and add formatting to messages if the recipient uses an email program that supports HTML. Luckily, most do.

Attached files
are listed here   Attach File button   Formatting toolbar

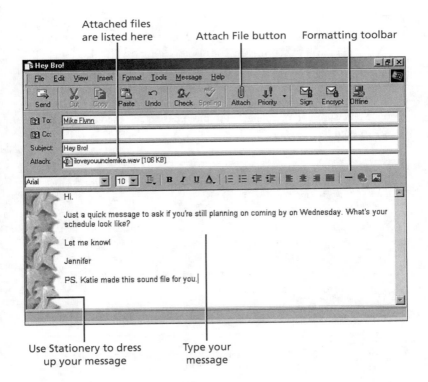

Use Stationery to dress   Type your
up your message   message

FIGURE 29.3   Creating an email message.

3. In the **Subject** box, type a description for your message.

4. Click in the text area and type your message. You can use the buttons on the Formatting toolbar to enhance your text with bold, italic, color, a change in font or font size, and so on.

5. To attach a file to your message, click the **Attach File** button. Select the file you want to send and click **Attach**. If you attach a graphic image, on the recipient's end it will appear in the body of the message (assuming you're using HTML format).

Compress That File! To reduce errors when you send large files, compress them first. See Lesson 14, "Compressing and Uncompressing Files," for help.

6. Make sure you're connected to the Internet, and then click **Send** to send the message.

 Check That Message! You can spell-check your messages before you send them, provided you have Office 95/97/2000 installed. Simply click the **Spelling** button on the Standard Buttons toolbar. To set up Outlook Express so that it spell-checks your mail automatically, open the **Tools** menu and select **Options**. Click the **Spelling** tab and select the **Always check spelling before sending** option.

 Wrong Address! If for some reason your message couldn't be delivered, you'll be notified via email.

To secure your messages, you may want to purchase a digital certificate from Verisign or some other third party. This third party takes information from you to verify your identity, and then issues a digital certificate (a file). This certificate is stored in Outlook, and part of it (the digital signature and a public key) is sent with the email messages you digitally sign by clicking the **Sign** button in the message window. The digital signature is used by the recipient to verify your identity; the public key can be used later on to send you encrypted messages, which you can open and view using the private key portion of your digital certificate. The first time you digitally sign a message, you'll be asked if you want to obtain a certificate. Click **Get Digital ID** and follow the steps to obtain one.

You can encrypt your message to protect it from being read while in transit by clicking the **Encrypt** button. However, if you don't have a digital certificate, you won't be able to read the contents of the message in your Sent Items folder. Regardless, once the message is fully received, it is automatically unencrypted by the receiver's email program so it can be viewed. If you have someone's public key (obtained from a message they digitally signed), then the encryption process is much more secure and private. Only the two of you will be able to read the messages you send to each other once you have exchanged digital certificates (attached your personal certificate to a message and received his digital certificate in the same way).

Checking for New Messages

By default, Outlook Express automatically checks for new email messages every 30 minutes and downloads them to your system. When new mail arrives, a small beep is sounded and a new mail icon (an envelope surrounded by blue arrows) appears on the status bar.

 Multiple Email Accounts?   When you set up your Internet connection, Windows automatically sets up one email account for you. If you have more than one email account, you'll need to set the additional ones up manually. For example, you might have an account with your ISP (jfulton@fake.net) and with a freebie mail server (jfulton@yahoo.com). Select **Tools, Accounts**. Then click **Add**, choose **Mail**, and follow the prompts. After you set up all your accounts, you can download messages from a single account by choosing it from the **Tools, Send and Receive** menu. If you click **Send/Recv**, all messages are downloaded.

You can check for new messages whenever you like. Follow these steps:

1. Click the **Send/Recv** button on the Standard Buttons toolbar.

2. If prompted, enter your email password and click **OK**.

3. Outlook Express sends any outgoing messages and checks for new mail. Incoming mail is placed in your Inbox. To view new messages, do either of the following:

- If the Outlook Express folder is displayed, click the **There are XX unread Mail messages in your Inbox** link to display the Inbox.

- From anywhere else in Outlook Express, select the **Inbox** folder from the **Folder list** to display incoming messages.

4. To view a message, click its header in the message list, as shown in Figure 29.4. The contents of the message appear in the Preview pane.

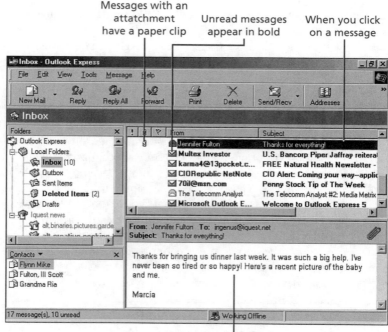

Messages with an attatchment have a paper clip

Unread messages appear in bold

When you click on a message

its contents appear in the Preview Pane

FIGURE **29.4** Checking your messages.

If you want to open a message in its own window, simply double-click it. You might want to do this to view a long message more clearly.

Saving File Attachments

If someone has sent you a message with a file attached to it, you'll need to detach the file before you can open and use it. Follow these steps:

1. Select the header for the message that contains the file attachment. A message with a file attachment has a paper clip icon next to the sender's name.

2. A paper clip icon also appears in the preview pane header. Click this icon and select **Save Attachments**.

3. Select the file(s) you want to save from the **Attachments To Be Saved** list.

4. To change the **Save To** location, click **Browse** and then change to the drive and folder where you want to save the attachment.

5. Click **Save**.

Replying to Messages

After you've received and read a message, you can reply to it. You can also forward the message to someone else, if needed. Follow these steps:

1. Click the header for the message to which you want to reply.

2. Click either **Reply** (to reply to the sender) or **Reply All** (to reply to everyone who received a copy of the original message). To forward the message to someone, click **Forward**.

3. The New Message window opens. The text of the original message is automatically copied into the text area. Type your reply or comments above this text.

4. In the reply, the message is automatically addressed to the sender (and all recipients, if you select that option). Click **Send** to send the reply. If you're forwarding the message, type the

address of the person to whom you want to forward it in the **To** box and click **Send**. (You can also click the **To** button and select an address from your Address Book.)

 Been There, Seen That   You can delete all or part of the original message if you feel that the recipient doesn't need to see it again. Just select the text and press the **Delete** key.

Deleting Old Messages

You should occasionally review your messages and delete the ones you no longer need. This reduces the amount of space your messages take up and makes Outlook Express more efficient.

To delete a message, follow these steps:

1. Select the messages you want to delete by pressing **Ctrl** and clicking them.

2. Press the **Delete** key or click the **Delete** button on the Standard Buttons toolbar.

3. If you use an IMAP mail server, your message is marked for deletion but isn't deleted yet. Open the **Edit** menu and select **Purge Deleted Messages** to remove messages from the server.

Deleted messages aren't *actually* deleted (except messages deleted from an IMAP server). Instead, they're moved to the Deleted Items folder. To empty this folder, choose **Edit**, **Empty "Deleted Items" Folder**.

You can set up Outlook Express so that it always empties the Deleted Items folder when you exit the program. Just open the **Tools** menu and select **Options**. Then click the **Maintenance** tab and select the **Empty messages from the "Deleted Items" folder on exit** option.

In this lesson, you learned how to send and receive electronic messages with Outlook Express. In the next lesson, you'll learn how to read and post newsgroup messages.

LESSON 30

Using Outlook Express News

In this lesson, you'll learn how to read and post newsgroup messages using Outlook Express.

Viewing and Subscribing to a Newsgroup

Newsgroups are the Internet equivalent of your company bulletin board. There are many newsgroups on various areas of interest, from deep-sea fishing to space exploration. No matter what your hobbies or special interests are, you can probably find a newsgroup that focuses on them.

Subscribing to Newsgroups

First you need to download the list of available newsgroups from your news server. Then select the newsgroups you want to view and download the posted messages in those groups. This is called *subscribing*. Follow these steps:

1. Connect to the Internet and start **Outlook Express**.

2. Click the newsgroup folder.

3. You're asked if you'd like to view a list of available newsgroups. Click **Yes.** (You may also be asked if you want to make Outlook Express the default news client. Click **Yes** or **No** as you prefer.) The Newsgroup Subscriptions dialog box appears, as shown in Figure 30.1.

To search for a group, type a keyword here

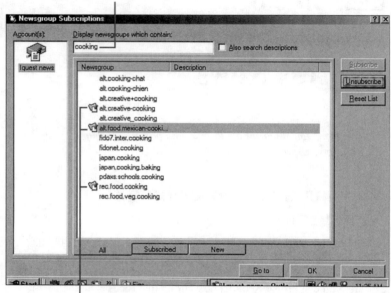

Subscribed-to newsgroups
have a newspaper icon

FIGURE 30.1   Available newsgroups.

4. Click a newsgroup and click **Subscribe**. To view a list of newsgroups on a particular topic, type that topic in the **Display newsgroups which contain** text box.

> **Try Before You Buy**   If you want to preview a news-
> group before you subscribe to it, select it and click
> **Go to**.

5. When you're through subscribing to newsgroups, click **OK**.

Viewing Messages

After subscribing to the newsgroups that interest you, you're ready to download the messages in a newsgroup so that you can view them:

1. Select a newsgroup you want to synchronize (download messages). Then either click its checkbox (to download new messages only) or click **Settings** and select the option you prefer (such as downloading all messages, or just their headers).

 Headers Only, Please   Downloading messages takes longer than downloading just the message headers. You may want to download headers for any new newsgroups so you can decide if they're right for you.

2. Click **Synchronize Account.** Outlook checks for new email and then downloads the messages/headers you requested. You're now ready to view the messages/headers in a newsgroup.

3. In the Folders list, select a newsgroup whose messages you want to review. Headers for that newsgroup appear in the upper-right pane.

4. Click a message whose contents you want to view. The headers for messages you haven't yet viewed are displayed in bold text. After you select a message, its contents appear in the lower panel. (If you downloaded only headers, Outlook Express will quickly download the content of any message you select, provided you're online.)

 Quick Viewing   To view the next message, press **Ctrl+>**. To view the next *unread* message, press **Ctrl+U**.

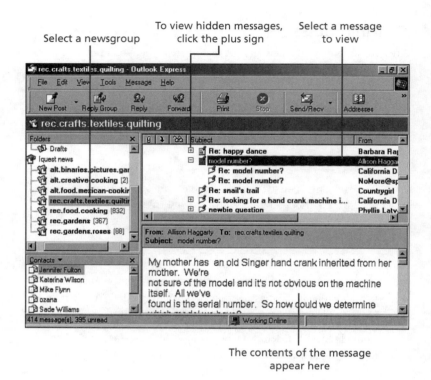

Select a newsgroup

To view hidden messages, click the plus sign

Select a message to view

The contents of the message appear here

FIGURE 30.2 Viewing newsgroup messages.

Messages that relate to each other are listed in a hierarchy called a *thread*. To view the messages in a thread, click the plus sign next to the first message for that topic. To hide the messages again, click the minus sign that appears.

Posting a Message

When you post a message, you have two choices: You can reply to an existing message, or you can create a message on a new topic and post it. To create a message on a new topic, follow these steps:

1. Select the newsgroup you want to post a message to.

2. Click the **New Post** button.

3. Type a subject.

4. Type your message in the large text box.

5. Click the **Send** button.

Post to Several Newsgroups   To post this same message to additional newsgroups, open the **Tools** menu and choose **Select Newsgroups**. Select the newsgroups you want to add and click **Add**. When you're through, click **OK**.

To comment on an existing message, follow these steps:

1. Select the message to which you want to reply.

2. Click the **Reply Group** button.

Respond Privately   If you want to send a private message to the author of a newsgroup posting rather than posting your reply publicly, click **Reply** instead.

3. Type your message in the large text box.

4. Click **Send**.

Wrong Message!   If you want to cancel your posting after you've sent it, select the message, open the **Message** menu, and select **Cancel Message**. Of course, if someone has already downloaded your message, this command won't remove the message from that person's system.

In this lesson, you learned how to subscribe to newsgroups and post messages. This is the last lesson. Have fun with Windows Me!

APPENDIX A

Configuring Hardware and Adding/Removing Windows Components

When you install Windows, it checks your system for hardware and configures it for use. However, if you upgrade your hardware or add something new, such as a modem, printer, or tape backup, you'll need to configure it for use under Windows. In this appendix, you'll learn how to do just that.

Configuring the Modem

You might use a modem to connect to the Internet or an online service, or to connect to your office network from home.

Adding a Modem

Adding a new modem to your computer is fairly painless. If you have an external modem, make sure it's turned on before you begin. If you use an internal modem, it's turned on when you turn on your PC.

To configure the modem for use, follow these steps:

1. Click **Start**, select **Settings**, and select **Control Panel**.

2. If needed, click **view all Control Panel options** and then double-click the **Modems** icon. The Add New Modem wizard appears. (If the Modems Properties dialog box appears, click **Add** to start the wizard.)

3. Turn on your modem and click **Next**. Windows searches for your modem.

4. Windows displays the name of your modem. If it's incorrect, you can click **Change** to display a list. If Windows doesn't detect your modem, click **Next** to display the modem list. After you've selected a correct modem name, click **Next**.

 My Modem Isn't Listed!   If you can't locate your modem on the list, click **Have Disk** and use your modem's installation disk to install it.

5. Select a COM port for your modem and click **Next**.

 COM Port   Short for communications port, this is the port through which your computer communicates with serial devices such as a modem or a serial mouse.

6. Click **Finish** to add the modem.

7. You're returned to the Modems Properties dialog box. Click **OK**.

Modifying Dialing Properties

Once your modem is installed, you'll want to view the dialing properties and make any necessary changes. Follow these steps:

1. In the Modems Properties dialog box, click **Dialing Properties**. The Dialing Properties dialog box appears, as shown in Figure A.1.

2. Select your country and enter your area code.

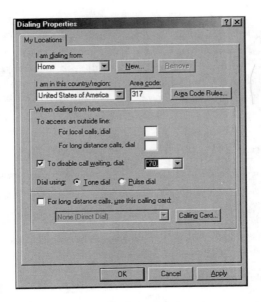

FIGURE A.1 Setting up your modem's properties.

3. If you need to dial a 9 or some other number to get an outside line, enter that number in the text boxes provided.

4. If you use call waiting, you'll want to disable it so that the modem won't try to answer an incoming call when you're online. Select the **To disable call waiting, dial:** option, and then select the appropriate code for your area from the drop-down list.

5. Select **Tone dial** or **Pulse dial** (rotary dial).

6. If you use a calling card to charge long-distance phone calls, enter that information as well. Select the calling card option, and then choose your card carrier from the drop-down list. Enter your card number by clicking the **Calling Card** button.

7. Click **OK**.

Multi-User   You can create multiple dialing properties when needed by clicking **New** and then typing in
the information for the other dialing locations. For
example, you can create **Home** and **Office** properties if
you use the same computer in both places.

Adding Other New Hardware

When you upgrade existing hardware or add new hardware, you should
follow these steps to configure it:

1. Click **Start**, select **Settings**, and select **Control Panel**.

2. If needed, click **view all Control Panel options** and then double-click the **Add New Hardware** icon.

3. The Add New Hardware wizard appears. Click **Next**.

4. Click **Next**. Windows checks your system for the new hardware.

5. Windows displays the name of the new hardware. Select the
   device from the list and click **Next**. (If the device isn't listed,
   select the **No** option before clicking **Next**, and Windows will
   search again.)

6. Click **Finish**.

Changing the Properties of an Object

Every object under Windows has its own properties—from folders to files
to applications. These properties tell you what the object is and what it
can do. You can view these properties at any time and change them as
needed. Follow these steps:

1. Right-click the icon for the object, or right-click its folder or
   filename.

2. Select **Properties** from the shortcut menu that appears. A
   Properties dialog box appears, as shown in Figure A.2. Each
   Properties dialog box contains tabs that are unique to that object.

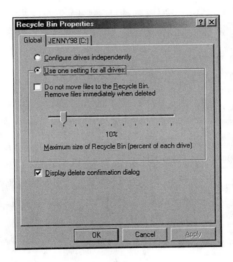

FIGURE **A.2**   A typical Properties dialog box.

3. Click the tab that contains the properties you want to view or
   change.

4. Change any options you need to (you might need to consult the
   hardware manual), and then click the **Apply** button to test those
   changes (if that button is provided in that particular Properties
   dialog box). Click **OK** when you're through.

Adding or Removing Windows Components

When you installed Windows Me, certain options and accessories were
installed as well. As you begin to use Windows, you may find that an
option you need wasn't installed. This is no problem, because it's easy to

install any Windows component you need. You can also remove components you don't intend to use and free up some hard disk space. Follow these steps:

1. Click **Start**, select **Settings**, and select **Control Panel**.

2. Click the **Add/Remove Programs** link.

3. Click the **Windows Setup** tab. The list of Windows components is displayed, as shown in Figure A.3.

Categories with a gray check
mark are partially installed

Categories with a gray check
mark are partially installed

A list of components
in the selected category

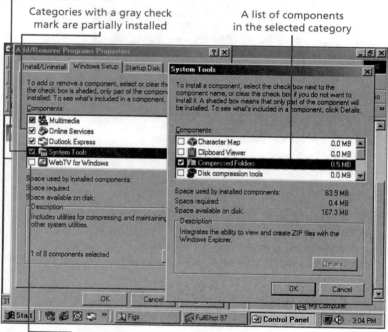

Categories without a
checkmark are not
installed at all

FIGURE A.3   Add or remove Windows components as needed.

4. Select the category for the component you want to install, and then click **Details**. Categories that include some components that aren't yet installed appear with a gray check mark. Categories in which all components are installed appear with a white check mark. For example, to install **Compressed Folders**, click the **System Tools** category.

5. A list of components for that category appears. Installed components appear with a check mark; those without a check mark are not yet installed. To add or remove any component, add or remove its check mark.

6. Select as many components as you want, and then click **OK**. You're returned to the Add/Remove Programs Properties dialog box.

7. Repeat steps 4 to 6 to add additional components. Click **OK** when you're done making selections.

8. You may be asked to insert the Windows CD-ROM; do so and click **OK** to continue. You may also see a message that you must restart your system. Close all your applications and click **Yes** to reboot.

After your system restarts, new components are ready to use and any components you removed are deleted.

INDEX

SYMBOLS

* (asterisk), wildcard file searches, 153

? (question mark), wildcard file searches, 153

A

accessing shared resources
full access, 129-131
home networks, 128-129
password dependent access, 129-131
read only access, 129-131
activating
Active Desktop, 262
Single-Click option, 105
windows, 30-31
Active Desktop, 6, 262-263
activating, 262
appearance, 20
channels, 21, 263
desktop icons, hiding, 262
features, 261
Gallery, site additions, 267-269
icons
hiding, 65
removing, 262

Internet connections, 261
Internet Explorer channel bar, hiding, 266
Item window, 21
moving items, 268
paper icon identifier, 79
Single Click option, 22
sizing buttons, 32-33
subscriptions, 264
channels, 263-266
starting, 264
Web sites, 267-268
switching to/from Classic Desktop, 263
turning on, 262
Web browser, 21
Web updates, 22
Web windows, display option, 34
Active Desktop Gallery, 264-269
Add Favorite dialog box (Internet Explorer), 259-260
Add Printer Wizard, launching, 196-197
Add/Remove Programs dialog box, 176, 182
adding
commands to Start menu, 87-88
Favorites folder (Internet Explorer), 259-260
narration (Movie Maker), 210

shortcut icons
    Desktop, 65-67
    Quick Launch toolbar, 68
    Start menu, 68
special effects to desktop, 82-83
tasks (Task Scheduler), 167-168
titles (Movie Maker), 206
Web sites to Links bar (Internet
  Explorer), 260
Windows 95/98 computers to
  home networks, 125-126
Address Book (Outlook Express),
  email address entry, 275-277
Address button (Windows Explorer
  toolbar), 41
Address toolbar, 24
  Address Box button, 43
  Go button, 43
addresses, Web sites, entering
  (Internet Explorer), 246-247
adjusting volume to system speakers,
  91-92
Airbrush tool (Paint), 230
Alt+Tab combination, open windows, scrolling, 30-31
AltaVista Web site, 254
America Online, 244
applications
  Desktop, quick display
    option, 27
  documents, printing, 200-201
  DOS
    configuring, 180
    installing, 179-180
  exiting, 195
  installing, 175-177
  launching
    by file association, 186
    Document menu, 187
    Quick Launch toolbar, 188
    Run command, 186
    shortcut icons, 188
    Start button, 186
    StartUp menu, 187
  uninstalling, 182

windows, opening, 30
Windows Me CD-ROM trial
  versions, previewing, 184
applying new skins (Media Player),
  223-224
arranging icons, 64-65
Assisted Support Page (Windows Me
  Help and Support), 62
attachments (email), 279
  saving (Outlook Express), 283
attributes (Taskbar), customizing,
  86-87
audio
  CD Player, 215
    pausing, 217
  collection files, 206
  Media Player, 220-221
  Movie Maker
    importing, 205-206
    recording, 207-208
  narration, adding (Movie
    Maker), 210
  Sound Recorder
    playing files, 234
    recording files, 235
    special effects, 235
  types (Movie Maker), 206
audio CDs
  controls (Media Player),
    215-217
  Extended CD format, 215
  playing (Media Player),
    217-218
  playlists, creating (Media
    Player), 218-220
autocheck (Outlook Express),
  281-283
Automatic Updates dialog box,
  95-96
AutoUpdate
  disabling, 96
  fixes, removing, 183-184
  function of, 94
  options, setting, 95-96
AutoUpdate command (Start
  menu), 11

B

Back button (Standard Buttons toolbar), 42
backgrounds
    colors, Color Box (Paint), 232-233
    desktop
        changing, 77-80
        system performance, 79
    images
        types, 77-80
        Web pages, 77-80
backups
    copying to other hard disks, 170
    creating, 169
    System Restore, executing, 170-171
    tape media, 170
    Zip disks, 170
Best of the Web button (Links toolbar), 43
.bmp images, 77
booting Windows Millennium, 5-6
borders, windows, sizing, 29, 34
browsers (Internet Explorer)
    addresses, entering, 246-247
    History button, 249
    home page, 246
    links, following, 247
    navigation buttons, 248
    refreshing display, 247
    searches, 255-258
    starting, 245
Brush tool (Paint), 230
business Web sites, searching (Internet Explorer), 258
bytes, 100

C

cable, Internet connections, 239
Calculator
    math functions, 235
    memory functions, 236
    scientific calculations, 236
call waiting, disabling for Internet connections, 244
Cancel Message command (Messages menu), 289
Cancel Printing command (Document menu), 203
canceling newsgroup messages (Outlook Express), 289
capacity
    floppy disks, 157
    hard disks, 157
cascading windows, 37
CD Player, 215-217
Channel bar (Active Desktop), 21, 265
Channel Guide button (Links toolbar), 43
channel subscriptions, 264
    Active Desktop, 263-266
    modifying (Internet Explorer), 272
    removing (Internet Explorer), 272
    synchronizing (Internet Explorer), 270-271
    updating (Internet Explorer), 272-273
check boxes (dialog box element), 51
Classic Desktop, 6
    address toolbar, 19
    appearance, 19
    mouse pointer, 20
    Start button, 20
    switching to/from Active Desktop, 263
    taskbar, 19
Classic view, folders, 103-104
clearing recent documents from Start menu, 89

clicking with mouse, 7
clients (networks), 120
Clip menu commands
    Set Clear Trim Point, 210
    Set End Trim Point, 210
    Set Start Trim Point, 209
Clipboard, 190
clips (Movie Maker)
    deleting, 208
    editing, 208
    playing, 212
    publishing on Web sites,
      213-214
    saving, 212
    sending via email, 212-213
    transitions, creating, 211
    trimming, 209
Close button, 29, 33
Close command (File menu), 195
closing
    documents, 195
    windows, 38-39
Color Box (Paint), 232-233
color schemes
    desktop, selecting, 80-81
    elements, 80-81
combo boxes (dialog box
  elements), 51
command buttons (dialog box elements), 52
commands
    Clip menu
      Set Clear Trim Point, 210
      Set End Trim Point, 210
      Set Start Trim Point, 209
    Document menu, Cancel
      Printing, 203
    Edit menu
      Copy, 192
      Cut, 193
      Paste, 192
      Select All, 135
    File menu
      Close, 195
      Copy Disk, 160

      Exit, 195
      Format, 159
      Import, 206
      New, 189
      Open, 189
      Print, 200-201
      Rename, 152
      Save, 194
      Save Project, 208
      Send To, 139
    menus
      selecting, 47-48
      shortcut keys, 48
    Message menu, Cancel
      Message, 289
    New menu, Compressed Folder,
      142
    Printer menu
      Pause Printing, 203
      Purge Print Documents,
      203
    Programs menu, Games, 8
    Settings menu, Printers,
      196-197
    shortcut menus
      default, 49
      right-click option, 48-49
    Start menu
      adding, 87-88
      AutoUpdate, 11
      Documents, 11
      dragging action, 89
      Help, 11
      Log Off, 12, 17
      Programs, 10
      Recent Document, 152
      removing, 88
      Run, 12, 186
      Search, 11
      selecting, 13
      Settings, 11
      Shut Down, 12-16
      sorting, 88
      Windows Update, 10

Tools menu
  Select Newsgroups, 289
  *Synchronize (Internet
    Explorer), 271-272*
compact software installations, 177
Compressed Folder command (New
  menu), 142
compressed folders, 141
  creating, 142-143
  decrypting, 145
  encrypting, 145
  files
    deleting, 146
    extracting, 146
    viewing, 144
  icon identifier, 142
  WinZip utility, 141-142
CompuServe, 244
configuring
  DOS applications, 180
  hardware, 294
  Internet, 240-244
    ISPs, 241-244
    online services, 244
  Maintenance Wizard, 165-167
  modems, 292
  multiple users (home net-
    works), 126-128
  Power Management, 72-74
connections (Internet)
  call waiting, disabling, 244
  configuring, 240-244
  dial-up, 239
  direct, 239
  ISPs, 241-244
  online services, 244
  shared modems on home net-
    works, 129
Contents (Help system), 55
context menus, 7, 48-49
control boxes (windows), 29
Copy command (Edit menu), 192
Copy Disk dialog box, 160
Copy To button (Standard Buttons
  toolbar), 42

copying
  Clipboard, 190
  data with mouse, 192-193
  files, 136-138
    Send To menu option, 139
    Send To option, 139
  floppy disks, 160-161
  folders, 136-138
    *Send To menu option,
      139-140*
  shortcut keys, 192
Cover Desktop button (Active
  Desktop), 33
creating
  compressed folders, 142-143
  file backups, 169
  folders, 148
  manual restore points (System
    Restore), 172
  system startup disk, 169
  toolbars, 26-27
cross-fade transitions (Movie
  Maker), 211
Ctrl+Alt+Delete combination, shut
  down dialog box, 16
Ctrl+C (Copy) keystroke, 48
Ctrl+V (Paste) keystroke, 48
Ctrl+X (Cut) keystroke, 48
Curve tool (Paint), 231
custom software installations, 177
Customize Links button (Links toolbar), 44
customizing
  folders, Web view (My
    Computer), 118-119
  Taskbar attributes, 86-87
  toolbars, 27
Cut command (Edit menu), 193

D

data, mouse
  copying, 192-193
  moving, 193
data files, 98

date/time, setting (Taskbar), 91
decompressing files, 145
decrypting compressed folders, 145
default printers, designating, 199
defragmenting hard disks (Disk
  Defragmenter), 163
Delete button
    Standard Buttons toolbar, 42
    Windows Explorer toolbar, 40
deleted files, restoring, 149
deleting
    clips (Movie Maker), 208
    email messages (Outlook
      Express), 284
    files, 149
        compressed folders, 146
        Recycle Bin, bypassing,
          151-152
        rescue of, 149
    folders, 149
    print jobs, 203
    tasks (Task Scheduler), 169
    Web sites from Links bar
      (Internet Explorer), 260
Desktop
    Active, 262-263
        appearance, 20
        channel bar, 21
        icons, removing, 262
        Internet connections, 261
        moving items, 268
        Single Click option, 22
        sizing buttons, 32-33
        subscriptions, 264
        switching to Classic from,
          263
        turning on, 262
        Web browser, 21
        Web updates, 22
    backgrounds
        changing, 77-80
        system performance, 79
    Classic, 6
        address toolbar, 19
        mouse pointer, 20

        Start button, 20
        switching from Active to,
          263
        taskbar, 19
    color schemes, selecting, 80-81
    icons, 19
        arranging, 64-65
        removing, 262
    maximized windows, quick dis-
      play option, 27
    screen savers
        function of, 68
        password protection, 69
        previewing, 85
        selecting, 68-70
        time settings, 69
    shortcut icons, adding, 65-67
    sounds, previewing, 85
    special effects, adding, 82-83
    themes, 78-80
        screen resolution
          settings, 85
        selecting, 83-85
    windows
        cascading, 37
        closing, 38-39
        tiling, 38
Desktop toolbar (taskbar), 24
dial-up connections, 239
dialog boxes
    Add Favorite (Internet
      Explorer), 259-260
    Add/Remove Programs,
      176, 182
    appearance of, 50
    Automatic Updates, 95-96
    Copy Disk, 160
    Display Properties, 78, 81-82
        Screen Saver tab, 69-70
    elements, 51-52
    Format, 159
    Gaming Options, 181
    Home Networking Wizard, 122
    Items to Synchronize, 271-272
    Log Off Windows, 17

My Picture Screen Saver
Options, 71-72
Newsgroup Subscriptions, 285
Open, 189
options, selecting, 50-53
Pattern, 79-80
Power Schemes, 72
Properties, 295
Save As, 194
shortcut keys, 53
Shut Down Windows, 14
Sound and Multimedia
Properties, 90
Sounds Properties, 90-95
tabbed, changing pages, 53
Taskbar and Start Menu
Properties, 23, 86
Taskbar Properties, 88
Volume Control, 91-92
Welcome to Windows, 5-6
What's This? button, 62-63
digital cameras, images, importing
(Image Preview), 114-115
digital certificates, email encryption
mechanism, 280-281
DirectPlay, voice chat, enabling,
180-181
disabling
AutoUpdate, 96
call waiting (Internet connections), 244
Disk Cleanup, hard disks, junk file
removal, 163-165
Disk Copy command (File menu),
160
Disk Defragmenter, 163
disk drives
floppy, 97
hard, 97
viewing (Explorer), 102-103
viewing (My Computer), 99
disks (floppy)
copying, 160-161
formatting, 158-160
labeling, 159

Display Properties dialog box
color schemes, 81
Screen Saver tab, 69-70
special effects, 82
wallpaper, 78
displaying
file contents via scrollbars,
35-36
Files list (Explorer), 109
Files list (My Computer), 109
folders
Classic view, 103-104
Web view, 103-104,
118-119
Folders list
Explorer, 106-109
My Computer, 106-109
History list (Explorer), 110-111
images (Thumbnails view), 115
MS-DOS prompt, 16
open applications on
Desktop, 27
personal images as screen
savers (Windows Me), 70-72
print queue, 201
toolbars, 25
Web windows (Active
Desktop), 34
Document menu commands, Cancel
Printing, 203
documents
closing, 195
creating (WordPad), 189-190,
225
editing (WordPad), 225
opening, 189-190
print queue, 200-201
saving, 193-195
Start menu, clearing, 89
text
formatting (WordPad), 227
typing (WordPad), 225-226
Documents command (Start
menu), 11
Documents menu, applications,
launching from, 187

DOS
> applications
>> *configuring, 180*
>> *installing, 179-180*
> files, naming restrictions, 98
> prompt, displaying, 16
double-clicking (mouse), 8
> speed adjustments, 93
downloading new skins (Media Player), 224
drag-and-drop (mouse), 7, 193
> data, moving, 193
> Explorer, 136
> files
>> *copying, 136*
>> *moving, 136*
dragging commands to Start menu, 89
drives. *See* disk drives
drop-down list boxes (dialog box elements), 51
DSL (digital subscriber line), Internet connections, 239

E

Ellipse tool (Paint), 231
ellipsis, menu bar indicator, 47
email
> account identities (Outlook Express), 277
> addresses
>> *Address Book (Outlook Express), 275-277*
>> *case-sensitivity, 278*
>> *format, 274*
>> *grouping (Outlook Express), 277*
> autocheck features (Outlook Express), 281-283
> clips, sending (Movie Maker), 212-213
> deleting (Outlook Express), 284
> encryption, digital certificates, 280-281
> file attachments, 279
>> *saving, 283*
> multiple accounts, 281
> replying to (Outlook Express), 283-284
> sending (Outlook Express), 277-281
> spellchecking (Outlook Express), 280
> stationery selection (Outlook Express), 278
emptying Recycle Bin, 149-151
encryption
> compressed folders, 145
> email messages (Outlook Express), 280-281
Eraser tool (Paint), 230
Excite
> search operators, 254
> Web site, 254
executing backups (System Restore), 170-171
Exit command (File menu), 195
exiting applications, 195
expanding Start menu, 13
Explorer (Windows Explorer)
> bar panels, display options, 111
> desktop appearance, 102
> disk drives, viewing, 102-103
> drag-and-drop, 136
> Favorites bar, 110
> files
>> *searching, 153-156*
>> *viewing, 102-103*
> Files list, display options, 109
> folders, viewing, 102-103
> Folders list
>> *display options, 106-109*
>> *replacing, 110-111*
> History list, viewing, 110-111
> launching, 103

Quick Print, 201
Search bar, 110
versus My Computer, folder
hierarchy, 101
Extended CD format (ECD), 215
extracting files from compressed
folders, 146

F

F1 key (Windows Me Help and
Support), 54
Favorites bar (Explorer), 110
Favorites folder (Internet Explorer),
adding to, 259-260
Favorites menu, starting programs
with, 187
fax images, viewing (Kodak
Imaging), 116-118
file associations, applications,
launching, 186
file compression
WinZip utility, 141-142
.zip file extension, 142
File menu commands
Close, 195
Disk Copy, 160
Exit, 195
Format, 159
Import, 206
New, 189
Open, 189
Print, 200-201
Rename, 152
Save, 194
Save Project, 208
Send To, 139
files
backups
copying to other hard disk,
170
creating, 169
tape media, 170
Zip disks, 170

compressed folders
deleting, 146
extracting, 146
viewing, 144
copying, 136-138
Send To menu option, 139
decompression, modifications,
145
deleting, 149
Recycle Bin, bypassing,
151-152
rescue of, 149
DOS naming restrictions, 98
email attachments, 279
saving (Outlook Express),
283
extensions, 98, 194
folders
compressing, 142-143
placing, 98
moving, 136-139
naming conventions, 98, 194
Recycle Bin, emptying, 149-151
renaming, 152
searching, 152-156
selecting, 134-136
individual, 134
noncontiguous, 135
starting programs with, 186
viewing (Explorer), 102-103
viewing (My Computer), 99
Files list (Explorer), icon display
options, 109
Files list (My Computer), icon
display options, 109
fill, graphics, adding to, 232
Fill with Color tool (Paint), 230
floppy disks
copying, 160-161
formatting, 158-160
labeling, 159
space, determining, 157
folders, 97
Classic view, displaying,
103-104

compressed, 141
    files, dragging, 142-143
    files, viewing, 144
copying, 136-138
    Send To menu option,
    139-140
creating, 148
deleting, 149
    Recycle Bin, bypassing,
    151-152
    rescue of, 149
Favorites, 258-260
    adding pages to, 259-260
files, placing in, 98
hidden contents, 101
hierarchy, My Computer versus
  Explorer displays, 100-101
home network shares, setting,
  125
moving, 136-139
My Documents, 12
My Pictures, 12
naming, 148
Recycle Bin, emptying,
  149-151
renaming, 152
selecting, 134-136
    individual, 134
    noncontiguous, 135
sharing on networks, 129-130
Single-Click option, activating,
  105
viewing (Explorer), 102-103
viewing (My Computer),
  99-101
Web view, displaying, 103-104
    creating, 118-119
Folders button (Standard Buttons
  toolbar), 42
Folders list (Explorer)
  Details view, 107-109
  display options, 106-109
  replacing, 110-111
Folders list (My Computer)
  Details view, 107-109
  display options, 106-109

fonts (WordPad), 227
foreground colors, Color Box (Paint),
  232-233
Format command (File menu), 159
Format dialog box, 159
formatting
  floppy disks, 158-160
  WordPad text, 227
forms (search engines), 252
Forward button (Standard Buttons
  toolbar), 42
Free Form Select tool (Paint), 229
Free HotMail button (Links
  toolbar), 44

G

Games command (Programs
  menu), 8
games, voice chat, enabling
  (DirectPlay), 180-181
Gaming Options dialog box, 181
.gif images, 77
gigabytes, 100
Go button (Address toolbar), 43
graphics
  creating (Paint), 228-232
  drawing tools (Paint), 228-231
  handles, 192
  links (Web pages), 247
  mouse, selecting, 191-192
  selecting, 192
grouping email addresses (Outlook
  Express), 277

H

handles on graphics, 192
hard disks, 97
  defragmenting (Disk
    Defragmenter), 163
  error scans (ScanDisk), 163
  file backups, copying to, 170

junk file removal (Disk Cleanup), 163-165

Power Management settings, 72-74

space, determining, 157

hardware, adding, 294

Help command (Start menu), 11

Help system. *See* Windows Me Help and Support

hiding

    channel bar (Internet Explorer), 266

    desktop icons (Active Desktop), 262

    icons (Active Desktop), 65

    taskbar, 23-24

history, Web sites, tracing (Internet Explorer), 248-249

History button (Standard Buttons toolbar), 42

History list (Explorer), folders, displaying, 110-111

Home Networking Wizard dialog box, 122

home networks. *See also* networks

    access levels

        full, 129-131

        password dependent, 129-131

        read only, 129-131

    computer names, 122

    folder shares, setting, 125

    installing, 121-122, 125-126

    Internet connections, setting, 122

    multiple users, configuring, 126-128

    NICs (network interface cards), 121-122

    notes, sending (Win Popup), 131-133

    printers, sharing, 125

    required equipment, 121

    shared modems, 129

    shared resources, accessing, 128-129

    Windows 95/98 computers, adding, 125-126

home pages, setting (Internet Explorer), 246

horizontal scrollbars, 29, 35-36

horizontal tiling (windows), 38

HTML (Hypertext Markup Language), 119

hyperlinks (Windows Me Help and Support), 54. *See also* links

I

icons

    Active Desktop, hiding, 65

    arranging, 64

    compressed folders, 142

    Desktop, 19

    File list (My Computer), arranging, 109

    removing, 262

    Single-Click option, highlight options, 105

    spacing, 82

    special effects options, 83

Image Preview (My Pictures)

    import options, 114-115

    slide show, 113

    view options, 112-113

images

    .bmp (bitmap), 77

    creating (Paint), 228-232

    faxes, viewing (Kodak Imaging), 116-118

    .gif, 77

    importing

        Image Preview, 114-115

        Paint, 229

    .jpg, 77

    Kodak Imaging, viewing, 116-118

Movie Maker, types, 204
My Pictures
  importing option (Image
    Preview), 114-115
  slide show option (Image
    Preview), 113
  view options (Image
    Preview), 112-113
screen savers, personal
  (Windows Me), 70-72
Thumbnails view, reviewing,
  115
Import command (File menu), 206
importing
  audio files (Movie Maker),
    205-206
  images
    My Pictures (Image
      Preview), 114-115
    Paint, 229
  video files (Movie Maker),
    205-206
Index (Windows Me Help and
  Support), keyword entry, 55-59
indexes, search engines, 252
InfoSeek Web site, search operators,
  254
installing
  applications, 175-177
  DOS programs, 179-180
  home networks, 121-122,
    125-126
  printers
    local, 196-197
    network, 197-199
  software
    pre-installation, 175
    upgrades, 175
InstallShield, 176-177
IntelliMouse, 9, 36
Interactive CD Sampler (Windows
  Me CD-ROM trial), 184

Internet, 239
  Active Desktop, 261-262
  connections
    Active Desktop, 261
    cable, 239
    call waiting, disabling, 244
    configuring, 240-241
    dial-up, 239
    direct, 239
    DSL, 239
    home network configura-
      tions, 122
    IDSN, 239
    ISPs, 241-244
    manual entry, 242-243
    modems, 239
    networks, 239
    online services, 244
    shared modems on home
      networks, 129
  games
    launching (Windows Me),
      188-189
    voice chat, enabling,
      180-181
  site addresses, entering,
    246-247
  streaming audio, playing (Media
    Player), 222-223
Internet Connection Wizard, 241
Internet Explorer, 239, 245-249
  addresses, entering, 246-247
  Channel bar, 265
    hiding, 266
    subscriptions, 263-266
  channel subscriptions, 263-266
    modifying, 272
    removing, 272
    synchronizing, 270-271
    updating, 272-273
  disconnecting, 246
  downloaded content, offline
    viewing, 270
  Favorites folder, adding to,
    259-260

History button, 249
home pages, setting, 246
launching, 245-246
links, 247
Links bar, favorites
adding, 260
deleting, 260
navigation buttons, 248
page history, tracing, 248-249
Radio toolbar, streaming audio,
250-251
refreshing display, 247
search engines, 255-258
starting, 245
Web site searches, 257-258
Internet service providers. *See* ISPs
Internet Start button (Links
toolbar), 44
ISDN lines, Internet connections,
239
ISPs (Internet service providers)
connections, 240-241
manual entry, 242-243
existing accounts, transferring,
242
Microsoft Referral Service, list
selection, 241-242
selecting, 240-244
Items to Synchronize dialog box,
271-272

J - K

.jpg images, 77
junk files, removing (Disk Cleanup),
163-165
keyboards, menu commands,
selecting, 48
kilobytes, 100
Kodak Imaging
images, viewing, 116-118
toolbar buttons, 117-118

L

labeling floppy disks, 159
launching
Add Printer Wizard, 196-197
applications
by file association, 186
Document menu, 187
Quick Launch toolbar, 188
Run command, 186
shortcut icons, 188
Start button, 186
StartUp menu, 187
Calculator, 235
Explorer, 103
Internet Explorer, 245-246
Internet games, 188-189
Movie Maker, 204
My Computer, 100
Outlook Express, 275
Paint, 228-232
Phone Dialer, 237
programs from Start menu, 9
Sound Recorder, 234-235
Windows Me Help and Support
F1 key, 54
Tours/Tutorials Page,
60-61
WordPad, 225
Line tool (Paint), 231
links
colors, 247
graphic, 247
text, 247
Links bar (Internet Explorer), 260
Links toolbar, 24
Best of the Web button, 43
Channel Guide button, 43
Customize Links button, 44
Free HotMail button, 44
Internet Start button, 44
Microsoft button, 44
Windows Media button, 44
Windows Update button, 44
list boxes (dialog box elements), 50

local printers, installing, 196-197
Log Off command (Start menu),
    12, 17
logging off users, 16-18
logging on as different user, 16-18
lost files, searching, 152-156
Lycos Web site, 254

M

Magnifier tool (Paint), 230
Maintenance Wizard
    configuring, 165-167
    Disk Cleanup, 163-165
    Disk Defragmenter, 163
    performance tuning, 162
    ScanDisk, 163
    scheduling, 165-169
manual restore points, creating
    (System Restore), 172
Maximize/Restore button (windows),
    29-31
Media Player, 220-221
    audio CDs
        controls, 215-217
        playing, 217-218
        playlist creation, 218-220
    opening, 220
    skins
        applying, 223-224
        changing, 216
        downloading, 224
    streaming audio, 222-223
    streaming video, 251
    video controls, 220-222
menu bar, 46-47
menus
    commands
        ellipsis, 50
        selecting, 47-48
        shortcut keys, 48
    expanding, 13
    menu bar, 46-47

personalized, 10, 13, 47
shortcut, right-click commands,
    48-49
Message menu commands, Cancel
    Message, 289
messages, newsgroups (Outlook
    Express)
        canceling, 289
        posting, 288-290
        threads, 288
        viewing, 287-288
Microsoft button (Links toolbar), 44
Microsoft Network (online service),
    244
Microsoft Referral Service, ISP
    listing, 241-242
Microsoft Windows Update Web
    site, 96
Minimize button (windows), 29-31
minimizing window sizes, 31-34
modems
    adding, 291-292
    dialing properties, modifying,
        292
    Internet connections, 239
    placing phone calls with,
        236-238
    shared, home network config-
        urations, 129
monitors
    Power Management, configur-
        ing, 72-74
    resolution
        desktop themes, 85
        modifying, 75-76
        pixel sizes, 75-76
mouse
    buttons, 93
    clicking, 7
    data
        copying, 192-193
        moving, 193
    double-clicking, 8
    drag-and-drop action, 7
    graphics, selecting, 191-192

IntelliMouse, 9
menu commands, selecting, 47
pointer symbols, 7
    schemes, 94
properties, modifying, 93-94
right-clicking, 7
single-click option, 8
speed settings, 8
taskbar, moving, 23
text, selecting, 191-192
window borders, resizing, 34
windows, moving, 36-37
Move To button (Standard Buttons toolbar), 42
Movie Maker
    audio files
        importing, 205-206
        recording, 207-208
    clips
        playing, 212
        transitions, 211
        trimming, 209
    features, 204
    image types, 204
    launching, 204
    narration, adding, 210
    projects
        editing, 208
        publishing on Web,
          213-214
        saving, 212
        sending in email, 212-213
    titles, adding, 206
    video capture cards, 204-205
    video files
        importing, 205-206
        recording, 207-208
    window appearance, 204
movies, opening (Media Player), 220-221
moving
    data with mouse, 193
    files, 136-139
    folders, 136-139
    scrollbars with IntelliMouse, 36

    taskbar, 23
    toolbars, 45
    windows, 36
        drag effects, 37
MS-DOS prompt, displaying, 16
MSN Gaming Server, 188-189
multimedia, opening (Media Player), 220-221
multiple email accounts, 281
My Computer
    desktop appearance, 99
    disk drives, viewing, 99
    files
        searching, 153-156
        viewing, 99
    Files list, display options, 109
    folders
        hierarchy, 100
        viewing, 99-101
    Folders list, display options, 106-109
    launching, 100
    Quick Print, 201
    refreshing display, 101
    versus Explorer, folder hierarchy, 101
    Web view, folder displays, 118-119
My Documents, 12, 148
My Picture Screen Saver Options dialog box, 71-72
My Pictures, 12
    image import options, 114-115
    slide show option, 113
    view options, 112-113

N

naming
    computers in home networks, 122
    files, 194
        conventions, 98
        DOS restrictions, 98

folders, 148
network printers, 199
narration, adding (Movie Maker), 210
Netscape Communicator, 239
Network Neighborhood, shared resources
  accessing, 128
  folders, 129-130
  locating, 129
network printers
  installing, 197-199
  naming, 199
  shared, 198
networks. *See also* home networks
  clients, 120
  Internet connections, 239
  peer-to-peer, 120
  servers, 120
  shared resources
    accessing, 128
    folders, 129-130
    locating, 129
  sharing functions, 120
  system administrators, 121
New command (File menu), 189
New Toolbar command (Toolbars menu), 26
Newsgroup Subscriptions dialog box, 285
newsgroups
  messages
    canceling (Outlook Express), 289
    posting (Outlook Express), 288-290
    threads, 288
    viewing (Outlook Express), 287-288
  subscribing (Outlook Express), 285-286
NIC (network interface card), 121-122
notes, home networks, sending (Win Popup), 131-133

O

objects, color fills (Paint), 232-233
online services, connecting, 244
Open command (File menu), 189
Open dialog box, 189
option buttons (dialog box elements), 52
Outlook Express, 274
  Address Book, 275-278
  email
    account identities, 277
    autocheck features, 281-283
    deleting, 284
    replying, 283-284
    sending, 277-281
    stationery selection, 278
  launching, 275
  newsgroup messages
    canceling, 289
    posting, 288-290
    viewing, 287-288
  Spellchecker, 280

P

Paint, 228-231
  Airbrush tool, 230
  Brush tool, 230
  Color Box, 232-233
  Curve tool, 231
  Ellipse tool, 231
  Eraser tool, 230
  Fill with Color tool, 230
  Free Form Select tool, 229
  graphics, creating, 228-232
  images, importing, 229
  launching, 228-232
  Line tool, 231
  Magnifier tool, 230
  Pencil tool, 230
  Pick Color tool, 230

Polygon tool, 231
Rectangle tool, 231
Rounded Rectangle tool, 231
Select tool, 230
starting, 228
Text tool, 230
paper icon (Active Desktop), 79
passwords, screen savers, 69
Paste command (Edit menu), 192
Pattern dialog box, 79-80
patterns, wallpapers, editing, 79-80
Pause Printing command (Printer menu), 203
pausing print jobs in print queue, 202-203
peer-to-peer networks, 120
Pencil tool (Paint), 230
performance tuning
    defragmenting (Disk Defragmenter), 163
    error scans (ScanDisk), 163
    junk file removal (Disk Cleanup), 163-165
    Maintenance Wizard, 162, 165-167
personalized menus, 10, 13, 47
Phone Dialer
    frequent numbers, 237
    launching, 237
    logs, 238
    speed dial, 237
Pick Color tool (Paint), 230
pixels, monitor resolution, 75-76
playing
    audio CDs (Media Player), 215-218
    clips (Movie Maker), 212
    desktop sounds, 85
    multimedia files, 220-221
    sound files, 234-235
    streaming audio
        Media Player, 222-223
        Radio toolbar (Internet Explorer), 250-251
    video (Media Player), 220-222

playlists, audio CDs, creating (Media Player), 218-220
point size, changing (WordPad), 227
pointers (mouse), 7, 94
Polygon tool (Paint), 231
posting newsgroup messages (Outlook Express), 288-290
Power Management, 72-74
Power Schemes dialog box, 72
Print dialog box, 200-201
print queue
    pausing, 202-203
    removing, 203
    reordering, 202
    resuming, 202-203
    viewing, 201
Printer menu commands
    Pause Printing, 203
    Purge Print Documents, 203
printers
    Add Printer Wizard, 196-197
    default designation, setting, 199
    drivers, 197
    home networks, sharing, 125
    jobs, previewing, 201
    local, installing, 196-197
    network
        installing, 197-199
        naming, 199
        shared, 198
    print jobs, deleting, 203
    print queue, 200-201
        jobs, reordering, 202
        pausing, 202-203
        resuming, 202-203
        viewing, 201
    stalled, 203
Printers command (Settings menu), 196-197
Prodigy Internet, 244
programs
    adding to Start menu, 88
    folders, 97
    starting (Start menu), 9
    taskbar, switching, 22

Programs command (Start menu), 10
Programs menu commands,
    Games, 8
publishing projects to Web sites
    (Movie Maker), 213-214
Purge Print Documents command
    (Printer menu), 203

Q - R

Quick Launch toolbar
    applications, launching, 188
    Display Desktop icon, 27
    program icons, adding, 24
    shortcut icons, adding, 68
Quick Print, 201

radio buttons (dialog box el-
    ements), 52
radio stations, streaming audio, play-
    ing (Media Player), 222-223
Radio toolbar (Internet Explorer),
    250-251
Recent Documents (Start menu), 152
    clearing, 89
recording
    audio files (Movie Maker),
        205-208
    narration (Movie Maker), 210
    sound files (Sound Recorder),
        234-235
    video files (Movie Maker),
        205-208
Rectangle tool (Paint), 231
Recycle Bin
    bypassing file deletion, 151-152
    deactivating, 151
    emptying, 149-151
    properties, 151
removing
    channel subscriptions (Internet
        Explorer), 272
    commands from Start menu, 88

hard disks, junk files (Disk
    Cleanup), 163-165
    toolbars from taskbar, 25
Rename command (File menu), 152
renaming files/folders, 152
reordering print jobs in print queue,
    202
replying email messages (Outlook
    Express), 283-284
rescuing deleted files, 149
resolution (screen), 75-76
Restart mode (Shut Down menu), 16
restarting computers
    (Crtl+Alt+Delete combination), 16
Restore button (Active Desktop),
    31-33
restore points (AutoUpdate), 171-172
restoring
    deleted files, 149
    system changes (System
        Restore), 172-174
    window sizes, 31
resuming print jobs in print queue,
    202-203
right-clicking mouse, 7
Rounded Rectangle tool (Paint), 231
Run command (Start menu), 12, 186
    applications, launching, 186

S

Save As dialog box, 194
Save command (File menu), 194
Save Project command (File menu),
    208
saving
    documents, 193-195
    email attachments (Outlook
        Express), 283
    projects (Movie Maker), 212
ScanDisk, error scans, 163
scanners, images, importing (Image
    Preview), 114-115

screen savers
    Desktop, selecting, 68-70
    password protection, 69
    personal images, displaying
        (Windows Me), 70-72
    previewing, 85
    time settings, 69
scrollbars
    file contents, displaying, 35-36
    horizontal, 35-36
    moving with IntelliMouse,
        9, 36
    open windows (Alt+Tab combi-
        nation), 30-31
    vertical, 35-36
Search bar (Explorer), 110
Search button (Standard Buttons
    toolbar), 42
Search command (Start menu), 11
search engines, 252-258
    accessing (Internet Explorer),
        255-257
    AltaVista, 254
    entering criteria, 253
    Excite, 254
    forms, 252
    indexes, 252
    Lycos, 254
    operators, 254
    people, 258
    search criteria, 253-254
    Snap, 254
    Yahoo!, 254
Search Page (Windows Me Help and
    Support), 59
security, compressed folders, 145
Select All command (Edit menu),
    135
Select Newsgroups command (Tools
    menu), 289
Select tool (Paint), 230
selecting
    color schemes for desktop,
        80-81
    desktop themes, 83-85

dialog box options, 50-53
files, 134-136
    individual, 134
    noncontiguous, 135
folders, 134-136
    individual, 134
    noncontiguous, 135
graphics with mouse, 191-192
ISPs, Microsoft Referral
    Service, 241-242
menu commands, 47-48
Start menu commands, 13
text
    mouse, 191-192
    words/paragraphs, 191
Send To menu
    files, copying, 139
    folders, copying, 140
    locations, 139
sending
    email (Outlook Express),
        277-281
    notes on home networks (Win
        Popup), 131-133
    projects via email (Movie
        Maker), 212-213
servers (networks), 120
Set Clear Trim Point command
    (Clip menu), 210
Set End Trim Point command
    (Clip menu), 210
Set Start Trim Point command (Clip
    menu), 209
setting
    AutoUpdate options, 95-96
    date/time, 91
    folder sharing on home net-
        works, 125
    Internet connections on home
        networks, 122
    printers, default designation,
        199
Settings command (Start menu), 11
Settings menu commands, Printers,
    196-197

shared modems, home networks, 129
shared resources
  accessing, 128
  folders, 129-130
  home networks, access levels,
    128-131
  locating, 129
shortcut icons
  applications, launching, 188
  custom toolbars, 27
  Desktop, adding, 65-68
shortcut keys
  creating, 188
  dialog boxes, 53
  menu commands
    Ctrl+C (Copy), 48
    Ctrl+V (Paste), 48
    Ctrl+X (Cut), 48
shortcut menu commands, 7, 48-49
Shut Down command (Start menu),
  12-15
  Hibernate mode, 16
  Restart mode, 16
  Standby mode, 15
Shut Down Windows dialog box, 14
Single Click option (Active
  Desktop), 22
    activating, 105
    icon titles, highlight options,
      105
    mouse, 8
    windows, opening, 30
sizing
  Active Desktop, 32-33
  borders on windows, 34
  toolbars, 25
  windows, 31
skins (Media Player)
  applying, 223-224
  changing, 216
  downloading, 224
slide shows, launching (Image
  Preview), 113
Snap Search Engine, 254

software
  exiting, 195
  installing, 175-177
  uninstalling, 182
  Windows Me CD-ROM trial
    versions, 184
sorting commands in Start menu, 88
Sound Recorder, 234-235
sounds. *See also* audio
  desktop, previewing, 85
  system events, changing, 90-91
Sounds and Multimedia Properties
  dialog box, 90
speakers, volume
  adjusting, 91-92
  mute setting, 93
special effects
  desktop, adding, 82-83
  window drag effects, 37
spellchecking email messages
  (Outlook Express), 280
Split Desktop with Icons button
  (Active Desktop), 33
stalled printers, troubleshooting, 203
Standard Buttons toolbar buttons,
  42-43
Standby mode (Shut Down
  menu), 15
Start button (Start menu), 9
  applications, launching, 186
  file searches, 153
  taskbar, 22
Start menu
  adding programs, 88
  commands
    adding, 87-88
    dragging action, 89
    removing, 88
    selecting, 13
    sorting, 88
  documents (recent), clearing, 89
  expanding, 13
  reorganizing, 87-89
  Run command, 186

shortcut icons, adding, 68
Start button, 9
Windows Me, personalized
    menus, 13
starting. *See also* launching
    Active Desktop, 262
    applications, 186-188
startup disk, creating, 169
Startup folder, adding programs to,
    187
stationery, email (Outlook Express),
    278
streaming audio
    playing (Media Player),
        222-223
    Radio toolbar (Internet
        Explorer), 250-251
streaming video (Media Player), 251
submenus, right-pointing arrow, 47
subscriptions
    channels
        *modifying (Internet
            Explorer), 272*
        *removing (Internet
            Explorer), 272*
        *synchronizing (Internet
            Explorer), 270-271*
        *updating (Internet
            Explorer), 272-273*
    newsgroups (Outlook Express),
        285-286
    starting, 263-266
    Web sites, 267-269
switching
    between windows, 30-31
    programs on taskbar, 22
Synchronize command (Tools menu-
    Internet Explorer), 271-272
synchronizing channel subscriptions
    (Internet Explorer), 270-271
system administrators (networks),
    121
system events, sounds, changing,
    90-91

System Restore
    backups, executing, 170-171
    record dates, 172-174
    restore points, 170-171
    system changes, undoing,
        172-174
system startup disk, creating, 169

T

tabbed dialog boxes, pages,
    changing, 53
tape media, file backups, 170
Task Scheduler, tasks
    adding, 167-168
    deleting, 169
Taskbar
    appearance, 22
    attributes, customizing, 86-87
    date/time, setting, 91
    hiding, 23-24
    moving, 23
    options, 86
    programs, switching, 22
    Start button, 22
    Start menu, 87-89
    status area, 23
    toolbars, 23-26
    Volume icon, 92
Taskbar and Start Menu Properties
    dialog box, 23, 86
Taskbar Properties dialog box, 88
text
    file search criteria, 154-156
    mouse, selecting, 191-192
    Web pages, searching (Internet
        Explorer), 257
    WordPad
        entering, 225
        fonts, changing, 227
        point size, changing, 227
        selecting, 226
text boxes (dialog box elements), 50
text links, 247

Text tool (Paint), 230
themes (desktop)
 screen resolution settings, 85
 selecting, 83-85
threads in newsgroups, 288
tiling windows, 38
time/date, setting, 91
title bar (windows), 29
titles, adding (Movie Maker), 206
toolbars, 40, 251
 Address, 43
 Channel Guide, 43
 creating, 26-27, 89
 displaying, 25
 Links, 43-44
 moving, 45
 removing from taskbar, 25
 sizing, 25
 Standard Buttons, 42-43
 title display option, 26
 Windows Explorer, 40-41
Tools menu commands
 Select Newsgroups, 289
 Synchronize, 271-272
Tours/Tutorials Page (Windows Me
 Help and Support), 60-61
transitions (Movie Maker)
 clips, creating, 211
 cross-fade, 211
trimming clips (Movie Maker), 209
troubleshooting
 folder display, hidden contents,
  101
 stalled printers, 203
 Startup Menu, 5
 system startup disks, 169
turning off Recycle Bin, 151
typical software installations, 177

U - V

Undo button (Standard Buttons toolbar), 43
uninstalling
 applications, 182
 updates, 183-184
Up button (Standard Buttons
 toolbar), 42
updates
 channel subscriptions (Internet
  Explorer), 272-273
 uninstalling, 183-184
URLs (uniform resource locators),
 246-247
users, multiple
 home network configuration,
  126-128
 logging off, 16-18
 logging on, 16-18

Verisign, digital certificates, 280-281
vertical scrollbars, 29, 35-36
vertical tiling windows, 38
video
 collection files, 206
 Media Player, 220-221
  playing, 220-222
  supported formats, 220
 Movie Maker
  importing, 205-206
  recording, 207-208
video capture cards (Movie Maker),
 204-205
viewing
 disk drives
  Explorer, 102-103
  My Computer, 99
 downloaded content, offline
  (Internet Explorer), 270
 files
  Explorer, 102-103
  in compressed folders, 144
  My Computer, 99

folders
>Explorer, 102-103
>hierarchy (My Computer),
>>100
>My Computer, 99-101

images
>Kodak Imaging, 116-118
>My Pictures (Image
>>Preview), 112-113

newsgroup messages (Outlook
>Express), 287-288

print queue, 201

screen savers, 85

slide show, My Pictures (Image
>Preview), 113

topics (Windows Me Help and
>Support), 55-57

troubleshooter links (Windows
>Me Help and Support), 58

Views button (Standard Buttons
>toolbar), 43

voice chat, Internet games, enabling
>(DirectPlay), 180-181

volume, speakers
>adjusting, 91-92
>mute setting, 93

Volume Control dialog box, 91-92

Volume icon (Taskbar), 92

W

wallpapers
>patterns, editing, 79-80
>themes, 78-80

.WAV files (Sound Recorder),
>234-235

Web (World Wide Web), 239
>integration on Active Desktop,
>>262-263
>viewing pages, 239

Web browsers, 239
>Active Desktop, 21

Internet Explorer, 239, 245-246
>Channel bar, 265
>disconnecting, 246

Netscape Communicator, 239

Web pages
>backgrounds, applying, 78
>folders, customizing (Web
>>view), 118-119
>text searches (Internet
>>Explorer), 257
>toolbars, access, creating, 26-27

Web sites
>Active Desktop Gallery,
>>267-269
>addresses, entering (Internet
>>Explorer), 246-247
>AltaVista, 254
>business searches (Internet
>>Explorer), 258
>clips, publishing to (Movie
>>Maker), 213-214
>entering addresses, 246-247
>Excite, 254
>Favorites folder (Internet Explo-
>>rer), adding to, 259-260
>Links bar (Internet Explorer),
>>260
>links, following, 247
>Lycos, 254
>Microsoft Windows Update, 96
>navigating between, 248
>page history, tracing (Internet
>>Explorer), 248-249
>people searches (Internet
>>Explorer), 258
>refreshing display, 247
>saving as favorites (Links bar),
>>258-260
>search engines
>>AltaVista, 254
>>Excite, 254
>>forms, 252
>>indexes, 252

Internet Explorer search page, 255-257
Lycos, 254
search criteria, 253-254
Snap, 254
Yahoo!, 254
text criteria, 257
subscribing to, 267-268
video, playing (Media Player), 220
Windows Me Help and Support (Assisted Support Page), 62
WindowsMedia.com, 224
Yahoo!, 254
Web view (My Computer) folders, displaying, 103-104, 118-119
What's This? Button, dialog box options, 62-63
wildcard characters, file searches, 153
Win Popup utility, notes sending over home networks, 131-133
windows
    Active Desktop, display options, 34
    borders, sizing, 34
    cascading, 37
    closing, 38-39
    elements, *29-30*
    maximized, unable to move, 37
    menu bar, 46-47
    minimizing all, 33-34
    moving, 36
        drag effects, 37
    opening, 30
    sizes, 31
    switching between, 30-31
    tiling, 38
Windows 95 computers, home networks, adding to, 125-126
Windows 98 computers, home networks, adding to, 125-126

Windows Me
    CD-ROM trial samples, previewing, 184
    Internet games, launching, 188-189
    personalized menus, 13
    screen savers, personal images option, 70-72
    uninstalling, 183
Windows Me Help and Support
    Assisted Support Page, 55, 62
    F1 key, launching, 54
    Home Page, 57-58
    hyperlinks, 54
    Index Page, 55, 58-59
    Search Page, 55, 59
    Tours/Tutorials Page, 55, 60-61
    Web page-based, 54
Windows Update button (Links toolbar), 44
Windows Media button (Links toolbar), 44
Windows Update command (Start menu), 10
Windows Update, uninstalling, 183-184
WindowsMedia.com Web site, 224
WinZip utility, file compression, 141-142
WordPad
    documents
        creating, 225
        editing, 225
        typing text, 225-226
    formatting
        fonts, 227
        point size, changing, 227
    launching, 225
World Wide Web. *See* Web
Yahoo! Web site, 254
Zip disks, file backups, 170
.zip files (WinZip utility), 141-142

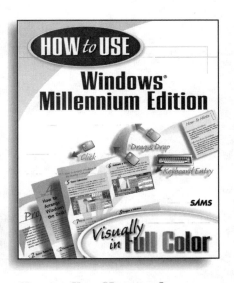